PLOT BASICS

PLOT YOUR NOVEL OR SCREENPLAY IN EIGHT SEQUENCES

PAUL TOMLINSON

Copyright © 2017 by Paul Tomlinson

All rights reserved. This book may not be reproduced or transmitted, in whole or in part, or used in any manner whatsoever, without the express permission of the copyright owner, except for the use of brief quotations in the context of a book review.

For country of manufacture, please see final page.

ISBN: 978-1-976098-75-8

First published September 2017
Publisher: Paul Tomlinson

www.paultomlinson.org

Cover image and design © 2017 by Paul Tomlinson

Contents

Introduction: Plot versus Character — 1
    Do You Need This Book? — 1
    Plot First, Write Later. Or Not — 2
    Dramatic Writing — 4
    What is Plotting? — 4
    What Makes a Great Story? — 4
    What's the Difference Between Story and Plot? — 5
    What is a Story? — 5
    What is a Plot? — 6
    Plot versus Character — 7
    What About Genre? — 8

What Does a Plot Look Like? — 10
    You Must Be Joking! — 10
    The 'Rule of Three' — 11
    Once Upon a Time There Were Three Bears... — 12

Quarters — 14
    The Love Story — 15
    Murder Mystery — 16
    The Thriller — 16
    The Action / Adventure — 17
    The Flawed Hero — 18
    What's the Worst Thing That Could Happen? — 18
    What Use is Any of This? — 20
    Does This Sound Right to You? — 21

The Eight Sequences: An Introduction — 24
    A Summary — 25
    Diagram — 26
    What Goes in Each Sequence? — 27

Act I: Setting Up and Setting in Motion — 31
    Promises, Promises — 31
    Fight, Fight, Fight! — 31
    The Beginning, Middle, and End of the Beginning — 32
    The Major Dramatic Question — 33
    Begin at the Beginning — 33

Sequence 1: Set-up, Foreshadowing & Challenge — 34
    1. Vivid Opening Image or Paragraph — 35
    2. The Hook: Grab Me or Seduce Me — 35

3. The Opening Scene: Action or Slow-Build?	38
4. Choosing the Right Type of Opening Scene	39
5. Genre	41
6. Setting	42
7. Introduce the Hero	45
8. Theme	52
9. The Hero's Internal Problem or 'Lack'	53
10. Foreshadowing – Coming Soon: Conflict!	53
11. Opposition: The Antagonist	55
12. The Challenge or Inciting Incident	59

Sequence 2: Responding to the Challenge — 62

1. Initial Reaction to the Challenge	63
2. The Hero's Greatest Fear?	64
3. Refusal of the Call – The Reluctant Hero	65
4. Backstory	66
5. Subplots: The B-story & Other Secondary Plotlines	68
6. Consequences of the Refusal	71
7. Pressure to Accept the Challenge	71
8. Lock-in – Why Doesn't the Hero Run Away?	72
9. Introduce Other Major Characters	73
10. Stakes – A Potential Disaster	78
11. Motivation – The Hero's Point of View	79
12. Decision – Accepting the Challenge	79
13. The Hero's Goal	80
14. The Major Dramatic Question	81
15. Crossing the Threshold	82
16. Major Turning Point	82

Act II: The Middle — 84

The Functions of Act II — 84

Sequence 3: Responding to the 'Strange New World' — 86

1. First Test – The Threshold Guardian	88
2. First Impressions of the 'New World'	89
3. Initial (Emotional) Reaction	90
4. The Hero as an Outsider	91
5. Mistakes and Transgressions	91
6. Tests	92
7. Learning	93
8. Allies and Enemies	93
9. Recruiting	94
10. Beginning of the B-story Relationship	95
11. First Actions Towards the Goal	96

12. Planning the First Attempt – How to Be A Success	97
13. Pinch Point I – 'Page 45'	98
14. First Action of the First Attempt	99

Sequence 4: First Attempt, First Failure & Consequences — 100
1. The First Attempt	101
2. First Failure	101
3. The Antagonist Counter-Attacks	102
4. Consequences of the Failure	103
5. Co-protagonist / Team Confront Hero Over Failure	103
6. The Hero Denies There is a Problem	103

The Midpoint — 105
(i) What the Hero Learns About the Story Situation	107
(ii) The Wrong Goal or a Change of Goal	108
(iii) Conflict with Antagonist & Thematic Argument	108
(iv) The Hero's Personal Growth	109
(v) The Relationship or B-Story	109

Sequence 5: Reaction to Midpoint & Raising the Stakes — 111
1. Emotional Reaction to the Midpoint	112
2. Reluctance to Go On	113
3. Decision & New Commitment	113
4. Hero Tries to Prove Himself	114
5. Hero Redeems Himself	115
6. Active Hero	115
7. Active Antagonist	116
8. Planning the Second Attempt	116
9. Pinch Point II – 'Page 75'	116
10. Hero Wants a Second Chance	117
11. Bonding and Increased Intimacy	117
12. Unite Against the Villain	118

Sequence 6: The Second Attempt: The Crisis — 120
(i) Preparation for the Ordeal	123
(ii) Opposition	124
(iii) The 'Underworld' or Villain's Lair	124
(iv) The Supreme Ordeal	126

Act III: The End – Climax & Resolution — 131

Sequence 7: The Climax — 134
(1) Reacting to the Crisis – A Decision or Dilemma	134
(2) Antagonist Forces a Response from the Hero	138

(3) A Discovery or Revelation	138
(4) Highest Stakes	139
(5) The Reader Learns of an Increased Threat	140
(6) Thematic Argument – Points of View Restated	140
(7) The Final Battle	140
(8) The Battle Begins Badly for the Hero	141
(9) The Hero Learns of the Increased Threat	142
(10) Hero Discovers a Way to Fight Back	142
(11) Outcome of the Battle	142
Types of Ending	143
Building a Climax	144
How to Get Endings Wrong	150
Sequence 8: Resolution and Denouement	**152**
(1) Reaction to the Climactic Events	153
(2) Resolution	154
(3) Validation and Closure	154
(4) New Equilibrium	155
(5) Denouement	156
(6) Final Image or Paragraph	156
The Series Novel or Screenplay	157
Symmetry and Plot Cohesion	**158**
Sources & Bibliography	**161**
Index	**165**

Introduction: Plot versus Character

This is a book about plot. The clue is in the title. When you are writing a novel or a screenplay, you don't need characters, but you do need plot. All those children's stories, fairy tales, myths, legends, and folktales that we grew up with didn't concern themselves with 'character growth.' They just got on and told us a story. Characters just get in the way of a good story. You know what they're like, always chattering away: Where's my backstory? What's the nature of my psychic wound? I need a development arc! Me, me, me. And before you know it, you've lost sight of your plot and you're wondering why the middle of your story is sagging.

I'm only half-kidding here. I do think that if we get too caught-up in thinking about character, we risk forgetting how important it is to get plot right.

Plot is the most important thing in a story. You can have characters fresh out of Flatland, and dialogue straight out of the poorest daytime soap opera, and readers will still enjoy your story – as long as you have a strong plot. Check out the novels that have made it on to the bestseller lists over the years, and you'll find many that have cardboard people spouting 'on the nose' dialogue – but millions of readers still bought them. Because they had an attractive premise that was explored via an effective plot. Of course, *some* bestseller writers create three-dimensional characters to people their plots, but the bestseller that features characters without a plot is so rare as to be almost non-existent.

The same with movies, though it's easier to see the importance of plot when films fail. A film can have great actors, special effects, locations, and snappy dialogue, but fail to engage an audience because there is no real plot as such. No one really cares why the characters are doing what they're doing and saying what they're saying. Readers and movie-goers like strong plots.

Plot matters. Yes, you will want to have three-dimensional characters and sparkling dialogue. And deep themes and fully-realised settings. But none of these will sell your story if it doesn't have a fully-functioning plot.

Do You Need This Book?

Do you really want another book on writing? And if you do, do you need *this* one? Let me tell you what I'm going to include in the following pages, and then you can decide.

My aim is to give you an 'aerial view' of plot structure, of the very basics, so that you can see what should go where and how the different parts fit together. We'll start with a long shot, and then zoom in closer to examine the parts in more detail.

I'm going to show you how you can break your story into manageable chunks, using a 'three-act, eight-sequence' model that was developed for screenwriting.

Why would you use a screenplay model for writing novels? Plotting for screenplays has been studied and developed continuously since the early days of cinema and has been refined to the point where you can find a complete, simple model for constructing an effective plot. There hasn't been a similar development of a theory for plotting novels. I don't believe that there *is* a great deal of difference between plots for films and those for novels, since both developed from dramatic theories originally developed for theatre. I don't intend to spend any time covering the historical development of plot theory because I want to concentrate on practical tools.

I am not going to tell you that the eight-sequence model is *the* way to plot a story, but it is *one* way. It is a tool that I think you will find useful. And it is flexible enough that you can use it in conjunction which any other theories of storytelling that you find helpful, whether it's the 'hero's journey,' or *Plotto* or whatever.

By showing 'what goes where' this model for plotting also tells you what you need to have in place in order to write an effective story. The raw ingredients that you will need. This should enable you to look at your initial story idea, and evaluate it to see whether it has everything necessary to create a successful plot for a novel or screenplay. And it will give you some pointers of what you need to add or develop if your story comes up short after this first analysis.

I should make it clear from the outset that I am only covering plots for long-form stories here: novels and feature-length screenplays. It can probably be adapted for full-length theatrical plays as well, but that is not an area where I have any experience. Short stories, television episodes, sitcoms, and one-act plays require a different approach and are beyond the scope of this book.

Plot First, Write Later. Or Not

You should write down your basic plot *before* you begin writing. I can almost hear the wailing and gnashing of teeth from certain quarters. From those who claim that working out the plot beforehand 'stifles my creativity,' and from those who proudly declare 'I am a pantser!' Please give me another 30 seconds of your time before you reach for the remote and flip channels.

By 'plotting your story,' I do not mean writing a twenty-page outline that sets down every detail of your story from beginning to end. If you're writing a novel or the first draft of a screenplay, that level of outlining *can* stifle your enthusiasm for a project: Who wants to write a story they've already told?

No. What I *am* talking about is a couple of pages or so where you set down the main plot points of your story – that is the six major turning points plus the climax. That's all you need. And it is actually pretty easy to figure these things out, based on a plot pattern that almost all popular stories share.

I am not saying that there is a *formula*. There is no magic recipe for creating a novel or a screenplay. But popular stories do share some common features – an overall pattern or shape. This is something that many successful writers pick up subconsciously from their own reading. And it is something that readers expect, without even being aware of it. There are other story patterns, but this one is easy to understand and easy to explain.

Still not convinced? How about if I told you that a few hours spent preparing your underlying plot would enable you to sit down and write your novel or screenplay more quickly? Or if I told you that it almost guarantees that you'll never suffer from writer's block, because you will always know what comes next and why? And that it means your first draft will be structurally sound, and only need minor edits before you do your final polish? And that it will help you figure out what to do if things go wrong? And that it can make your writing time more rewarding and enjoyable because if you feel that you know what you're doing, it's bound to be more fun? Unless you enjoy feeling lost and confused and inadequate to the task.

There's none so pure as a reformed whore, or so they say. I'm probably only semi-reformed. I used to hate plotting. Before I started using this plotting technique, it would take me a year or eighteen months to complete the first draft of a novel-length story. And I'd end up with something that I wasn't entirely happy with. In my gut, I'd know that this poorly formed thing didn't really work, but I was never sure why. And I would start many, many projects that I could never finish. Novels and screenplays that would just fizzle out because I didn't know how to complete them. I had notebooks full of great ideas that I did not know how to develop into finished stories.

In 2015, as an experiment, I used the eight-sequence plot model to write a 1930s murder mystery. It was a genre I enjoyed but had never thought about writing. I knew it was probably the most plot-centred genre of story, based on the unravelling of an intellectual puzzle, rather than on the emotional interaction of characters, so I thought it was an ideal way of testing out my newly-acquired plotting skills. I wrote 65,000 words in three months – from initial idea to final edit. And I did this while working full-time, out of the house for ten hours a day. I self-published it on Amazon and made some money from it. Not a lot, but some. It's called *The Sword in the Stone-Dead*.

In theory, then, you can use this method to write two or three or four novels (or screenplays) a year. Maybe more if you are writing full-time. And the more you write, and successfully complete, the better writer you'll become.

There will probably still be times when I decide to sit down with a blank page and no plan, and just write as it comes. But if I end up with a misshapen lump of a story, I can use the eight-sequence model to take it apart and restructure it. And if it fizzles out before I finish it, I can use the eight-sequences to figure out what went wrong with it, and maybe get the story back on track. And if writing 'by the seat of your pants' is the only way that you can do it, you too can use this book when you come to edit your first draft or to try and fix a failed draft.

Plotting your novel or screenplay in this way is quick and easy. A handful of plot points placed in the correct order, and you're done. And four of those plot points will carry you through that awfully long middle section of your story, lifting it up out of the dirt and stopping it sagging.

Plotting is easy. I'm laying it out in a short book. You can read it in a single evening. Read on – you've almost nothing to lose, and lots to gain.

Dramatic Writing

I regard both novels and screenplays to be examples of *dramatic* writing. 'Drama' was originally a Greek word meaning action, and is derived from a verb meaning *to do* or *to act*. I'm not interested in stories where characters sit around *thinking* about doing things, I want to see them make a decision and then go out and take action to bring about whatever they have decided to achieve. For that reason, I'm going to be concentrating on plotting the external and visible action in a story, rather than the internal aspects of character.

In the following pages, I don't make much distinction between movies and novels, and some of the ideas I talk about come from texts on writing stage plays. As far as plot structure is concerned, I don't believe there is a great deal of difference. A story is a story.

What is Plotting?

Plotting means putting the events of your story in the order that will create the most dramatic effect. And by 'dramatic effect,' I mean something that creates a strong response in the reader. Plot is what causes a reader to respond intellectually, emotionally, and/or physically to your story. It appeals to the head, heart, or gut. Ideally, it will appeal on all of these levels. The more levels of appeal a story has, the more potential buyers you have for it.

Ask people why they read fiction or watch movies, and most will tell you that they want to *escape* from their everyday lives while being entertained. People talk about being 'lost' in a book as they sit in an airport lounge or during their daily commute to work. If they go to the movies, they are transported to another world for a couple of hours. Stories provide people with an experience that allows them to get away from the real world for a while.

Plot is the basic underlying structure of a story. It is what gives a story form, and helps you deliver the experience viewers and readers crave. Certain things *have to* appear in a particular sequence, and at particular points in a story. That is what plotting is about.

There is no such thing as an original plot, so you aren't required to come up with something new and clever for the structure of your story. What you *do* have to do is come up with your own story events to fulfil the purpose required by each major plot point in the structure. This book is about how to do that.

What Makes a Great Story?

We want a beginning that hooks or intrigues the reader, making them want to read on and find out what happens next. A middle that *builds* – in terms of action and tension and emotion – keeping the reader turning the pages, and increasing their desire to find out how the story will end. And we need a big finish. Something dramatic and surprising, yet which satisfies the reader's expectations as they were set-up at the beginning of the story.

And afterwards, we want a feeling that the story was actually *about* something important. It wasn't just a series of interesting events, but rather it was something where the outcome had a significant impact on the lives of the characters – something that causes the reader to think about the implications of what they have just witnessed, in relation to their own lives.

Plot contributes towards this, and it is the most significant contributor. But we should also acknowledge that other things go towards making the most successful stories: a cast of larger-than-life characters; high stakes; a 'high concept' premise; a situation that is 'the same only different,' that successfully meets genre expectations; dialogue that reveals character and moves the plot along, yet seems fresh and realistic; a meaningful theme; setting and social milieu... a whole host of secondary features that you need to get right. But none of these matter if your plot sucks.

What's the Difference Between Story and Plot?

What is a Story?

Stories are a way of communicating something. They do not communicate factual information on an intellectual level, we have non-fiction for that, instead they provide an emotional experience. They make the reader *feel* something. The better the story, the stronger our reaction to it. Some people will disagree with that, and argue that manipulating the reader to bring about an emotional response is what cheap, sensationalist fiction does: 'proper' fiction does something much more subtle. This may be true, but I'm not interested in writing proper fiction. I want to write stories that people enjoy reading. Stories that give them an emotional experience. I *do* want to manipulate the reader and make them feel something – but I want to do it in a way that they don't realise they're being manipulated. Because that's what I want to happen when I *read* a story.

Life is complex. Every day we're faced with dozens of difficult situations – relationships with family, friends, and colleagues; issues at work; financial pressures; health worries – and we never get time to focus on just one thing and sort it out properly. We are always performing a kind of juggling act, trying to keep our overlapping web of problems from overwhelming us completely. And for many of life's problems, there is no answer.

Stories, on the other hand, are simple: they concentrate on only one or two issues in a character's life; they let us see the character concentrate their efforts on fixing one problem, and they let us see that most problems actually *do* have a solution. And while things in real life happen at random, without any apparent logic or reason, everything in a story has a purpose. Everything happens for a reason.

Stories, however lifelike they might appear, offer a simpler, more structured, and therefore reassuring, view of life. Their relative simplicity is part of their appeal.

I'm going to offer two definitions of what a story is, to help us in our explorations of story and plot. Here's the first one:

A story is an account of how an individual responds to change in his or her life.

Often you will see a story defined as being how a character deals with a *problem* in their life. But the situation a character faces doesn't *have* to be a problem. They can just as easily be faced with a positive opportunity for change. People go for the 'problem' definition because a problem implies struggle and conflict, and we have all been told that a good story requires conflict. But I'm going to stick with the slightly broader definition, because it includes 'problem' stories and other types.

The second definition is:

A story is a series of causally-linked events designed to convey meaning.

In real life, events occur at random, leaving us to try and make whatever sense we can of things. In a story, everything happens for a reason. Something happens. In response to this, a person decides to perform a particular action. That action has consequences, which in turn act as a new stimulus that causes this person – or another person – to respond by choosing an action. The first event in a story might be random, an accident, or a coincidence, but after that every event is a response to something that has gone before. Everything that happens – every decision and every action – happens for a reason. There is a chain reaction of cause and effect, sparked off by that first event. Because events in a story are all causally-related, we can see meaning in what happens – we can understand *why* particular situations arise, and *how* characters attempt to deal with them. We find stories reassuring because in a story everything makes sense.

Stories also give us characters who make decisions and take action based on those decisions. We see someone who tries to determine the course of his own life, and this encourages us to believe that we can choose the direction that our own lives take, that our fate is not pre-determined and unalterable. This is why we like to see stories about decisive characters who set out to *do* something. For this reason, what I am covering here is the sort of plot that works well in a genre or 'popular' novel, but tends to be anathema to those who want to write 'proper' mainstream fiction, where characters tend to spend a lot of their time navel-gazing and *not* taking action.

What is a Plot?

Words in English often have more than one meaning. You may think this is a bad thing, especially if you hate bad puns, but great poetry, prose, and humour all make use of the fact that we can have one word that means different things, and different words for the same thing, so we shouldn't complain too loudly.

'Plot' has a number of meanings that have their origins in Old English and Old French, or so my dictionary says. It means a small piece of land to be used for a building or garden. Or for burying a body. You dig? It means a secret plan to do something wrong or illegal. And it means to mark a route on a map or a position on a graph. All of these, in some way, relate to the meaning that we are interested in: the 'main sequence of events in a play, novel, or film.'

'Story' is one of those awkward terms. We tend to think that a novel, or a movie, or a play, or whatever *is* a story. But that is not, strictly speaking, true. These things *tell* a story, and they use a plot to do it. There are two key differences between story and plot: one relates to the order in which events happen, and the other relates to the reasons why things happen.

Story is what happens – the sequence of events in its chronological sequence.

Plot is those events placed in a sequence by the storyteller to achieve a desired dramatic effect.

This sequence will usually be different from their chronological sequence, and some events may be missed out or skimmed over. Alfred Hitchcock said that drama was 'life with the dull bits cut out.' In theory, the same events could be placed in a different order to achieve a different dramatic effect. Writers do not have to set down events in the order in which they happen. We can begin in the middle of the action – *in medias res* – and then go back and show what led up to, what caused, the current action to take place. We can use flashback to reveal events that happened before our story takes place, but which have an impact on what is currently happening. We can begin a story at the end, and then reveal what happened to bring about this ending. A whodunit typically has two sequences: a story going forward in time which shows the detective investigating the murder, and the gradual piecing together of an earlier series of events that culminated in a murder.

We are going to concentrate on how to construct a good plot so that we can tell a great story.

Plot versus Character

We are often told that there are two types of story: the plot-based story and the character-based story. Mainstream – or 'proper' or 'high-brow' or 'art-house' – stories are usually character-based. Exploration of character is regarded by critics and academics as being 'better' or 'classier' than the exploration of events in a plot. Genre fiction is all plot-based. By definition, it is based on 'generic' plot situations and characters who perform functions within those situations. Genre fiction is usually looked down upon by critics. And regarded as a guilty pleasure by academics. Being 'plot-based' means that genre stories don't feature much in the way of character development. And this is because they don't need to because it is not relevant to the emotional response the story is seeking to evoke. Some people believe that a film without character development is a bad film, but a look at the most popular – and even award-winning – films of all time quickly dispels that myth. Plot-centred genre stories aren't better or worse than flawed-hero stories – they're just stories of a different type. Pretty much the same is true of novels.

'Which is more important, plot or character?' seems to be a question that has been around at least since the days of Ancient Greece. For the record, the Greek philosopher Aristotle said that plot is more important than character, though he was writing about a particular type of drama performed in a particular setting at a particular point in history, so we shouldn't necessarily take his word as gospel, or quote him out of context. But I think, on balance, that he was right. Plot has to come first.

Even though good plots sell movies and novels, most story theorists (or 'gurus' if you prefer) tell you how to write character-based stories. The best screenplays ever written, they say, feature flawed heroes. They will list them for you: *Casablanca, Rocky, Jerry Maguire, Rain Man, Tootsie, As Good as it Gets, Good Will Hunting, Dead Poets Society*... All of these movies feature in my top 100 movies, but the 'flawed hero' is not the only genre of story I like. I enjoy whodunits and crime thrillers; horror, fantasy, and science fiction; caper stories, and a bunch of other sub-genres. And most of them are *not* character-based stories. These are the kinds of stories I wanted to write, but when I went looking for a book on how to create this type of plot, I couldn't find what I was looking for. Probably because what I was looking for was the secret formula for a best-selling novel or a blockbuster movie.

Putting this book together, I tried to include only material that was directly relevant to plot. Separating this stuff out wasn't easy, and some people would argue that it was a fool's errand, because you can't separate plot from the other two key aspects of story, *character* and *theme*. To some extent they are right: you do need an understanding of character and theme to write an effective story. But you need to have an understanding of plot first, and that's what we're about here.

What About Genre?

I've mentioned genre fiction a few times already and said that a lot of popular fiction is genre fiction. And that most genre fiction is plot-based rather than character-based. Popular movies too are often genre movies. If you want to write a romance, or a whodunit, or a thriller, or whatever, you might be wondering how you go about plotting one of those. What use is a book on *general* plot structure going to be to you if you want to write in a *specific* genre? The answer to that is: All genre stories are variations on the general plot structure that we're going to explore in this book. Each of the eight sections or sequences that we'll cover exists in every story of every type. Within individual genres, the specific kinds of incidents that will occur in those sections, and the specific types of characters who appear in them, will be different. But at the fundamental level of plot, all stories are the same.

How can I be sure of that? Genre fiction as we know it is a relatively recent occurrence. It began during the Victorian era, developing out of Gothic fiction and melodrama, but only really became defined when American movies and pulp fiction magazines began to target specific audiences. If all genres evolved from a single point – the genre-less novel, that came from the genre-less play, that came from the genre-less poem – then suggesting that there is a single meta-plot isn't such a mad idea.

Virtually all genre stories – and a significant proportion of non-genre stories – feature a main character who is trying to achieve something. They want to *do something*. As mentioned above, often they are trying to solve a problem or deal with an opportunity. They are trying to get something; or rescue or regain or retrieve something; they are trying to make something happen, or prevent something happening. Or they are trying to return a situation to the way it was. They are trying to create something or destroy something. They are trying to get to a place, escape from a place, or stay in a place. They are trying to catch someone, or avoid being caught. They are trying to uncover a mystery or a secret, or protect it from those who would uncover it. There are dozens of variations, but they all feature someone who is trying to do something. To successfully complete some action. The thing they are trying to achieve may be physical – to get a bag of gold coins – or it may be something less tangible: to get someone to fall in love with them; to remedy a particular injustice, or to prove that they as an individual are not a failure.

What all these stories have in common is that they show a character who is dealing with change in their life: trying to adapt to it, make it happen, reverse it, or avoid it.

Joseph Campbell in his *Hero with a Thousand Faces* argued that virtually all mythical stories from all of the different religions and cultures in the world were based on a single structure, which he termed the 'monomyth.' Campbell presented his monomyth as a 12-stage 'hero's journey' or quest. And Christopher Vogler adapted this for modern writers in his book *The Writer's Journey*.

The quest model is a useful one, but I find it a little confusing at times. It's easy to see how you can apply it to a literal quest, like *Star Wars* – George Lucas was a big Campbell fan – but it is harder to see how to use it for, say, a romantic comedy like *When Harry Met Sally*. The 'hero's journey' still applies, but you have to approach it as a metaphor, and that just adds a level of complexity that can cause confusion. I have nothing against the 'hero's journey' – I used it in my fantasy novel, *Slayer of Dragons* – but I do think that a sequence of 12 major plot points is too much to try and accommodate in a movie or novel.

I'm in favour of keeping things simple, but I will refer to some elements of the hero's journey, so you can see where the model I am describing fits with what you might already know from that model.

I'm not going to write in any detail about individual genres, as that would be a subject for a book on its own, and possibly several. I am going to cover the basics of plot without spending time on the differences between, say, the detective thriller, the romance, and the Western. The basics we cover here can be applied to, and adapted for, any of the popular genres or subgenres of plot-based story. I'm going to talk about plot pure and simple, because once you have the basics of plot nailed down, you can go ahead and add all of that additional character development arc and genre iconography stuff you want, knowing that you are building your screenplay or novel on a firm foundation, or using a robust framework, or whatever you want to call it.

First, catch your plot.

What Does a Plot Look Like?

This line is your story (it's a storyline):

|———————————————————————————————|

One-hundred-and-twenty minutes of screen time or 300 pages of a novel, or whatever. Your task, should you choose to accept it, is to plot your story along this line for maximum dramatic effect. You need to figure out what should go where in order to keep your reader turning the pages. We know that the first part of the story is going to be the *beginning*. We know the last part is going to be the *end*. And all the rest is *middle*.

People say that the Greek philosopher Aristotle came up with the theory of three-act structure and that it was used in all those great Ancient Greek plays that we know and love. Not true. *The Poetics,* written about 335BC, is the oldest surviving work on dramatic theory, and the ideas Aristotle set down in it form the basis of much of modern dramatic theory. Aristotle was the first – that we know of – to write about dramatic structure. He did *not* say that a play should have three acts. All he said was that a story should have a beginning, a middle, and an end. They are not acts; they are just bits of the plot that serve particular functions. Having said that, most people refer to them as the three acts, so we're stuck with this terminology, so we may as well use it. But in our hearts we will know: *They are not really acts!*

You Must Be Joking!

An Englishman, an Irishman and a Scotsman walk into a bar, and the barman says: What is this, some kind of joke?

You've heard that before. It's an old joke, but in just 22 words it demonstrates the classic structure of a joke: *Setup, rising tension, climax.*

If you wanted to plot the shape of a joke on a graph, it would look something like this:

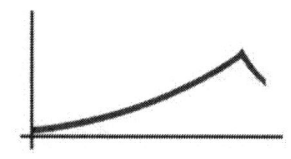

The horizontal axis represents time, and the vertical one represents the dramatic or emotional intensity. This 'inverted check-mark' can also be used to represent other types of story. I first saw it in Janet Burroway's *Writing Fiction: A Guide to*

Narrative Craft. This, in essence, is what your plot should look like. Your story increases in dramatic impact, has a climax, and then a brief 'tailing off,' so that your reader or audience doesn't have time to be bored or let down by a long anticlimax.

In *The Megahit Movies,* Joseph Michaels Stefanik studied the film *Jaws* and drew a graph of his own perceived emotional level at each point in the movie's running time. He came up with a spiky, up and down graph that looks like a sound wave visualised by an MP3 player or an oscilloscope, but it does – broadly speaking – have an underlying trend that looks like our inverted check-mark. The most significant difference is that the story begins with heightened emotion: there is the first shark-attack, a prologue that is a 'hook' that grabs the attention of the audience and pulls them into the story. Something like this:

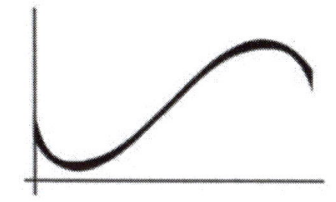

The 'Rule of Three'

There are a couple of other things to note about the joke above that will come up later when we look at the plots for novels and screenplays. First of all, there is the 'rule of three.' Englishman, Irishman, Scotsman. There are longer jokes that feature these three, or three other nationalities, or maybe a priest, a rabbi, and a duck. But there is always three of them. In fairy stories, too, there are the three little pigs; and Cinderella and her two aesthetically-challenged sisters vying for the hand of the prince. Why? Call it economy or elegance. 'Elegance' in the context of achieving the maximum effect with the minimum expenditure of effort or fuss. Three is the minimum number of times you can repeat something to establish a pattern or rhythm, and anything more than three is overkill. Two could just be a coincidence, three is a pattern. Four just becomes tedious.

I remember sitting in a cinema watching the movie *Vantage Point,* which retells the same events from different viewpoints. It's an interesting idea. But when the movie flashed back to the events for the fourth time, the audience around me groaned out loud. Not just a few people – lots of them. And those that didn't groan, nodded in agreement with those who did. The rule of three.

The last thing I want to say about that specific joke above is that it relies on the listener being familiar with the pattern of Englishman, Irishman, Scotsman jokes. We've all heard so many of them that we almost groan out loud when we hear someone open a joke this way. (Leaving aside the issue of the perpetuation of national stereotypes). We expect a long rambling story where the Englishman does something bland, the Scotsman does something penny-pinching, and the Irishman does something involving a misunderstanding. The joke above pulls the rug from under us – surprising us, the first time we hear it – by subverting our expectations.

It can do this because we *have* expectations. As recipients of jokes, we know how they're supposed to work.

Exactly the same thing is true of stories. Our readers have read so many novels and seen so many movies, that they know how plots are supposed to unfold. This is particularly true of popular and genre stories.

Once Upon a Time There Were Three Bears...

We learn how stories work when we are children, having pestered the adults around us to keep reading the same stories over and over again. We are attracted by the pattern and the rhythm and the twists and turns in the story, and every time we hear them, we are satisfied by the way the story ends. How many times in your life have you heard, or read, or seen *The Three Little Pigs?* Or *Cinderella?* If someone put you on the spot, you could probably sit and tell these stories, even without the text in front of you.

The fact that a children's story is so brief – something like 32 pages in a picture book – means that their plots exist in the purest, simplest form. There's no room to make things unduly complicated. If you Google 'how to write a children's book,' you will find a lot of advice, but it will all boil down to a plot structure that looks something like this:

1. Introduce a character with a problem or mystery
2. Place obstacles between the character and the goal he seeks
3. The character reacts to the obstacles, causing new obstacles to arise
4. The character reacts to the new obstacles, creating even bigger obstacles until all seems lost
5. Then an unexpected solution is found.

1 and 2 are the set-up. 3 and 4 are the rising tension. 5 is the climax. And 3, 4 and 5 are the *three* attempts that the central character makes to solve his problem: the first two attempts fail, the final one is successful. A house of straw, a house of sticks, a house of bricks. Two girls with big feet, and the slender-footed Cinderella. When it comes to plotting, this is the 'secret formula' that everything is based on. Setup, rising tension, climax and the 'rule of three.'

That gives us almost all we need to understand story plotting. To recap, we have a main character who must deal with some sort of change in his or her life: a problem or an opportunity. We know that our story will have a beginning, a middle, and an end, and that they will correspond to setup, rising tension, and climax. And that the hero will make three attempts to deal with his situation; the first two will fail, but the final one will bring about a resolution.

This is the aerial view I promised you. And you've been looking at it since you were a child. It's that simple.

I want to add one more thing before we zoom in on the next level of detail. As far as I'm aware, this idea first appeared in Syd Field's 1979 book *Screenplay: The Foundations of Screenwriting.* Field said that a screenplay has a beginning, a middle and an end, which he referred to as three acts – and he said that Act I (the beginning) was the first quarter of the story; Act II (the middle) was the middle two quarters; and Act III (the end) was the final quarter.

On our 'story line' it looks like this:

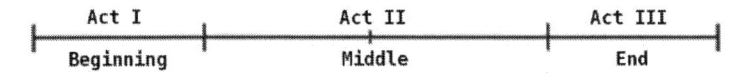

```
|      Act I      |       Act II       |     Act III     |
|----------------|--------------------|-----------------|
|   Beginning    |       Middle       |       End       |
```

This idea has been around for such a long time now that it may not seem like a big deal, but dividing a plot up into four quarters like this is a really helpful concept. In the next chapter, we will forget about the three acts, which aren't really acts, and look at the four quarters in more detail. Then later we'll split them down into the eighths that give us our 'eight sequence' plot model.

Quarters

Plotting involves figuring out what should go where so that your story achieves the maximum dramatic effect. You also have to arrange things such that events unfold in a way that can be understood and appreciated by your reader, which means meeting certain expectations people have about what a story should be like.

At this point, I'm going to abandon the idea of stories having 'acts.' The fact is, in films and novels, there are no acts as such. From here on, we're going to talk about the four quarters of a story. And then we'll look at splitting them into eights. Bear in mind that the quarters and eighths are *approximate* measures, not absolutes. They're serving suggestions.

Four Quarters

To recap: the *beginning* of a story is the first quarter. The *middle* is made up of two quarters. And the *end* is the final quarter.

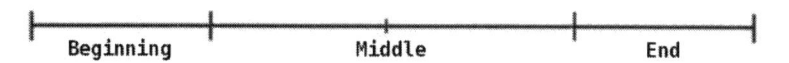

|—————————|—————————|—————————|—————————|
   Beginning   Middle   End

Taking our cue from Aristotle, we can say that each of the quarters should serve a specific function in the story. Let's start with some basic ideas:

- Bad
- Worse
- Worst
- Climax & Resolution

At first glance, this looks too basic to be any use at all, but sometimes it helps to pare things back to their simplest level.

Going back to what we said about the hero making three attempts to achieve his goal or resolve his situation gives us another way of looking at the four quarters:

- What the hero wants
- First attempts don't work
- Second attempts end in disaster
- Final attempt, outcome and resolution

Here's another variation:

- Introduce a problem or opportunity
- Ignorance/denial – Hero doesn't know, or denies, the scale of the problem or the nature of his 'lack' (unconscious incompetence)

- Midpoint – Revelation/Realisation – Hero knows what he doesn't know. Awareness
- Trying to deal with the true problem or 'lack' – Conscious incompetence
- Mastering the situation – Conscious competence

If you're still not seeing anything helpful in this, maybe it'll help if we apply it to some real types of story.

The Love Story

Boy meets girl, boy loses girl, boy gets girl. Beginning, middle, and end, as the old cliché has it. This can be broken down into four quarters plus a midpoint:

- Boy and girl meet
- They deny their attraction
- (Midpoint) They admit their love
- Happy together, then disaster forces them apart
- Happily ever after

or

- Boy and girl meet
- Girl is reluctant to accept boy
- (Midpoint) Boy wins girl over
- Happy together, then boy loses girl by doing something stupid
- Boy and girl are reconciled, and live happily ever after

This is one of the most common plot patterns, found in both genre romances, and in the relationship subplots of many other stories. It can be used for the relationship between the hero and his lover (or, to use an older term, 'romantic interest'), and it can be used for a platonic relationship between the hero and a friend or ally. A 'buddy movie' and an 'odd couple' story are also variations on this basic pattern.

Two people meet, providing an opportunity for a relationship. Although there is some attraction between them, there are also opposing feelings, and the two are initially antagonistic towards one another and/or afraid to show their feelings. At the midpoint, their conflict is (apparently) resolved, and they enjoy a brief moment of happiness together. Then someone does something stupid, or there is some misunderstanding, or external events force them apart, and the relationship seems to be over. Then, in the end, the situation is resolved and they can go forward as lovers or as friends. This works as both a main plot and for the relationship subplot of a story.

Even at this level of four quarters and a midpoint, you can see how the story as a whole progresses. We can see what is referred to as rising action, or rising tension, as the stakes are raised at key points. The story moves from absence of love to denial of love; to realisation and acceptance of love; to love in jeopardy, ending in a crisis when the relationship seems to be over forever; and finally to love triumphant.

Murder Mystery

A murder mystery, or 'whodunit,' is an intellectual puzzle: a problem is presented at the beginning of the story, and the hero must solve it through investigation and rational thought. The first half of a mystery usually explores what seems to have happened: this is the version of events that the murder wants people to believe, as it steers suspicion away from him (or her). The second half of the story shows the detective reinterpreting the evidence in a new and unconventional way so that he can demonstrate what really happened. The detective's efforts during the second part of the story initially seem to make the situation much more complicated than it first seemed, until a point is reached where it seems impossible to make any sense of the whole mess. It is usually at this point that the detective announces he has the solution and calls all of the suspects together in the drawing room to explain his findings.

- A body is discovered
- The detective investigates, clues point towards a culprit
- (Midpoint) The suspected culprit is found dead, second victim of the murderer
- The detective re-evaluates the evidence, investigates more, to establish a second theory, but what he discovers seems to make the situation even more baffling and impossible to solve.
- Final solution – murderer identified and brought to justice.

The Thriller

Alfred Hitchcock perfected the man-on-the-run thriller, placing an innocent man in the midst of a conspiracy that usually involved a villain determined to get hold of a 'MacGuffin' that was the key to the fate of the free world.

- Innocent man accidentally mixed up in a conspiracy
- Hero is a victim, pursued by the villains
- (Midpoint) Hero discovers the nature of the conspiracy and decides to be proactive and stop it
- Hero takes the fight to the villain, becoming hunter rather than hunted
- Hero outwits villain, beating him at his own game.

The hero moves from a position of innocence to being unjustly accused and pursued; deciding that he cannot escape the injustice of this situation, he decides to turn and fight: defeating the villain is the only way to prove his own innocence; he pursues the villain, and finally outwits him. Again we have a pattern of rising action, of increasing stakes and suspense.

The James Bond novels and films are another form of thriller, involving a professional hero rather than an innocent amateur.

- The villain puts an evil plot into motion; M gives Bond the assignment of stopping the villain
- Bond pursues the villain and takes action to block the villain's plot

- (Midpoint) The villain is more powerful than Bond suspected.
- Bond is captured by the villain and usually tortured as well.
- Bond outwits and outfights the villain, puts a stop to the evil plan, and usually blows up the villain's hideout.

In this variation, Bond is the hunter before the midpoint rather than a victim and becomes – or appears to become – the victim after the midpoint. The Bond stories, while fitting in the thriller category, also have much in common with our next type, the action / adventure story. For my purposes, a story is a thriller if it centres on some form of conspiracy, and this is what differentiates Bond stories from straightforward action or adventure stories.

The Action / Adventure

I believe that an action story is different from an adventure story because it features a different type of character as the hero. An action story concerns a 'warrior' hero who competes to achieve a particular goal – he wants to *win*. An adventure story features an 'adventurer' – a character whose main goal is seeking thrills: he does what he does for the adrenaline rush, and he competes, for the most part, with himself and with the obstacles in the world around him. The difference between these two characters exists in the 'why' rather than the 'what' – the actions they undertake can be the same, and they usually involve some sort of quest, but their *motivations* are different.

In other types of story, the hero often begins as a victim of circumstances – he is acted upon, rather than choosing to take action – until the midpoint of the story; at the midpoint, he moves from being passive to being active. In action and adventure stories, there is no room for a passive hero: he is active from the get-go. Act I is often shorter in this type of story, as any reluctance to act is quickly overcome. The hero might fight against what he must ultimately do – he may be forced into action against his will – but he will be active while he's doing it!

- Introduce the hero and his objective: something to win or conquer
- Initial actions towards the goal, resulting in setbacks
- (Midpoint) The hero realises the goal is more difficult (and more important) than he expected
- On the brink of failure
- Final efforts and success

Action and adventure stories often require the hero to discover additional reserves of stamina and strength. He often meets an ally or love-interest, but he is reluctant to admit his feelings towards them. They may offer to assist him at the midpoint, but he rejects the offer, mistakenly believing that a true hero must act alone, or believing that he must protect the other person from any form of risk because they are not up to facing it. Only when things reach crisis point does he recognise the importance of having help from, or love for, others – from this he gains what he needs to finally succeed.

Up to this point, I have discussed only genre plots, but what about the so-called character-based story? Do those stories also follow the same plot pattern? These stories often feature a main character who is in need of redemption. He or she needs to learn some lesson, to undergo some kind of character growth or self-discovery, in order to achieve happiness and success in life. *Tootsie, As Good as It Gets,* and *Casablanca* are examples.

The Flawed Hero

The basic plot structure of these stories is the same as for our genre examples – the difference is that the hero must resolve an *inner* problem – or opportunity for change – rather than an external one. Michael Dorsey in *Tootsie* must learn to treat women with respect; Rick Blaine in *Casablanca* must rediscover his commitment to a just cause and be selfless rather than selfish, and the Jack Nicholson character in *As Good as It Gets* must experience empathy with another human being. Each of these characters is flawed or wounded, and must overcome this in order to become a whole, functional person.

- Introduce a flawed hero and demonstrate their flawed behaviour
- Hero denies flaw – but flawed behaviour causes problems in his life and the lives of others
- (Midpoint) Hero recognises and admits his internal flaw
- Hero attempts to overcome flaw, but it is difficult; he falls back into old behaviours, with catastrophic results
- Hero overcomes flaw and happy ending. (Or, hero fails to overcome flaw and tragic ending)

This flawed hero character development arc can be used in genre stories too. Often both partners in a romance undergo some kind of growth or develop new self-awareness, as they move from being alone to being in a partnership. A crusading hero must learn the difference between revenge and justice. A warrior must learn that not all situations can be resolved through confrontation, he must also learn compassion.

The character development arc does not appear in all genre stories and is less likely to appear where a character appears in a series of books. Though even here, the character arc may be developed over three or six or more books in a series. Where a character arc is used in a genre story, it is a subplot and is usually closely-linked to the relationship subplot. A character's progress along the development arc is demonstrated through his relationships with other people.

What's the Worst Thing That Could Happen?

A piece of advice you will often see in 'how to' books for writers is 'know your ending.' This suggestion causes some people to run for the hills, waving their arms and yelling 'If I know how my story ends, there's no point in me writing it!' And then there are some people who will write that part of the story first, and write the rest of their story with the ending in mind. 'You wouldn't begin a journey without knowing your destination,' these people say. Both types of people are wrong – and they're sort of right as well.

Writing a novel or a screenplay isn't really comparable to going on a journey. Instead, think of it as creating a guidebook and map so that a reader or viewer can go on a journey. When you start writing, you might not know exactly where the journey will end up, and you may have to try a couple of places before you can pick the one you'll think is most effective for your travellers. At the same time, you can't just set off into the wilderness without some idea of the sort of place you might like to end up.

The ending of a story is implied at the beginning and is further defined by the genre of the story. Write a romance without a 'happily ever after' and you're going to struggle to find readers. And no Hollywood studio is going to invest hundreds of millions of dollars in your blockbuster screenplay if your hero dies in the third act and the US of A is overrun by foreign zombies.

Having said that, you want your reader or viewer to think it's *possible* that this sort of ending *might* happen.

Just before the climax of the story, the hero will suffer a *crisis* – his darkest hour. He has suffered through 'bad' and 'worse' and has arrived at *'worst.'*

Throughout a story, a writer should be asking 'what is the worst thing that could happen at this moment?' – and then making that thing happen, or at least making the risk of it happening seem real. Your characters should be in constant physical or emotional jeopardy at various levels of severity. But at the end of the third quarter, we have to ask, 'what is the worst possible thing that could happen to the hero given what he has gone through thus far?'

It must appear to the reader or viewer that everything the hero had, and everything he has gained during the story, is going to be lost. It should feel like this to the hero too. At this point in the story, it should seem as if the villain has won. Or the two lovers are further apart than they have ever been, with no hope of reconciliation. The crisis should be the farthest from a happing ending that you could imagine.

Unless you plan for it early, creating a crisis situation on a scale that feels appropriate – with the right thing(s) at stake – for the story you are telling can be tricky. It's much better to think about it while you're in the 'four quarters' stage, and to set down the bad, worse, and worst moments. This will help you create the rising action and rising tension that a screenplay or novel must have.

A quick recap:

- *Bad* = inciting incident/challenge at the end of Quarter 1
- *Worse* = midpoint failure of first attempt at the end of Quarter 2
- *Worst* = crisis/darkest hour; failure of second attempt at the end of Quarter 3

A weak ending in a film or novel is usually the result of the crisis not being sufficiently strong. It is not enough that we feel sorry for the hero – we should feel *devastated!* We should be upset and angry on his behalf.

In part, this *worst* situation is such that the hero has done the best that he can to succeed, but his best has proven to be not good enough. We should feel that he has done everything he could, but his circumstances – the odds against him – were too much for him to overcome. Another feature of this moment of the story is that the crisis is where the hero discovers the one thing that is more important to him than anything else – including his own happiness, and possibly his own life. This is the thing that he is prepared to sacrifice himself for – and that is what he has to do in the final attempt at the climax of the story.

The crisis and climax at the end of a story should arise organically from the challenge that is set up at the beginning. The first quarter is where we promise the reader something special, and the final quarter is where we deliver on that promise. The beginning implies the ending. The challenge offers the hero an opportunity to achieve something that will bring happiness and fulfilment – or at the very least, an escape from misery. The crisis and climax are where that something is most obviously at stake, and where the outcome of a single action will decide the hero's fate.

The crisis point – the *worst* point – of a story is not the point at which the hero fails to achieve something: *it is much worse than that.* After the midpoint, the hero does actually appear to achieve this 'something' – he experiences those feelings of happiness and fulfilment. But at the end of Act II, he loses it. He may lose it as a result of his own actions, or because of something the antagonist does, or from a combination of the two. It is usually best if he is at least partly responsible for the loss himself.

They say it is better to have loved and lost than never to have loved at all – but that's not how it feels when your heart has just been broken. The absence of love is all the more intense for having experienced it. Give your hero a taste of happiness – then whisk it away from under his nose. To be a writer, you have to have a sadistic streak – at least when it comes to your fictional people.

Before you begin writing, you need to know what your *worst* moment is – not necessarily the exact form it will take, because you can discover that as you write, but your beginning defines your end. You can't *not* have it in mind.

What Use is Any of This?

I believe that thinking about your story in terms of four quarters and a midpoint can be a really useful tool. If you write those five things down, you have virtually written out the logline for your screenplay. And you have the beginnings of your synopsis and the headings for the main sections of your outline. If you have an idea for a story, you can break it down and see if you can come up with these five elements. If you can't, the missing bits will give you an idea of what you need to add to the idea to turn it into a viable starting point for a novel or screenplay.

Four quarters and a midpoint are detailed enough to give you an overall structure for your story, without being so detailed as to inhibit your creative freedom. They may be all you need before you begin writing. Other writers may want to go on and break these elements down further: we'll look at the first stage of doing that in the next chapter when we look at dividing the quarters into eighths.

Wherever you are in your writing process, you can come back to these five elements and see whether what you are writing is fulfilling the required functions for that quarter of the story. If you're stuck, it can help you see if you've gone too far off track, or it can give you a clue about where you should be heading next.

Does This Sound Right to You?

How do I know that this model for plotting stories is right? How do I know it will work? I said at the beginning that this wasn't the only way to explore plot, that it was only a tool that you may find helpful. But hopefully, as you've been reading, you will have recognised this pattern – not just from stories you've read or movies you've seen, but also from your own life. It is based on theories about how human beings deal with crises or other significant changes in their lives. A problem, a change, a disaster, an opportunity enters a person's life. Initially, they may be unaware that this is their problem. They may ignore it, deny it, try and force it or blame it on someone else, or they may be completely ignorant of it. But eventually, they are forced to do something to deal with it. They decide to tackle the situation. End of Act I.

They take their first steps but are in a state of unknowing: they don't yet know the extent of what they don't know. Act II begins with them trying to deal the situation, without fully understanding its nature and scale. Then at the midpoint, they have a realisation or revelation: they achieve a new awareness. Now they know the full extent of their problem.

In the second half of Act II, they begin to take action based on this new awareness. They may feel overwhelmed by the situation and suffer a period of self-doubt, but with a little encouragement from others they recommit themselves to dealing with the situation. They become a kind of enthusiastic but unskilled underdog, and this almost proves their undoing. All seems lost. End of Act II.

By the end, our underdog has become a seasoned veteran: he has learned many difficult lessons and is now ready to make one last attempt at success.

This is a pattern we see when someone falls in love; when they lose a job; when they start a new job; when a loved one dies; when someone suffers an illness or injury. It is the pattern of how people deal with major events in their life. Stories mirror that pattern, and that's one of the reasons why stories can resonate so deeply – they echo our experiences.

- A problem or new opportunity upsets the balance of my life
- I am the victim of my circumstances, and accept that I must suffer
- (Midpoint) I accept responsibility for my problem and choose to take action rather than continue suffering
- I fight, but I am an inexperienced underdog and I make mistakes
- I apply what I have learned and achieve relief and/or success

The psychiatrist Elisabeth Kübler-Ross wrote about this pattern of experience in her book *On Death and Dying* (1969). She described 'five stages of grief' which I will summarise as:

1. *Denial* – A person, in a state of shock and confusion, refuses to believe a terminal diagnosis, and clings to false hope for a preferable outcome.
2. *Anger* – Unable to maintain their denial, the individual becomes frustrated and angry: Why me? They become angry and may seek to blame people around them.
3. *Bargaining* – This involves the hope that the individual can avoid death by negotiation: Let me live and I will change my life.
4. *Depression* – The lowest point for the individual, when they give up all hope and withdraw and often don't want to see or interact with others: I'm going to die, what's the point?
5. *Acceptance* – The individual comes to terms with the inevitable and achieves a sense of peace, understanding that they cannot prevent what is to come, and so must use whatever time they have left to best effect, and to prepare themselves.

Kübler-Ross was writing about the experience of people who had been given a terminal diagnosis, and of the reactions of their close family. Her theory has been criticised for being not universally applicable – some people don't go through these stages – and for being too linear: people do not progress cleanly from one stage to another, they can fall back into an earlier stage, and some stages can overlap. But her model has been accepted and extended to the experience of all kinds of life-changing events: I first came across it in a work context, when it was used to help people come to terms with major changes in working practices which were having an impact on morale in a team.

Kübler-Ross's original five stages, and the change model adapted from it, are usually presented in terms of a curve. A sixth stage is sometimes added – 'Integration' – to show that having accepted the change, people go forwards having made it a part of their lives:

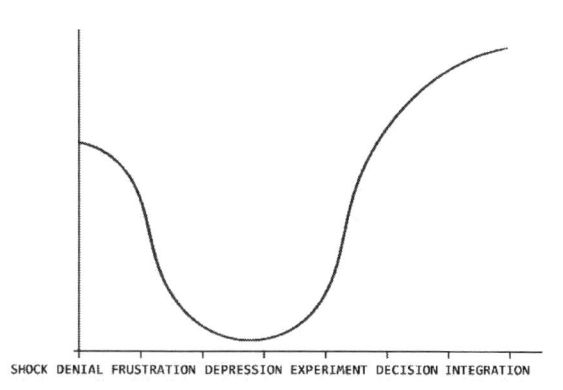

SHOCK DENIAL FRUSTRATION DEPRESSION EXPERIMENT DECISION INTEGRATION

You have probably already spotted the similarity between this s-curve and the one we saw earlier for the plot of the movie *Jaws*. We can imagine it as plotting the emotional journey of our hero, from the initial surprise of the challenge or opportunity; then a downward trajectory as his initial attempts at resolving his situation fail; and then ultimately battling up from the low-point towards a positive ending. Our reader or audience will be going on the same journey with our main character.

Four quarters and a midpoint allow us to construct the 'bird's-eye view' of our own plots. Whenever you are first planning your story, or at any point where you are struggling to figure out where your plot is going, I would recommend setting everything else aside and coming back to this very simple model. Have you defined your bad, worse, worst, and climax? Have you figured out what happens at the midpoint? The midpoint is an important turning point in the story, and we will look at it in depth later. But now let's look at adding the next level of detail by dividing our quarters into eighths.

The Eight Sequences: An Introduction

How do you create a plot for a 120-minute movie or an 80,000-word (or more) novel? That's a lot of pages to fill. The 'eight sequences model' says that in the main plotline of any full-length film or novel, there are seven key moments or 'turning points' – and everything else either builds up to, or happens as a consequence of, one of these moments.

If you can identify these seven key moments in your story, then you've got your plot sorted.

Divide your story up into eight roughly equal parts, and there will be a turning point or mini climax at, or near, the end of the first seven parts. The eighth part is where you tie up the loose ends after the seventh turning point: this seventh point is the climax of the story and its highest point.

Each of the seven key moments serves a specific function in the story. And they each occur in roughly the same place, regardless of the genre of your story. This is as close to the 'secret formula' as we're going to get!

The development and teaching of eight-part structure are credited to Frank Daniel, while he was the head of the Graduate Screenwriting Program at the University of Southern California. František Daniel was a film director, producer and screenwriter born in Kolín, Czechoslovakia in 1926. He died in 1996. He produced and/or directed more than 40 films, before he emigrated to the United States in 1969. He wrote two books on filmmaking: *Cesta za Filmovým Dramatem* (*The Path to Film Drama*, with Miloš Kratochvíl, 1956), and *Stručný Přehled Vývoje Evropských Dramatických Teorií* (*A Compact Overview of European Dramatic Theories*, 1957). As far as I am aware, neither of these books have been translated into English and Daniel never published the theories on screenwriting that he taught: the information we have comes from people who were students of Frank Daniel.

Paul Gulino's *Screenwriting: The Sequence Approach* is the best known of the books about plotting screenplays using eight-sequences. Chris Soth also teaches this approach, and has published *Million-Dollar Screenwriting: The Mini-Movie Method*. Alexandra Sokoloff writes about it in *Screenwriting Tricks for Authors: Stealing Hollywood*. And you can find articles about it on ScriptLab.com

Big films, Gulino writes, are made up of little films. He defines a sequence as an eight- to fifteen-minute segment of a movie that has its own internal structure, and says that it differs from a standalone 15-minute movie in that the conflicts and issues raised in it are only partially resolved, and even if an issue is resolved, it often opens up a new issue which will become the subject of a later sequence. Gulino says that the 15-minute sequence exists because of the way films used to be distributed in the early days of cinema. A film reel held about a thousand feet of film: when it was projected, this lasted for around fifteen minutes. When the reel ended, the projectionist had to load a new spool so that the story could be continued: the audience had to wait while he did this, so filmmakers used to end a reel with some incident that ensured that people remained seated so they could find out what happened next. These end of reel incidents weren't necessarily cliff-hangers, like those in the old weekly movie serials, but they were something which captured the attention. TV shows do the same thing to make sure we come back after the commercial break.

A full-length feature film filled between six and eight reels: 8 x 15 = 120 minutes. This sounds like it could all be made-up, but here is a quote from the 1913 manual *The Technique of the Photoplay* by Epes Winthrop Sargent, in which he talks about the 'multiple reel' film:

"While this is undoubtedly the story of the future, its special technique is still so new that few definite rules may be laid down.

"Some companies want stories in which each reel or part shall be capable of being used as a single reel independently of the other reels or parts. This is because a story may be found not strong enough in interest to run for two or three reels and yet one or more of the parts may be made into good single reel releases.

"The more general demand, however, is for a series of reels with a continuous subject, each reel terminating with a minor climax with the grand climax at the end of the last reel. For this no better example can be given than the play of the stage. At the end of each act there comes a definite stoppage of the action at a point which leaves the audience eager for the continuation."

Gulino acknowledges that as films became longer, and particularly with the advent of talking pictures in the late 1920s, screenwriters adopted the approach to plotting used by playwrights which developed out of the five-act structure. He also notes that ten to fifteen minutes has generally been quoted as the average length of the human attention-span.

The Eight Sequences: A Summary

Here is my own summary of the eight-part structure:

1. Set-up and Challenge
2. Reluctance and Commitment (Decision)
3. Preparation and Minor Actions
4. First Attempt & Failure (Action)
5. Planning (Decision)
6. Second Attempt and Crisis (Action)
7. Climax / Third Attempt (Decision & Action)
8. Conclusion

Placing this on our story line gives us something like this the diagram on the next page:

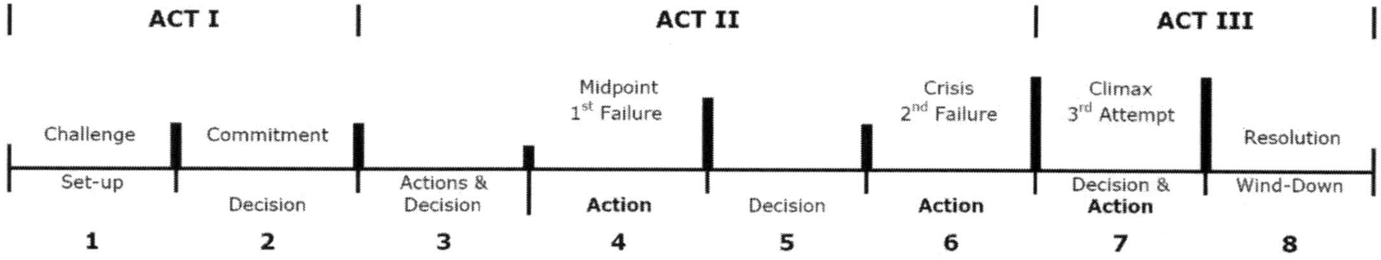

ACT I

Challenge	Commitment	Actions & Decision
Set-up	Decision	
1	2	3

ACT II

Midpoint 1st Failure		Crisis 2nd Failure	
Action	Decision	**Action**	
4	5	6	

ACT III

Climax 3rd Attempt	Resolution
Decision & **Action**	Wind-Down
7	8

From: *Plot Basics: Plot Your Novel or Screenplay in Eight Sequences* © Paul Tomlinson 2017

I think this diagram gives a helpful breakdown of the shape of a plot, with its broad indications of 'what goes where.' At the end of each of the first seven sequences, there is a turning point, indicated by a thicker line. The emotional or dramatic significance of each of these turning points will vary, with a tendency towards more dramatic turning points as we approach the end of the story – these are indicated by the height of the lines above the baseline. The overall shape of the 'graph' above resembles a stretched out version of the Kübler-Ross change-curve we saw earlier, with the issuing of the challenge at the end of Sequence 1 being the equivalent of the 'shock.'

Generally speaking, there will be a slight dip in the level of drama or emotion at the end of Sequence 3 and the end of Sequence 5. In both cases, things seem to be going well for the hero, and he is poised to take action towards his story objective, and he feels reasonably confident of success. The dip at the end of Sequence 3 prepares the way for the heightened drama of the midpoint at the end of Sequence 4. And the dip at the end of Sequence 5 prepares for the heightened drama of the crisis at the end of Sequence 6.

The 'action' – whatever this consists of in the context of the story – occurs more frequently as the story progresses, with each major action phase being preceded by a decision phase.

What Goes in Each Sequence?

(1) *Setting up the Situation*. The hero and his world are introduced, and he is given a 'challenge' or 'call to adventure' or an opportunity for change. This is the 'inciting incident' or catalyst that starts off the chain of events that will form the story.

(2) *Responding to the Challenge – Decision*. The hero may initially deny the situation he is faced with, or be reluctant to accept the challenge he has been presented with. An external action – by an opponent or by an ally – serves to push or pull the hero into making a decision. He accepts the challenge and chooses a goal which he believes will provide a solution to his predicament. Here we also learn what is at stake for the hero. What terrible fate will await him if he fails? What is the worst possible thing that could happen to him? At this point, set-up of the story is complete and the 'major dramatic question' has been asked: Will the hero succeed? Sometimes there is a secondary question: Has he chosen the right goal to be successful?

(3) *Actions Taken in Ignorance*. The hero doesn't really know what he is doing, and he doesn't really know what he is up against. He begins by doing the obvious things that anyone would do in his situation. This sequence answers the question 'Why doesn't he just go to the police? / run away? / get out of the house?' He may also attempt one or more quick fixes, showing that he has underestimated the difficulty of the situation. These easy options don't work, and we see his options being reduced and the chances of failure increasing. The audience may be aware of something that the hero doesn't know: we may know that he has chosen the wrong goal; we may know that he has a lack of knowledge, skills, or experience that he will have to overcome before he can succeed; we may know that he has been set-

up and manipulated by someone; we may know that his closest ally has betrayed him... We have rising action, tension, or suspense in this section. The audience should be aware that the hero has taken on more than he can cope with, or that he has made some fatal or tragic error that will guarantee his failure – but the hero doesn't know this yet. The hero realises he has to come up with a more considered plan of action, which he does – but it is based on an incomplete knowledge of the nature and scale of the problem he faces. The odds for its success don't look good. The climax of Sequence 3 is the point at which he takes the first action of what will be, in effect, his First Attempt to achieve the story objective.

(4) *The First Attempt: Action Taken in Ignorance 2.* The hero tries harder to achieve his goal, putting into effect the main action he has planned for his First Attempt. But we know he's still doing the wrong thing or going for the wrong goal or doing things for the wrong reason. The hero may suspect that there is a problem, but he will deny it. People around him may know that the hero is the problem, but he will refuse to accept this. His actions will have consequences that make his situation worse rather than better. The hero will probably have provoked the villain or rival into taking action against him. He may have put other people at risk. Again we have rising action and suspense, building towards the midpoint of the story. The First Attempt fails, and it usually fails because of some action (or inaction) by the hero.

(Midpoint) *A Moment of Revelation or Discovery.* The hero learns what the audience has known or suspected for a while; the problem is bigger than he imagined; he has chosen the wrong goal; he has some sort of lack that is preventing him from succeeding; he is ignorant of something that he needs to know. The midpoint is like a pivot point, where things could go one of two ways. In a tragedy, the midpoint is often a 'false victory' – the hero thinks his actions are working and believes that he doesn't need to change; he just needs to fight harder. In a 'happy-ending' story, the midpoint is usually a 'false defeat' – something terrible happens or is learned, and the hero feels that he will never be able to succeed; the odds are too high, the challenge too great. But actually this midpoint defeat is a learning opportunity – only by going through this experience can he gain the knowledge, skills, experience, wisdom, self-knowledge, or whatever he needs in order to succeed.

(5) *Responding to the Midpoint.* Typically this is a character-focused moment; a pause for reflection and re-evaluation. It is a decision phase. The hero needs to decide whether or not to continue with his story quest, in the light of what he has just learned. The hero may suffer a crisis of confidence: I can't do this, it's too much for me. I'm not brave, smart, good-looking, skilful enough. An ally or lover will usually support the hero during this, and help him to overcome his self-doubt. I believe in you, I know you can do this. With their relationship centre-stage, we often see a glimpse here of what the hero's life *could* be like if he successfully completes his story quest. This effectively raises the relationship stakes, bringing hero and ally or lover closer together, and making the bond between them stronger. The hero *does* decide to continue, and may choose a new goal at this point if he was previously going for the wrong goal; or he may go for the same goal but now for the right reason, if he had been acting selfishly before. In either case, he makes

a recommitment to achieving success. And the hero begins planning his Second Attempt. The major dramatic question is restated, though success now seems less likely than it did in Sequence 2. The hero's response to the midpoint is often a decision to be more pro-active – he will take the fight to his opponent, rather than carry on reacting to whatever the opponent throws at him: he moves from passive to active. At the same time, the opponent or villain may also change his goal: he no longer wants to prevent the hero from succeeding, he wants to completely destroy him. The stakes have been raised. Sequence 5 climaxes with the hero taking the first action of the Second Attempt.

(6) *The Second Attempt.* Sequence 6 contains the main action of the hero's Second Attempt. This part takes us from the hero's re-commitment and renewed optimism, to a point of catastrophe or crisis, when the Second Attempt fails. This failure, which marks the end of Act II, is the major crisis of the story, and is the hero's 'darkest hour.' At this point he appears to have lost everything that was important to him; he has brought harm to people he cared about and has effectively handed victory to his opponent. The opponent or villain may have used the hero's own weakness against him, forcing the hero to make – in a moment of desperation – an unwise move that was bound to fail. In Sequence 2 we had a glimpse of the 'worst possible thing' that could happen to the hero. At the crisis point, we see this actually happen – only much worse! Early in the story, he didn't really know what was most valuable to him; during the course of his adventures he has come to realise what he really cares about; and now at the end of Sequence 6, he has lost that and more. The catastrophe has to be so bad that the hero feels that all is lost – that he will never achieve his story goal, and that his relationship with his ally or lover has ended for good: he must feel that he has nothing left to lose.

(7) *Responding to the Crisis and the Third Attempt (The Climax).* Sequence 7 is the beginning of Act III. It begins with a decision phase – the hero must decide how to respond to the crisis and failure of the previous sequence. He faces a dilemma, a choice between two courses of action. He must also make this decision alone, as he doesn't have the co-protagonist – the ally or lover – to support him this time. As we are close to the end of the story at this point, the decision phase is kept reasonably short as we want to move quickly into action again. The hero has been pushed to a point where he is prepared to make the ultimate sacrifice in order to prevent the villain or opponent from succeeding. He is no longer acting out of selfish motives, he doesn't care what happens to himself, and he is prepared to do whatever it takes to bring about the right outcome. He will sacrifice his own love, his sanity, his physical self: he is prepared to die, figuratively or literally, to save the thing that is most important to him. This 'thing' will usually be something tangible that represents a human value or virtue; 'justice,' for example. Sequence 7 is the final battle or a do-or-die struggle, the Third Attempt, and involves a coming together of whatever has gone before. The climax of this sequence is the climax of the story as a whole, and should be the most dramatic and emotional point in the story.

(8) *Resolution and Denouement.* The outcome of the battle, the major dramatic question is answered. Endings can be tragic, happy, or ironic, but they must answer the question: Did the hero succeed? Sequence 8 ties up any loose ends, answers any remaining questions about the fate of secondary characters. It shows us the consequences of the success (or otherwise) of the Third Attempt. And it gives a hint of what the new 'everyday world' will be like for the hero: he is not the same person he was in Sequence 1, and he will not be returning to a life that is the same as it was. He may return to the same place and the same job, but something important will have changed. You can also have a final 'twist in the tail' in Sequence 8, if that is appropriate for your story, or if you want to set up the possibility of a sequel. Sequence 8 is effectively a post-climax 'winding down,' with no action, and – at most – only a 'what shall we do now?' decision to be made. This sequence should be kept relatively short.

In the following chapters, we look at each of the eight sequences in more detail, and we'll also see how they relate to the traditional idea of the 'three acts.'

Act I: Setting Up and Setting in Motion

Act I, the *beginning,* in the 'three-act structure' is the first quarter of a story and is made up of Sequences 1 and 2. It can be longer or shorter than one quarter of your story: in some stories, it may be half this length (an eighth of the total length of the novel or screenplay), in others, it may need to be up to a third of the total length. Do whatever feels right for the story you are currently writing. But if you're still setting up your story past the midpoint, chances are something has gone wrong. The first two sequences should set-up your story and set it in motion. You need to introduce all of the important elements that the reader will need in order to understand and appreciate your story. The beginning sets up a situation and sparks off the chain of events – actions and reactions – that will provide the 'rising action' that makes up the middle of the story, and that will propel the story forward. And it sets in motion the forces that will collide at the end of the story.

Promises, Promises

Nancy Kress, in *Beginnings, Middles and Ends,* says that the beginning of a story makes implicit promises to the reader. On an emotional level you are saying: Read my story and you will be "... entertained, or thrilled, or scared, or titillated, or saddened, or nostalgic, or uplifted..." And on an intellectual level, you promise the reader a new perspective on the world or an introduction to a new and interesting world. These promises are made at the beginning of the story; the middle develops the promise; while a satisfying ending delivers on the promise. Endings feel satisfying, Kress says, only because the beginning set-up the implicit promise in the first place.

Fight, Fight, Fight!

Dwight V. Swain, in *Techniques of the Selling Writer,* says that the function of the beginning is to "... let your reader know there is going to be a fight – and that it's the kind of fight that will interest him." A story is generally about some who wants to do something – remember the Greeks saying that drama is action? A story is about a character who wants to get or keep something, or who wants to escape from or prevent something. To get. To keep. To escape. To prevent. These are verbs. At school you were probably taught that these are 'doing' words. A story has someone who wants to do something. It also needs something that stands in the way of this character's success: there needs to be some obstacle or opposing force that means there is a risk of the character failing to achieve their desired purpose. Desire and danger are two of the key factors in a story. The third, according to

Swain, is decision. The hero of a story is someone who makes a decision to take action, even when they know that there is risk involved in doing so. The beginning of a story has to introduce those three elements: desire, danger, and decision. In fact, that almost defines the first quarter for us. Who is the story about? What do they want? What stands in their way? What risk do they face if they decide to take action?

There is a danger here of assuming that we are talking about physical risk here and that by 'fight' Swain is referring to something like a bare-knuckle brawl. But when we talk about danger, the thing at risk is actually some positive human value: it could be love, or justice, or dignity, or any one of a dozen other things. The risk faced by the character may be physical, but it could also be to their emotional or mental well-being. There is as much danger and conflict in a love story as there is in an action-adventure story – perhaps more. But the stakes are different, and the 'fight' takes place in a different arena. The 'arena' is another thing that has to be established at the beginning of the story: where and when is the story taking place? The genre too needs to be defined, though there's every chance that was done by the title and cover of your book or the movie poster. But still, the beginning has to be in the style of the genre. Each genre has a whole set of implicit promises that the reader expects you to deliver on.

In discussing plot there is a tendency to think about a story being about a person with a *problem*. Many stories deal with exactly that. But there doesn't have to be a problem at the centre of every story. Sometimes the thing that the hero is dealing with is an opportunity: should he accept it? What will be the implications if he does? The key thing is that something new comes into a character's life – this is the catalyst or inciting incident we will talk about shortly – and this new thing means that the character has to deal with change. A change is not necessarily a problem, but it is something that we need to understand and accept and integrate into our lives. One of the things that draws us to stories is that they show us how other people deal with change in their lives. Change is a universal experience.

The Beginning, Middle, and End of the Beginning

It has been said by more than one writer that a story is like a fractal or a set of Russian dolls. The same pattern is repeated on smaller and smaller scale. A story has a beginning, middle and end. So does each quarter, each sequence, each scene sequence, each scene, and each beat within a scene. The first act, or beginning, of our story, will have its own beginning, middle, and end. Early in Act I, we meet the protagonist and we see the world in which he or she lives. In the middle of Act I a change is introduced, that upsets the equilibrium of the hero's life. In the last part of Act I we see how the hero responds to this change, and we see them make a decision to take a specific action. They decide to do something.

The Major Dramatic Question

Once the hero has made a decision to act, the story set-up is done and we move from the beginning into the middle – from Act I into Act II. At this point, we have

– implicitly – asked the central question of our story: Will the hero succeed in resolving his situation? This question – sometimes referred to as the major dramatic question – is not answered until the ending of the story, until Act III. Part of the reason your reader keeps turning the pages is to find out the answer to this question. Everything that follows is directly related to this question; every action and every line of dialogue bring us closer to the answer. If we are honest, the answer to this central question isn't in much doubt. Of course, the hero will defeat the villain; the murderer will be identified; the lovers will be reunited. The real reason we keep turning the pages is that we want to learn *how the hero succeeds*. And the fact that we want to see him suffer along the way, though we never admit that to anyone. We want to see what he has to overcome in order to succeed. And we probably want to understand why achieving this objective is so important to him. Why does he risk his life, health, happiness, and/or sanity? The how, what, and why are what the middle, the second act, are all about.

Begin at the Beginning

The best place to begin your novel or screenplay is at a point just before change is introduced into your hero's life. That change will be the 'inciting incident' or 'call to adventure' or 'gauntlet' or 'challenge,' and will happen before the end of the first sequence of your story. This incident may be the culmination of a number of smaller incidents that cumulatively cause the change in the hero's circumstances. If you start your story way, way before the inciting incident takes place, you risk boring your reader who is sitting there waiting for something significant to happen. Conversely, if you begin at the moment of change, you may confuse the reader: they don't know who the change is happening to or why it is significant to them. You need to prepare the way a little bit. And if you open *after* the change has taken place, you may find yourself having to shoehorn in great chunks of exposition or backstory.

That is enough overview, let's get into the detail of the two sequences that make up Act I.

Sequence 1: Set-up, Foreshadowing & Challenge

The *function* of Sequence 1 is to introduce vital elements, foreshadow the coming conflict, and build up to the inciting incident (or 'challenge' or 'call to adventure'). The first sequence is probably the most important of any novel or screenplay: if these pages don't work, there is every chance that the rest of the story won't be read at all. Within a very short time, the reader will know whether the story is working, whether or not it is being properly set-up. These pages must capture the reader's attention and make them want to read on. Little wonder, then, that these are the pages that writers rewrite and polish the most. When we begin reading a story, we have a number of questions: Who is the story about? What kind of story is it? What is it about? What is the hero trying to achieve by the end of the story? Why does he need to achieve it, and why now? Who or what stands in his way? What happens if he fails? In other words: Who is the story about, what do they want, and why do I care? With that in mind, there are a number of things that you should try and include as soon as possible. Some of them are elements of the story that need to be included, and some are effects that you need to achieve.

I've listed 12 things in total, and I have numbered them for ease of presentation. With the exception of the first one, these can occur in just about any order you like. The 1 to 12 sequence I have here is one possible way of doing it – but many of them overlap, and some of them occur simultaneously. The sequence here is really only so that I can introduce them in some sort of logical order in this guide. Some of these things are optional, but if your story has them, Sequence 1 is (probably) where they should be introduced. Some of them can wait until Sequence 2 if that works better for your story, but those marked * really ought to be in Sequence 1.

1. Vivid Opening Image or Paragraph*
2. Hook*
3. The Opening Scene: Action or Slow-Build?*
4. Choose the Right Type of Opening Scene*
5. Genre*
6. Setting*
7. Introduce the Hero*
8. Introduce the Value / Theme
9. The Hero's Internal Problem or 'Lack'
10. Foreshadowing – Coming Soon: Conflict!*
11. Opposition: The Antagonist
12. The Challenge or Inciting Incident*

All of this may make Sequence 1 seem even more daunting, but it shouldn't. Knowing what these pages need to achieve, you can construct them so they deliver what people will be looking for. This sequence can be rewritten as often as necessary to get them right. Initially, it may be sufficient simply to make only a few notes regarding what scenes are meant to achieve: the best opening for a story is sometimes not discovered until the first draft has been completed. Let's look at each of the 12 elements of Sequence 1 in detail.

1. Vivid Opening Image or Paragraph

First impressions count – this applies as much to stories as it does to people. In a book store, a reader may open your book and read the opening sentences to see if it is the sort of thing they want to read. On line, they might look at your sample chapters before deciding whether to buy. You want your opening paragraph to make it easy for them to say 'yes.'

Films and television are *visual* media and can use an image to capture the attention of the viewer. Or a blurred or abstract image to intrigue them and draw them in. Or a black screen with sound over it, so that people wonder what it is they are not seeing. It could be a 'wide shot,' establishing the world of the story, or it could be an extreme close-up of one tiny detail that symbolises that world, or hints at the action to come. It may be a 'still life' or a tableau. It may be an action. Quick movement, slow movement, or no movement – whatever is most appropriate for your story. The image can reveal the location of the story, the time period – including historical period, season, or time of day; the genre; the tone – is it a comedy or a tragedy? – and the mood. The image can also be a representation – a metaphor – for the story to come. It might show an action that demonstrates, in miniature, the conflict that will be played out in the main story. Or it may symbolise the value (or virtue) that will be at stake. Or the vice that will be fought or argued against in what is to come. The opening image can also be contrasted with an image at the climax of the story, or the closing image – showing a 'before and after.' These images can show the change that the hero has undergone or the change that he has brought about in his world. Or has failed to bring about. Films and television episodes can begin with an action prologue or 'teaser,' in which case the 'opening image' may be the first image of the scene immediately following the prologue.

A novel can use all of these same techniques, but obviously you will need to evoke the image, making the reader see it in his or her mind's eye.

The opening may include the hero, or it may not. It might show his world during a moment of peace, before the arrival of some disruptive element. Or it may instead show something that is about to impact on the hero's world and upset its balance.

Alice Orr, in *No More Rejections,* gives five options for the opening sentence of your novel:

i. A startling exclamation in dialogue
ii. An intriguing statement
iii. A comment on something or someone strange

iv. A comment about an unusual aspect of setting
v. A brief statement alluding to a disaster or pending disaster

She also suggests that this opening sentence should be a simple declarative one.

The opening could be something that is weird, that intrigues the reader and makes them what to find out more. Or it could be the beginning of a sequence of action that captures their attention so that they want to discover how it turns out. The important thing is to make your opening paragraph vivid. Create an image and evoke an emotion. Choose something that is appropriate for the genre and tone of your story.

2. The Hook: Grab Me or Seduce Me

What is going to make the reader want to keep reading? Many stories are rejected by readers, producers, and agents before they have read to the bottom of the first page because there was nothing that made them want to read on. You have to make them turn that first page. Some writers deliberately structure their stories – whether screenplay or novel – so that there is something at the bottom of the first page that will make the reader want to turn over. Like a mini cliffhanger. I've probably spent too much time watching Hollywood movies, but I like to 'grab' a reader and pull them into my story. I always want to start with something startling or intriguing or violent or loud. Dialogue is a good way to start, people love to listen in on conversations. Or you can start with action – *in medias res* (in the middle of things) as Horace put it.

A narrative hook is something which catches the attention of the reader. Science fiction writer Harry Harrison's novel *The Stainless Steel Rat* opens with a hook. Harrison told me that he was practising writing narrative hooks and wrote one that hooked him: he had to write the short story to see what happened. The short became a novel, and the novel became a series that we wrote, on and off, for the rest of his life. He explained to me what a narrative hook was:

> *Back in New York, when I was still an artist, I knew all the writers, and we would sit around and talk. One of the things we discussed was the narrative hook. The first page of a pulp story [manuscript] has the name and address of the person to be paid for the story up in the left-hand corner; in the right-hand corner, we have the number of words in the story. That's the money! Then, we jump to the middle of the page – because we need a lot of white for the editor to write on – the title, double-space, 'by' any name at all, double-space, then the first paragraph. And it's all double-spaced. At this point you end up with six, or seven, or eight lines on the front page of the manuscript. The narrative hook is something that will hook the editor into turning that page. There's so much crap coming in front of him that is so rotten: eergh! He looks at it and throws it away. But if you get him to turn the page, he says: God, I turned the page! I'll buy it!*

Harrison was exaggerating – he did that sometimes – but not by much.

We will look at different types of opening scene under item 3 below. Action is a good way to open a story: straight away your story has a sense of forward momentum that – if done well – pulls your reader along. In Hollywood movies, there is often an action prologue for this reason – the pre-credits or credits sequence. Even when there is no action prologue, there should be a sense of impending action. Something is coming. There has to be a sense of forward movement.

The hook, or 'grabber,' has been criticised for being unsubtle and overused. Michael Hauge, in *Writing Screenplays That Sell* said that "...no one likes to be grabbed. It's a jarring, unpleasant experience. A far better way to approach the opening of your script is to realize you've got to seduce the reader..."

The thing that keeps a reader turning the pages after the opening is suspense, but it isn't always possible to create suspense at the very beginning: here you often have to rely on arousing the reader's curiosity. Dwight V. Swain gives us five possible ways to achieve this:

i. Uniqueness
ii. The unanticipated
iii. Deviation from routine
iv. A change about to take place
v. Inordinate attention to the commonplace

Wells Root, in *Writing the Script,* offers one possibility that does allow you to open with suspense. He gives an example described by playwrights Howard Lindsay and Russell Crouse, in which the curtain goes up on an empty living room setting: and a man enters...

...carrying a box marked DYNAMITE. He places it carefully under a centre-stage sofa. Lighting the fuse, he pushes the box gently out of sight. Then he disappears backstage where he came from. After a moment, the characters in the play enter the living room and launch into their opening dialogue.

As Root says, the audience will stay in their seats until that dynamite is discovered. This example sounds like one of Alfred Hitchcock's, but the 'plant' in such a scene doesn't have to be something as melodramatic as a bomb: it could be anything that is likely to 'blow up' at some later point in the story. This is an example of the audience knowing something the characters on stage don't, which is a much-used technique for gaining – and keeping – reader involvement.

Your opening sentence and opening paragraph have to draw the reader into the story. How you do this depends on the type of story you are telling. You might introduce a person or location or situation that the reader will want to find out more about. Or you could present them with a puzzle they will want to see unravelled, or an intriguing question they will want to know the answer to. Or you could amuse them. Or startle them. A word of warning: I would avoid trying to *confuse* your reader. That could just turn them off and make them put the book down forever. Better to give them a subtle hint that *something is not quite right.* Secondly, be aware that when your story opens, your audience will want to know who the 'hero' of the story is as soon as possible. For the most part, modern audiences expect an individual hero with whom they can identify and empathise, or at least be intrigued by. If you spend a lot of time on a different character at the beginning this could confuse things. It's easier if you're writing a first person protagonist in a novel, because by implication you've introduced them the moment they begin telling the story, and they can talk about any character they like, which at the same time will be revealing something about their own character: *Auntie Maureen was the loudest person I ever met. Even her lipstick was loud...*

The best way to figure out how effective openings work is to examine the first paragraphs of successful and popular novels or the opening scenes of movies, both in the genre in which you intend to write and in other genres. This is one area where you are probably best advised to look at modern novels rather than classics. Readers today expect a much snappier opening than those employed by, say, Charles Dickens. These expectations are based on a lifetime of watching movies and television, where stories begin quickly. Except in certain rare circumstances, you cannot afford to have a slow build-up with a great deal of non-essential detail.

All of which advice is probably enough to put anyone off trying to write the opening of a story. How can you sit down and write an opening that achieves all of these things? The answer is that, except in occasional fortunate circumstances, you can't. No one can. Opening paragraphs are the most frequently rewritten parts in anyone's story, and you often can't find the right opening until you've completed the first draft. Just start with something that works okay, and come back and fix it later. Or if that doesn't work, type this:

`[Opening paragraph]`

And then carry on and write the next paragraph. My first drafts are littered with square brackets that say things like *[Insert fight scene]* or *[Joe says something hilarious]* or *[Research 1930s coaches]* or *[word beginning with 's' that means sounding like a snake]*. If something isn't in my head ready to go down on the page, I try not to stop and worry about it, otherwise I risk being 'blocked' until I can remember the word 'sibilant'; or I'll waste an hour looking at images of coaches on Google, and then I'll get distracted and go off and search for some new fonts, and then someone I'm following on YouTube will have posted a new video...

3. The Opening Scene: Action or Slow-Build?

There are basically two ways to open your story: begin with action, or begin with calm and have a slow build-up to action. Which you choose will depend on what type of story you are writing.

Action. With some genres, we are plunged into fast-paced or suspenseful events from the outset. The story begins in the middle of some action that is already underway, or it shows a complete action, such as a robbery. If you are writing an action-adventure story, this is the obvious opening to choose. More than half of Hollywood movies are action-oriented, relying on strong visuals and simple dialogue: this makes them easy to translate and sell into foreign markets.

Slow-Build. In other stories, it is more important to introduce the reader to the hero and his everyday world, before showing the events that upset the balance of that world. The storm that hits the world may be on the horizon, and we may see it gradually approaching. Or it may be brewing within the world itself, pressure building and building until an explosion is inevitable. We will look at the hero in his ordinary world in more detail under the heading 'setting' below.

Over the next couple of pages, we will look at some different techniques you can use for creating both action and slow-build openings.

4. Choosing the Right Type of Opening Scene

There are five types of opening scene:

  i. Prologue
  ii. Flash-forward
  iii. True Beginning
  iv. Montage
  v. Narration

Prologue

A prologue is usually a self-contained scene that takes place before the main action of the story. It may take place many years before, or just a few hours. Either way, it shows events that will have a direct impact on the main story. One exception to this is the pre-credits sequence in an action-adventure movie, which may simply be designed to show how much of a kick-ass dude the main hero is – e.g. James Bond or Indiana Jones. The prologue could show the villain at work, doing bad things that will have an impact later: this happens quite often in horror movies, where we see some terrible thing being released or created or arriving on the scene, doing something nasty, and then heading off towards some peaceful unsuspecting community. *Halloween* opens with the serial killer's first murder, committed years before. *Jaws* opens with a shark-attack, which is the first in a chain of events that will lead directly to the climactic confrontation between the hero and the monstrous Great White.

The prologue may show some other sort of incident or danger that will soon impact on the hero's life. If the audience sees something that the hero doesn't know about yet – a literal or metaphorical storm that is about to wreak havoc on his world – then the reader is placed in a 'superior' position: they have information the hero doesn't. This use of dramatic irony sets up anticipation and tension: the audience is waiting for the storm to hit. *48HRS* opens with convicts escaping from a chain-gang, an event that sets off a chain reaction which ends up with cop Nick Nolte teaming up with convict Eddie Murphy. A less extreme variation of this type of opening is one which shows events that foreshadow or symbolically represent the conflict that is to come. This type of prologue doesn't show the actual 'storm' that is heading the hero's way, but instead shows a similar type of storm, usually on a smaller scale.

There is another form of prologue which I would advise against using – this is the 'bookend' or framing device. Here you start in one location and time period, and then jump to the main story which takes place in another location and at a different time period, sometimes in flashback. At the end of the story, we are returned to the first location and time period. One of the (many) problems with this device is that it draws attention to the fact that the story is being 'told,' as opposed to giving the impression that it unfolding now, in real time, in front of the audience. If we want to draw our readers in, so that they become 'lost' in our stories, we should avoid anything that distracts them from what is happening.

Flash-Forward

You don't have to start telling your story at the beginning of the chronological sequence of events. You can begin with something that happens in the middle, and then – through exposition or flash-back – fill in the details of what happened to bring about the action we saw in the first scene. With this sort of opening, the story is already in motion, and the background details aren't filled in until later. You will often see this in TV shows. They start with some intriguing action that typically ends up with a major character lying shot and bleeding, and then you will see a caption that says '24 hours earlier,' and we'll see the events leading up to the shooting. And all the time we are sitting anticipating the events we have already seen and wondering whether the shot character is going to survive or not. The movie *Confidence* is a great example of this technique in practice. *Reservoir Dogs* and *The Usual Suspects* are variations on the same thing. At first glance, this might look like an example of the framing device I have just advised you not to use, but it is slightly different in that the main action of the story eventually 'catches up' with the time and location of the opening prologue.

True Beginning

For some stories, it is appropriate to start at the beginning. It could be one character turning up on another character's doorstep. It could be the arrival of a letter or some other form of communication bringing bad news. Or good news. A birth or a death. Someone leaving or arriving. A new job... A beginning can be any event that triggers change in someone's life and which sets off a chain of events. This is like beginning the story with an 'inciting incident' – though there may be another one at the end of Act I. *The Silence of the Lambs* sees Clarice Starling begin work as an agent investigating serial killings. The advantage of having a newbie arrive in a situation is that it gives the writer a legitimate excuse to explain things for the benefit of the reader: we are learning things alongside Clarice, so it doesn't feel like a cheat. The old cliché has characters explaining things to each other that they already know, simply for the benefit of the reader: "As you know, professor, when litmus paper comes into contact with an alkaline..."

Montage

Sometimes you need to provide a lot of information, or many small bits of information, in order for the reader or viewer to be able to appreciate your story fully. Trying to put all of this into scenes, or having characters explaining it to each other, may not work, so you need another option. In a montage, rather than seeing a complete scene, we see a series of short actions or still images or a combination of the two. It may include newspaper headlines or snippets of news footage, or extracts from other documents. These build up to an image of a character and/or situation. The film *Soylent Green* opens with a series of photographs showing the development of the industrial world, leading to pollution of the environment, and the eventual over-population of the world, setting up the background against which the story is then told. Several hundred years of history are presented visually in a few minutes under the credits. *Tootsie* opens with a series of audition scenes in which Dustin Hoffman's character can't get a job because he's never quite right for the role – this brief sequence sets up the story as a comedy; and sets up Hoffman's character as an out of work actor who is desperate for work but who is never quite right physically for any character, thereby also setting up the hero's problem – he can't get work – and his desire: he wants to be the perfect person for the role.

In a novel, you also have the option of using extracts from letters, diaries, or other documents. This is a tricky way to open a novel, though, unless the extracts are vivid and startling enough to make the reader want to keep reading. Another option is to begin with a series of vignettes – brief actions that aren't quite full scenes in their own right, but which in combination serve to set-up the story.

Narration

You can have someone onscreen or in voice-over talking directly to the audience. This is frowned on by some story theorists because it tends to draw attention to the fact that you are watching a movie, rather than seeing the events unfold 'live' in front of you. In theatre, it was rare to have a character in a play address an audience directly – the actors were supposed to give the impression that the audience wasn't there: if they acknowledged their existence, it was known as 'breaking the fourth wall.' Even in novels, where first-person narrators are more common, the fact that you have someone telling the story – either their own story or someone else's adventures – draws attention to the fact that these actions have already taken place. Narration can also be regarded as telling rather than showing. But even bearing all this in mind, having a first-person narrator – at the beginning of the story, or throughout – can turn out to be the best technique for your particular story.

An opening narration – by Richard Burton, Liam Neeson, or Morgan Freeman, depending on which version of *War of the Worlds* you experience – can work well. The scrolling texts at the beginning of the *Star Wars* movies are a variation of this. A narration that carries on throughout a movie is more difficult, because it requires a voice that is worth listening to. The character speaking needs to be interesting, perhaps quirky, but never annoying. *Ferris Bueller's Day Off* is one successful example of a character we are happy to hear from.

You can, of course, mix and match these opening scene techniques. *Deadpool* manages to combine narration, flash-forward, and still images – or very slow-moving ones – into a unique and intriguing opening.

5. Genre

Genre is important because many readers only choose reading and viewing material in their favourite genre or genres. In the old days, it used to dictate which section your book or video got shelved in in the store, but that is less of an issue in these digital download days where you get to choose multiple subject keywords. It also matters because readers of a particular genre have certain expectations for the sorts of locations, characters, and situations in stories of this type. If you fail to meet those expectations, your story will be regarded as a failure by most of its readers. It is fine to mix genres, providing you have a good understanding of the two genres you are mixing – trying to mix more than two is unlikely to work. Trying to 'improve' or expand or subvert the genre is likely to alienate your readers. They are looking for something 'the same only different.' They want a well-told story with original elements, but within the accepted conventions of the genre. This is not to say that readers don't want surprises – they love surprises. But they have to be *genre-appropriate* surprises.

Switching genres midway is a definite no-no: if you start out as a Western and then introduce science fiction elements, the reader will feel cheated, unless you've established from the beginning that in this story world, both cowboys and aliens coexist. That should have been a great idea for a movie... If you are going to mix two genres, you have to make that clear from the start.

This isn't the place to go into the requirements for individual genres: that's a whole different kettle of worms. All I'll say here is: if you're going to write in a particular genre, make sure you know its conventions inside and out, and make sure it is a genre you *genuinely* love. Readers can always tell when you're faking it.

Your opening scene, or scenes, should be appropriate for your chosen genre. Give the reader what they expect from this type of story, what they came looking for, or you're unlikely to build your readership in the way you want. It might be too obvious to say this but... if you're writing comedy, then your opening scenes need to be funny – hell, your whole book needs to be a laugh-riot. If you're writing horror, then you need to begin with at least a hint of unease. Don't forget that everyone can be a critic these days, and you don't want a bunch of one- and two-star ratings from disappointed genre readers who never get beyond the opening pages.

6. Setting

First of all, the reader needs to know *where* and *when* the story is taking place. Physical location and historical period. If the story takes place at some time other than the present, or in some place other than our real world, this needs to be made obvious early in the story. Setting is not simply a painted backdrop against which the action takes place. Setting includes both physical and social elements, the 'milieu,' which can have a psychological effect on the people who live and work in that setting. What is the social hierarchy of the setting? Who is in charge? What sorts of people are present?

Setting can also have an emotional value. How you describe a place can establish the mood of your story. Does the story open on a crowded beach in bright sunshine? A dark alley after midnight? A suburban street, a decaying factory, or a mansion? As well as the man-made environment of buildings and machines, there are also natural elements such as the season of the year and the weather. Cold and frosty? Oppressively hot and humid? Rain? Wind? The more specific details you include, the better the reader will be able to see and feel your story setting. Don't forget textures and smells. This applies in a screenplay as much as a novel.

Often we first meet the hero in the 'ordinary world' in which he lives. This setting can help to characterise him – is he wealthy or poor? Professional or blue collar? Seeing where the hero lives helps us to understand his situation and life circumstances. A shabby bachelor apartment, a suburban home littered with children's toys and drawings, a sterile penthouse apartment – all indicate very different inhabitants. The things that people choose to surround themselves with – what makes them feel comfortable – tell us something about them as individuals. Quirky details can help bring a character to life. The hero's home or place of work can also help the reader identify with him, if it is similar to their own. Or perhaps something that they aspire to. Or perhaps the location is somewhere that reminds them of where they grew up.

Having said that, it is advisable to keep physical description to the absolute minimum. It is better to have a few *telling* details, that enable the reader to construct the rest of the picture themselves than it is to try and nail down every specific detail of a place. Because (a) readers like to contribute something themselves; (b) the details they add enable them to engage with the story more closely; and, (c) if readers see more than a couple of short paragraphs of description, they're likely to skim over them. Most modern readers don't like page after page of solid blocks of black text with no dialogue to break it up. This applies to novels as much as it does to screenplays. The one possible exception to this 'rule' is when you want to include a detail, but at the same time 'hide it in plain sight.' Clues in murder mysteries are often 'buried' in a pile of non-relevant descriptive detail.

The hero's 'ordinary world' is ordinary, but it should never be boring. There should always be a hint of the conflict to come (see *Foreshadowing* below). The purpose of showing the ordinary world is usually to give a sense of equilibrium in the hero's life before external factors come in to upset the balance. In which case, we are seeing the 'calm before the storm.' Or, we show the hero in the comfort of his everyday life, before he is hoisted out of it by events which drop him in a 'strange new world' where he is completely out of his depth. In this case, the ordinary world is designed to contrast with the world in which the adventure of the story will take place. We may also get a sense that the hero is *hiding* in his everyday world, afraid to face the adventure that is out there. Another function that the ordinary world can serve is to show a good place that the hero wants to protect and preserve. It may be the thing that he is fighting *for* when he goes off to tackle the bad guys. They pose a threat to the existence of this ordinary world. In this type of story, the hero often 'comes home' at the end of the story. Conversely, the ordinary world might be somewhere that the hero needs to escape from or to change significantly. Its ordinary state may be one of injustice or oppression. His world may be a metaphorical 'prison' that the hero needs to get out of. Or the world may be 'sick' – and the hero must go off on a quest to gain a 'magic elixir' that he can bring back and use the cure the sickness. This sort of 'Fisher King' mythology underlies the 'Hero's Journey' of Christopher Vogler's story model in *The Writer's Journey*.

The 'ordinary world' and the hero are closely linked in many stories. It will be a reflection of who he is as a person, and his circumstances within it are likely to be an indication of the weakness or flaw he will need to overcome during the course of his adventures. For example, if the hero is afraid of commitment, his everyday life will demonstrate that fact, and the story will force him to confront, and hopefully overcome, this fear. Although we may see the hero's ordinary world in equilibrium, we are likely to see that it is an uneasy or unhealthy equilibrium. The hero may seem comfortable there, but there is a sense that he isn't entirely happy being where he is. The hero is probably 'trapped,' and we should see some clue or demonstration of this. And we may get a sense of pressure building – such that he may not be able to put up with his current circumstances for much longer. He may be aware that he needs to escape to something better. Or he may have some vague sense that he can never be happy there until he has finally faced whatever inner demon haunts him. In other words, our man is ripe for an adventure – all he needs in that little push to set him off. And our story is about to give him exactly that. Part of the function of this 'ordinary world' is to show what the hero's life would continue to be like if the inciting incident didn't come along to upset the equilibrium.

The scene that introduces the hero in his ordinary world may foreshadow events that will take place in the 'strange new world' that is the setting for Act II. It may show a similar conflict on a smaller scale. Or we may see some entirely different action, but one which partially reveals the weakness the hero is going to have to overcome and/or the strength he is going to need to draw on. It will probably also demonstrate the value that will be at stake in the main plot. The setting – and the scene that introduces the hero in it – will demonstrate the hero's dominant characteristic: his attitude towards life, and the way in which he usually deals with problems.

Setting also includes the 'arena' in which the main action takes place – the 'new world' that the hero finds himself in when he begins his quest for a solution to his external problem. We will explore the 'new world' a little more when we get to it at the beginning of Act II.

With action-adventure heroes like James Bond or Indiana Jones, their 'ordinary' world is one of danger and excitement, which we are often introduced to in a prologue or pre-credits sequence. We see the hero in action, demonstrating heroic skills. Sometimes this is followed by a quiet scene in which we see our own everyday world, which the hero is going to protect from the villain. We are given a glimpse of what the hero is fighting for. Occasionally this comes later in Act I, just before the inciting incident, or even after it, so that we can see the impact of the inciting incident on 'our' world. Because it is our world, we are familiar with it and only need reminding of it, rather than introducing to it. In a whodunit, for example, the equilibrium may be upset before the story even begins – someone has committed a murder, and the corpse is discovered in Scene 1. The everyday world is implied by its absence – and the detective's job is to restore equilibrium by removing the cloud of suspicion that hangs over everyone by bringing the killer to justice.

7. Introduce the Hero

The storyteller's main goal is to evoke an emotional response in the reader. To make them *feel* something. We don't read a novel or watch a movie to see someone else have an emotional experience – we want to have that experience ourselves. I read that somewhere, I don't remember where, but it has stuck with me for a number of years and I think it is true. Some story theorists say that the emotions we experience as readers and viewers are received through the hero – we experience them *vicariously* – and this is achieved through identification with the hero. We put ourselves in his place, feeling what he feels. This happens as a result of our ability to empathise with other people. *Empathy* is our natural tendency to share what others are feeling – it is what makes our cheeks flush and our fists clench when we see someone else humiliated, or wince when we see them hurt themselves. We imagine what it feels like to be in their place. The argument goes that stories must be told subjectively, from the point of view of the hero, so that we can identify with them and have access to their emotions. An objective viewpoint on events would be external, unemotional, and uninvolved – the opposite of what a writer needs to achieve.

On the face of it, this argument makes some sense. And it may be *part* of the way we experience emotion evoked by story, but it is not the whole explanation. The fact is that we do not live our lives *through* others – moments when we feel empathy for others are relatively rare. Most of the time we are too wrapped up in our own feelings. Empathy is important – we need it to be able to see things from another person's perspective, otherwise we risk acting from purely selfish motives. Empathy is a quality that psychopaths lack: they are able to do what they do because they cannot imagine what their victims are feeling. But most of the time we experience our own emotions, not other people's. And the same is true when we are reading a novel or watching a film. We have a first-hand emotional experience of our own, not a second-hand one through one of the characters on the screen or page. We are more likely to watch what is happening to a character and feel *sympathy for* them, rather than *empathy with* them. It is a subtle difference. Some of the time we may feel the same emotion as the character in the story, but sometimes we feel a different emotion.

We might see a character on screen treated unjustly, to the point where they are completely humiliated – and we become *angry for them;* but the character on screen may stoically turn the other cheek. We don't have the same emotional experience as the character. We are angry at seeing another human being treated in this way. And we feel an element of frustration because we can't do anything to help the character. This is our emotional experience, not the character's. Similarly, there are occasions when we see something or read something in a story that makes us cry – even though no one in the story is crying. We are upset for them. Someone once said that if the audience cries, the hero doesn't need to.

Emotions – anger, love, hate, jealousy, despair (Spinoza identified 48 of them!) – are complicated things, but they are something that virtually all human beings have in common. Storytellers rely on the fact that there are certain types of situations that are almost guaranteed to evoke a particular emotional response, and they seek to create effective and specific examples of those situations. In stories, those emotions are generally evoked by situations that involve the hero (we worry about him), the ally or lover of the hero (we care about him/her because the hero does), or the villain (we hate him!).

It is a misconception, or an over-generalisation, to say that the reader must *like* the hero in order to identify with them. It is a bizarre quirk of the human mind that we are able to put ourselves in the position of people that we don't like, or whose actions we don't approve of. A situation we see all the time on television is someone breaking into a room and searching it to steal something – and no matter whether that character is a good guy or a bad guy, we find ourselves worrying that they will be caught red-handed. Wanting to do something 'naughty, to transgress, is a common human feeling, and so is the fear of being caught doing it. Fear of discovery – or of exposure or of humiliation – is, along with other fears of harm, the basis of tension and suspense, which are vital in storytelling. We don't actually have to *like* the hero. But we do need to be aware of what he is trying to achieve. What his objective is and – ideally – what his motivation is for achieving it.

Although I refer to the hero of a story as 'the hero' in this book, the main character (or protagonist) does not have to be a hero. Very successful stories have been written about characters who are definitely not 'good' people or characters which are anti-heroes. Examples include the Dirty Harry movies, *The Godfather,* and *Deathwish* and its sequels. You can even tell a story about someone who is truly monstrous – either literally or metaphorically. We do not need to identify with them, but we do need to be fascinated or intrigued by them. The key thing is that the reader must want to find out what is going to happen to this character. They must care whether or not he succeeds in achieving his story objective. We do not need to *approve* of his goal, his motivation, or his methods – but we do need to know what he is trying to do and why.

Of course, the current trend in popular and genre storytelling is to have a *likeable* hero that the reader can empathise and sympathise with. What does that mean in terms of plot structure? Making your character likeable is a good way of getting the reader involved in your story. If they like the character, they are more likely to want to see him succeed. We tend to like people who we recognise as being similar to ourselves, and who hold values of which we approve. 'Likeability' has been devalued somewhat in recent times. We are encouraged to click an on-screen button to 'like' something. People count the number of 'likes' they have accumulated. Our need for approval has been automated.

When a reader begins a story, one of the first things they look for is the 'hero.' It is difficult for them to become emotionally involved in a story until they know who they are supposed to be rooting for. This means that they are likely to attach themselves to the first remotely likeable person they come across. Like a baby chick imprinting on a rubber duck 'mommy.' This can sometimes work to your advantage. The movie *Witness* has the young Amish boy as its central character for the first scenes of the story. The sympathy the audience has for him is then transferred to the 'real' hero, Harrison Ford's John Book, when he becomes the boy's protector. That kind of transfer is tricky to pull off, but obviously it can be done. Hitchcock had even more fun with the idea in *Psycho*.

With stories about anti-heroes or 'avenging angels,' it often helps to have an ally or victim character that the audience can feel sympathy for. The hero himself may not be instantly likeable, but the fact that he cares for a sympathetic character makes him easier to accept as our 'hero.' There is an element of that in the original Holmes-Watson relationship. But in most stories, you are going to create a likeable hero, and you are going to make it easy for the reader by introducing this character early. He is either going to be in the opening scene, or in the first scene after the prologue.

Again, in order to make things easy for the reader, most modern stories – especially genre stories – are told subjectively. We see the action from the point of view of one or more viewpoint characters. As we have said, that doesn't necessarily mean that we experience the story *as* the hero, it is more along the lines of being a concerned observer who stands alongside the hero and sees everything as he sees it. As writers, we try and keep the reader as close to the hero as possible. When this isn't possible, as in the traditional 'whodunit' where the story works, in part, because we are not privy to the great detective's thought processes, the viewpoint character is the 'Watson' who sees everything the detective sees, but isn't able to make all of the deductions he does.

We've already mentioned narration, and the hero telling his own story in the first-person. That is a possibility and is the right choice for some stories and some characters. But for the most part, I would stick with a restricted third-person viewpoint. Restricted to standing at the hero's shoulder, seeing only what he sees. This gives you the option of occasionally standing beside another viewpoint character when the hero isn't around, without it seeming like too much of a cheat. Third-person omniscient – the view looking down from the gods – is something you can slip into occasionally if you need the equivalent of a wide shot of the scene in your novel, but I wouldn't try it for a whole novel. It is too distant – not emotionally involving. And it allows access to every character's thoughts and actions at all times, which is not always something that you want when you are trying to manage the reader's emotional response to a story.

And I wouldn't touch second-person viewpoint, unless you're writing a choose-your-own adventure story. *You sit down at the keyboard and notice that your coffee cup is empty. Do you (a) begin writing anyway, or (b) go into the kitchen, fire up the coffee machine, and then spend the rest of the morning alphabetising your canned goods...?*

People may accept second-person narration for a short story, or a brief section in a novel, but the fact that it is so rare means that it draws attention to the artificiality of the storytelling process, which has the effect of pulling the reader out of the story. The opposite of what you are trying to achieve. Don't use 'tricky' writing techniques and don't waste time. Get your hero on stage as soon as possible.

First Impressions

What impression does the hero make when we first see him? They say that you have something like thirty seconds or less to make your first impression when you go for a job interview. The same thing applies to the hero of a story. The generally stated 'rule' is that when the hero first appears, he should be doing something that allows him to demonstrate an admirable or likeable quality. This is the cliché Blake Snyder pokes fun at in the title of his book *Save the Cat!* The hero risks his own safety to save the cat. Villains kick the dog. Metaphorically, if you want to avoid cliché. Though if I remember correctly, Stephen King did actually have his villain kick the dog in *The Dead Zone:* I assume he was poking fun at clichés too.

When the hero first appears, we should see him in action. We should see what sort of person he is by what he does. We should never *tell* a reader how to feel about a character, we should let them form their own opinion based on the evidence before them. What someone is doing, their location and choice of clothing and props can all tell us something about them. How they speak and what they say also characterises them. What someone says and does is much more important than a page of physical description. Today it is rare for a writer to spend more than a couple of lines on the physical description of a character. Give the reader something uniquely memorable about the character, something that makes an impression – and that preferably evokes an emotional reaction – rather than serving up a slab of text that sounds like a witness describing the guy who just robbed the liquor store.

I'm not saying that you shouldn't know your character's hair colour, eye colour, height and brand of aftershave. Write them down for your own reference, so that you can refer to them and avoid having the character's eye colour change during the story – and add to these details as you make up new things about the character. But you don't need to include all of those details on the finished page. Because here's the thing: readers will ignore your character descriptions. Cover artists will ignore your character descriptions. And casting directors will ignore your descriptions. Sam Spade, portrayed by Humphrey Bogart, was described by his creator as a 'blond Satan.' And if I tell you that one famous action-adventure hero was described as looking like musician Hoagy Carmichael, would you know who I was referring to? Google an image of Hoagy Carmichael and see if you can figure it out. Spoiler alert: He doesn't look much like Sean Connery or Daniel Craig...

When I read, I always 'see' characters in my head. But when I re-read a book and hit the character description again, I'm usually surprised to find that the image in my head doesn't match what was on the page. My impression of the character caused me to see someone who looked different physically. I'm sure I'm not alone in this. When I'm writing, I also see the characters in my head. Often during the planning stage, I will think of the type of actor I think would play the part in a movie. I try to have two or three people in mind for each, so that I don't end up writing a character as, say, Jack Nicholson, because then I could fall into the trap of writing dialogue in his voice and using his facial expressions, which some readers will spot instantly. My over-the-top Shakespearean actor, Leo Fulbright, in *The Sword in the Stone-Dead* is a big man with a full beard. I initially describe him as a red-haired Viking. He's arrogant and does a lot of bellowing. I thought I was basing him on British actor Brian Blessed, with a soupçon of Kenneth Branagh, but as things went on I realised I was also seeing him as the late James Robertson

Justice with a little bit of Orson Welles. What I'm trying to say is, you need to give the *impression* of this type of person and allow the reader to provide the additional details that best enable them to see the character in their own mind's eye. Use whatever material you need – collect images of actors from the Internet or wherever if that helps – but use them to distil an essence that you can include on the page, rather than trying to make the reader see every detail that you see.

We've already said that where we encounter the hero – his ordinary world – affects how we view him as a person, so we don't need to mention that again. Again, use images if that helps you get a feel for a place, but again reduce this down to the essence. The other thing to remember in writing the hero's first appearance is that he hasn't just popped into existence for our entertainment – he had a life before this scene. What was he doing? Where was he going? Where was he coming from? He was probably planning to do something but is distracted from his purpose by the incident at the heart of the first scene. This incident draws our attention because it has distracted his.

In creating a likeable hero, we should – initially – see mainly his positive qualities. Don't reveal flaws or weaknesses until later, after the audience has become acquainted with him. Ideally, we should see the character as someone we recognise as being 'like us' in some way, but at the same time, we should see them as a unique individual. It's that 'same only different' rule again. We tend to prefer characters that are superficially like us – or like our idealised images of ourselves – in terms of age, appearance, and social background. But we also want our heroes sufficiently different from us to be interesting. This applies to the hero's home setting and employment too – keep it familiar, yet intriguingly different.

Creating characters is a subject for a book on its own, so we'll limit ourselves now to looking at some ways of creating a likeable hero using plot techniques.

How to Make People Like You

Having introduced your hero through his actions, you then need to keep attention focused on him so that the reader can get to know him better. The following are story situations that you can use in this process. Some of them can also be applied to the hero's very first appearance, but I'm grouping them here for ease of reference.

Make the Reader Feel Sorry for the Hero. Creating sympathy for the hero is one of the most effective and widely used techniques for establishing identification. Most of us will side with the underdog and want to see him triumph, it's that empathy/sympathy thing again – we've all felt like underdogs at some point in our lives. The way to create this sort of situation is to make the hero be the victim of some kind of undeserved misfortune or suffering. This misfortune can result from a specific incident, or from the hero's basic situation at the start of the story. Often we will see a hero who is not completely happy with the life he has. He is in some way 'making do,' having put his dreams on hold and putting up with a frustrating situation, either out of some sense of duty or simply because of apathy. The reader will feel sorry for a hero who is suffering and will hope he escapes or turns the tables on those who are causing his suffering, but there is a risk that the hero will seem weak if he is shown to be a victim. Readers prefer heroes who are strong and in control of their own lives, so it may be necessary to show that the hero had no choice but to become a victim of this particular tormentor. Or to show the hero's courage and/or sense of humour in the face of his suffering.

Make the Reader Worry About the Hero. Place the character in a situation where there is a threat to his life or physical safety, or in a situation where there is the threat of capture, exposure, embarrassment, or defeat. This creates tension and causes the reader to hope the hero will quickly escape this risky situation. Again there is a risk of making the hero look like a weak victim, and so care must be taken.

There are a number of other specific qualities which the hero might display:

Self-confidence is a quality we all probably wish we had more of, and we find it attractive in fictional characters, whether it is confidence in dealing with other people – the charismatic leader-type – or confidence in one's ability to take whatever action is necessary, regardless of danger, odds or moral implications. Or confidence to express one's feelings publicly, without worrying about the social acceptability of such a display – such confidence is particularly attractive to those of us who worry about 'making a scene'.

Competence. Make the hero good at his job – detectives in thrillers and gun-slingers in westerns are usually good at what they do, even if their methods are occasionally unorthodox.

Dependability. When the hero says he'll do something, he keeps his word no matter what. Or if he does break his word, he'll have a very good reason for it, and will do his utmost to make up for it later. This doesn't mean the hero can't lie – he can fib all he likes about events in his past, but if he promises to do something in the future, he can be depended on to do it. A promise, kept or broken, is a strong motif in fiction, and the idea of a 'gentleman' keeping his word is still important in stories about heroes. Accusing someone of breaking their word still carries a lot of weight in fiction.

Positive Attitude/Enthusiasm. The hero's attitude towards others and himself can help win the reader's sympathy. When things go wrong, a hero shouldn't complain and blame everyone but himself, he should take responsibility for his own mistakes, refer to his worsening circumstances with wry humour, and work out a way to solve his latest problem. And when he does achieve some kind of victory or performs some good deed, he doesn't boast about it and is embarrassed when others praise him. If someone criticises him, whether fairly or unjustly, he doesn't argue with them and defend himself, he trusts that the proof of his intentions will come across when his actions are successful. But if he sees someone else criticised unfairly, he will defend them. The hero always has sympathy for the suffering of others and tries to see things from other people's point of view. He may become angry, but he will always try to listen to a person's explanations. And he's willing to trust people, even when they've proved by previous actions that they aren't trustworthy.

Courage. Heroes take physical, social or financial risks to do what they believe is right or necessary. When a hero has the courage to risk losing his job rather than keep quiet about a scandal, the reader both admires and fears for his safety.

Fair play. The hero can never do anything underhand or sneaky to win: if he cheats or does something cowardly, he loses sympathy. This is what made the good guys in westerns always wait for the bad guy to draw first; what made the good guy in a swashbuckler always let the bad guy pick up his sword after disarming him; and what stopped the good girl in a romance from using sex to keep her man.

Volunteer. If a hero is faced with a challenge which requires great courage and which won't bring him much by way of glory or reward, the reader will feel sympathy for him if he volunteers. But if the adventure ahead will bring him fame and/or fortune, then the reader will have more sympathy for him if he doesn't volunteer, and modestly waits to be called on.

Self-Sacrifice. The hero is someone who is willing to sacrifice his own needs on behalf of others. Most people think a hero must be strong or brave, but these qualities come second to his willingness to give up something of value – perhaps even his life – to help a cause or group. This sacrifice is linked to the question of What's at stake? And the idea of character growth or change. Many heroes experience a kind of 'death and rebirth,' symbolically giving up some cherished aspect of their old life as the price of entering a new one. Sacrifice only results in reader sympathy if it is felt that the cause the hero is willing to die for is important and right. The reader must feel that the hero has no other choice and that his sacrifice will bring a genuine and worthwhile improvement for some other person or persons. If there is an alternative, the reader will expect the hero to choose it, otherwise his death will seem a stupid waste rather than a noble act. There is a link here with the idea of the volunteer too: if the hero chooses martyrdom because he knows that a glorious death means he will be remembered as a hero forever, his motive for choosing sacrifice is not sympathetic.

A Weakness or Flaw that Makes Him Vulnerable. Another way of making the hero sympathetic is to give him a normal human trait which the reader will recognise and identify with – such as feeling awkward around someone he's attracted to, or nervous in a high-pressure social situation such as a test or job interview. The hero's character weakness might also be something the villain can exploit later, providing the potential for suspense and a near-defeat for the hero towards the end of the story. The hero's weakness might be as simple as lack of knowledge or experience. Or difficulty in controlling his temper. Or perhaps it is self-deception, lying to himself about something in order to justify pursuit of an unwise goal – this self-deception could lead to a plot complication at a critical point. Or the hero might be indecisive, causing him to miss a great opportunity. The hero may also have a more series character flaw – sometimes referred to as a 'tragic flaw' – that usually arises as a result of some secret, traumatic incident in the hero's past. You should probably introduce the hero's main flaw – if he has one – in Sequence 2, where it has a function in the plot, unless you can introduce it in Sequence 1 in a way that makes him seem vulnerable in a good way. Otherwise, you might just want to give a hint of his flaw at this point, and concentrate on the hero's positive qualities, rather than negative qualities and flaws.

One final way of making the hero sympathetic is as a result of his goal and his motivation, which we will come to shortly.

8. Theme

Here we learn what *value* is at stake in the story. The writer decides here what is 'good' behaviour that will be rewarded, e.g. 'justice' or 'freedom,' and what is 'bad' behaviour that will be punished, e.g. 'injustice' or 'tyranny.' Early in the story, there is often a line of dialogue or an incident that reveals the question that the story will explore – the 'thematic' argument that it will prove. Someone, probably not the hero, poses a question or makes a statement. It will be subliminal rather than blatant, and will only become obvious in retrospect or on re-reading. At the heart of every story, there is a value at stake. The hero represents or personifies the positive side of this value – the virtue – and the villain or rival represents the negative value, the vice. These two opposing viewpoints effectively provide a 'thematic argument' in the story. The argument is settled, or proved, when one side wins and the other side loses.

One of the finest examples of this, written over 400 years ago, is William Shakespeare's *Othello*. Othello is a warrior who has achieved success as a result of his bravery in war. He is very much in love with his wife, Desdemona, and she with him. Iago is jealous of Othello's success, and so sets out to destroy him and take his place. He determines to do this by convincing Othello that Desdemona has been unfaithful to him. Iago provides 'evidence' that proves this. Driven into a jealous rage, Othello murders Desdemona. Iago's guilt is uncovered and he is sentenced to death. Iago's jealousy destroys him and takes away any chance of achieving the success he coveted. Othello's jealousy destroys him and the person he loved most. This being a tragedy, both hero and villain finish up badly – proving the thematic argument that 'jealousy destroys the jealous man and the thing he loves most' – or something along those lines.

Back in the first half of the 20th century, playwrights were advised to begin with theme – to decide up front what 'moral argument' their story was going to prove. During the latter part of the 20th century, the advice – especially to screenwriters – tended to be: Ignore theme as it will arise organically out of whatever you write. The argument was that you couldn't help but introduce a theme, subconsciously, through your choice of what constitutes 'good' and 'bad' behaviours. I think the right approach lies somewhere between the two. I don't think you should ever try and force a moral into a story because the chances are that what you write will be too obviously trying to prove a point. Theme belongs in the subtext – it should be between the lines of dialogue, not in speeches that are 'on the nose.' But I do think you should be aware of what value – virtue versus vice – is at stake, as this can guide you in the direction of the incidents that will provide the greatest dramatic effect in your story. If you know what is at stake – for the hero and his world, and for the reader – you can better work out what sort of thing to include to place that value in jeopardy.

Theme is a tricky thing to get a handle on. I would recommend Stanley D. Williams' book *The Moral Premise* if you want to explore it further.

9. The Hero's Internal Problem or 'Lack'

The hero doesn't just appear one day in order to put a stop to the villain's evil plan: he is meant to be a living, breathing human being with a life of his own. One way to make him seem more human is to give him problems of his own – situations that existed before the story opened. There is usually something missing in the hero's life. This is sometimes referred to as the hero's *lack*. The thing he most often lacks is a fulfilling relationship with another adult. Usually, this means there's no romance in his life. Another possibility is being in the wrong job – having failed to find a vocation that makes the best of his abilities and provide a sense of personal fulfilment. Sometimes the hero has achieved material success or excelled in a particular job or sport, but still lacks a sense of personal fulfilment.

The external 'story problem' caused by the villain or opponent will also provide the hero with an opportunity to do something about this lack. It may turn his lack into something that he can no longer live with or ignore. As the story opens, the hero has had this problem or lack for some time, but has never felt motivated to do anything about it. He has been coping with it or ignoring it or denying it. There should be a sense, early in Act I, that his unhappiness is reaching a point where he is going to have to do something about it. The hero's lack can be something that helps the reader identify with him. Most of us have felt dissatisfied with our jobs at some point in our lives. And we all know what it is like to feel lonely and in need of a soul-mate. It could be that he has been separated from his family and/or friends because of a relocation or a divorce. There is often some event in the hero's backstory that is the cause of his present lack. Or some unpleasant event that was caused by it. There is some unresolved issue – the exact nature of which we may not learn until Sequence 5 when he unburdens himself to someone he has come to trust.

The lack may be caused by the hero's flaw or weakness, some aspect of his personality that negatively affects his behaviour. We might get a hint of this early in Act I – 'something' is holding him back, preventing him from finding happiness and fulfilment in his life – but we won't normally reveal his negative characteristics until the reader has had a chance to get to know him and like him. We also need to introduce his *external* conflict before we get to his internal one. The hero's lack is something that he cannot overcome on his own. That is why the challenge is so important in his life – though he will only see this in retrospect – because it forces him to interact with someone – an ally or a lover – who can help him overcome his lack.

10. Foreshadowing – Coming Soon: Conflict!

'Conflict' comes from a Latin word for the act of striking together, and is used to indicate when two things are incompatible or in opposition. Think of opposing forces in collision. Imagine two trains hurtling down the track towards each other, neither one able to give way to the other. That's the sort of feeling you need to evoke in the first act of your story. From very early on there should be a sense of impending collision. In Act I one of the promises a writer makes to the reader is: Stay in your seat, there is a conflict coming, and it is going to be worth seeing.

We can't actually *have* the main conflict of the story begin until the end of Act I, when a challenge is issued to the hero and he commits himself to fighting to achieve something. Until then, we have to keep the reader's attention by introducing them to our two freight trains, and showing them being set on a collision course. They may only be moving slowly to begin with, but they're going to pick up speed, and eventually... *bam!* In Act I we advertise, as strongly as possible, that *conflict is coming!* How blatantly we do this depends on the type of story we are telling. If our story opens with action, then we're already showing minor conflicts, and can give an indication that these are connected to, or may lead up to, a much bigger conflict. For example, someone may undertake an act that is bound to trigger a reprisal. We are looking for the snowball that sets off the avalanche.

Conflict doesn't have to involve physical confrontation – it can be an emotional or mental struggle. A battle of wills. Conflict, as we have already mentioned, also exists within an individual. Imagine someone who is painfully shy who wants to ask a classmate out on a date. There are family feuds; romantic misunderstandings; financial challenges; all manner of small-scale conflicts and dilemmas.

If our story has a 'slow-build' opening, it is especially important to weave in suggestions that something important is going to happen soon. There needs to be a shadow hanging over things, or some sort of deep undercurrent. A force building that must eventually explode into action of some kind. Watching someone fight to control their temper can be just as dramatic to watch as an eruption of violence – more so if the circumstances are set up correctly. In the first few pages of a story, you need to plant the idea that change is coming. However calm the ordinary world looks, *something is not quite right.* A situation is developing. This will probably be related, in part, to the actions of an opponent or rival. And in part to the hero's internal conflict. At this early stage, the hero is not yet motivated to do anything about either his external or internal problems – he is doing his best to cope with them or ignore them. He may not even be consciously aware of the existence of either. One way to demonstrate this is to have the hero trying to complete some small-scale task and failing to attain the desired outcome. As he expresses his frustration – or represses these feelings – we see this as symbolic of a much deeper frustration and unhappiness.

Leading the reader to anticipate that conflict will erupt in the near future is an excellent way of capturing their attention and keeping them turning the pages. Conflict is a fundamental part of storytelling and, as we mentioned earlier, having promised this conflict, you have got to deliver on the promise later, and we will look at some ways you can do that in later sequences.

11. Opposition: The Antagonist

The antagonist is the second most important character in a story. His function is to provide opposition – to challenge the hero. He *actively* opposes the hero, preventing him from achieving his external objective. The actions of the antagonist place the hero under immense pressure – and we see the best, and worst of people, when they feel threatened. Conflict is the basis of drama – without it, there is no story. Alfred Hitchcock said that the better the villain, the better the story. Hero and villain must be worthy opponents for one another. We judge the hero by the size of the obstacles he must overcome to achieve his objective, admiring most those who tackle incredible odds. The outcome of a story is less important than the *struggle,* because it is the struggle that provides the reader with a sustained emotional experience and an insight into character, rather than the winning or losing of a battle. Hero and villain must be closely matched to ensure that their final confrontation is seen to be closely fought.

The hero and the antagonist must have goals that are mutually exclusive – there can be no middle-ground or compromise option. If the hero succeeds in achieving his goal, the villain or rival – as a consequence – must fail. And vice versa. Each will want to ensure that the other fails. If the hero advances a step towards his goal, there must be a counter-thrust from the villain, causing a setback for the hero. And vice versa. It is the steps the villain takes in order to thwart the hero's plans that provide the complications of the plot. As the adversaries act and react, the conflict rises and keeps the reader anxious to know the outcome.

The hero's antagonist, nemesis, or rival – the 'villain' if there is one – may not appear on stage in Act I. But the reader should become aware of his presence and his actions. In some types of story, it is important that the identity of the villain is kept secret until the end of Act II, or even into Act III. He often remains offstage, and we see instead the actions of his 'soldiers' and his second-in-command, his henchman. The antagonist doesn't have to be a 'villain' in the traditional sense – he can be a rival seeking the same promotion or the hand of the same romantic interest, or he can be an opponent in a sport or some other contest. The only requirement of the antagonist is that he is someone whose goals bring him into conflict with the hero. Romance genre stories typically have no central villain as such: there may be a rival for the heroine's affections, but the main antagonism occurs between the hero and the heroine: they serve as both the 'love interest' and antagonist for each other.

Where there is a villain or opponent, he should not be created as some guy in a black hat who does bad things for the sake of creating opposition in the story. Always remember that the villain is the 'hero' of his own story: he should be created with much the same attention to detail as the hero. The villain has a strong motivation of his own for doing what he is doing. He has his own backstory, and often feels he is 'owed' by society for some past 'injustice' he believes – or imagines – that he suffered. As the story opens, the villain has an objective and has chosen an external goal which he believes will enable him to achieve this objective. And his plan to achieve this goal is already in motion.

The challenge or inciting incident is usually caused by the actions of the villain – or his foot-soldiers – and is the first time that an action in the villain's plan *directly* impacts on the hero's life. Earlier stages of the villain's plan may have had a negative impact on the hero's everyday world, but the inciting incident is when the hero can no longer ignore what is happening. Someone once referred to it as the 'Popeye moment' – that point at which the hero says "That's all I can stands, I can't stands no more!"

The antagonist represents a point of view that is direct opposition to the hero's. If the hero strongly believes in justice, for example, the antagonist operates in a manner that is totally unjust. If the hero believes in serving others, in battle or in society, then the villain is totally self-serving. The antagonist is, for this reason often described as the hero's shadow. Where the hero represents light, the antagonist is darkness. Many stories, as we have already seen, present their theme in the form of an argument between two opposing points of view. Even the simplest of tales often demonstrates that 'bad' behaviour is wrong and should be punished, and 'good' behaviour is right and should be rewarded. Stories tend to reinforce the values of the dominant culture. Except when they deliberately do not...

When we move from children's picture books to novels and plays, the thematic argument becomes more subtle, and we have stories of opposites such as justice/injustice or justice/revenge. In Shakespeare's *Othello,* the theme is jealousy versus trust. In *Star Wars,* freedom versus oppression. And then we can move on to stories where the argument is not so clear-cut: the 'right' and 'wrong' are not so clearly defined. Here we have stories where the hero is forced to choose the 'lesser of two evils' or perhaps the 'greater of two goods.' Sometimes there is no 'right' answer, and we have to make a choice and then live with the consequences. These stories are difficult to write – and read – but are often the most rewarding.

The hero-villain relationship is central to the thematic argument. At the simplest level, the hero represents virtue and the villain represents vice. But as we have said, the villain also represents the hero's own shadow – his dark side. The villain embodies an aspect of his own character that the hero is afraid of and denies. Where the villain often feels he is owed by society – and intends to take what he believes is due to him; the hero often feels a sense of guilt, and that he must 'atone' for some crime or sin committed in the past. At some point, he failed to live up to his own high standards, and so feels that he is a failure. His opinion of himself is dominated by this one past mistake. No-one likes to feel guilty, and the hero feels angry if someone unwittingly reminds him of this event – even though he beats himself up about it all the time. The villain represents who the hero is afraid he could become if he drops his vigilance and allows himself to wander along the 'wrong path.' The villain openly demonstrates behaviour the hero knows he is capable of himself, and he is ashamed of this part of himself.

It is important that the antagonist is a visible, specific character, rather than an abstract concept. If the hero is battling the 'evils of society,' those evils should be personified in the form of a single, recognisable individual. The villain can't be a group – such as 'the Mafia' or 'the Nazis' or 'the Triads' or whatever – he must be a single person from within that group who represents their activities and their values. A personal, one-to-one confrontation is much more effective than having the hero facing unfocused opposition. The reader needs to be able to focus their fear and hatred on a single person!

As previously mentioned, creating a villain who is a visible individual does not necessarily mean revealing that individual's identity. But the reader should be aware of the existence of the villain as a result of his actions. Or through the actions of his agents. We often see more of the villain's henchman than we do of the villain – think of the steel-jawed 'Jaws' in the James Bond films, or 'Oddjob,' or Darth Vader. Hero and villain may not meet until the midpoint of the story, or perhaps not until Act III at the climax when they have their face-to-face showdown. The first time we really become aware of the antagonist as an opponent to the hero is at the moment of the challenge or inciting incident. We may not know who the opponent is, but we become aware that there are forces of opposition. This adds a hint of danger – the idea of a threat to the hero's everyday world or his well-being. The inciting incident upsets the balance of the hero's world, forcing him to make a decision – to choose how he will respond.

Our subject here is the function of character within the plot, so this is not the place to go into detail about creating a villain – but I will include a few notes below about the sort of qualities that make a villain villainous. By design, these are usually mirror-opposites of the qualities of a hero.

Creating Antipathy for the Villain

Getting the reader to hate the villain is easier than getting them to like the hero: nasty actions are far more memorable and dramatic than nice ones! Here are some of the techniques which can be used for making the reader loathe the villain:

Abuse of power. The typical villain is attracted to power for its own sake, and as a result may be a sadist or a bully. A sadist deliberately causes physical or mental harm to another person, and the appeal of this action to the sadist is the sense of control – of power – they have over the body or mind or life of another person. The reader will hate someone who enjoys causing pain, whether that pain is physical torture or some form of emotional domination or abuse.

Motive. The villain or rival has his own goal and motivation. His goal and the hero's are mutually exclusive. The villain or rival will actively try to ensure that the hero fails. If a hero has an admirable motive, the reader wants him to succeed in achieving his goal. The reader must want the villain to fail, so the motivation given to the villain must be far from admirable. The villain should act out of pure selfishness, and his victims should be people who don't deserve to be hurt. Actions in themselves are not guarantees for creating reader antipathy – an assassin can seem almost sympathetic if his intended victim is made evil enough – would the reader side with the would-be assassin or with Hitler? Similarly, Hamlet's desire to avenge his father's death cause him to plot Claudius' death, but his motive means that we sympathise with Hamlet, not Claudius. Motive helps us assign a character's relative place within the moral spectrum, which makes possible heroes who are con men, thieves and adulterers.

Betrayal. A hero must keep his promise or suffer pangs of guilt if he is forced to break it. The villain feels no such qualms. Villains break their promises and betray trusts. If we tell someone something in confidence and they reveal our secret to everyone, we feel betrayed and no longer trust that person. A person who does not keep his word, who breaks an oath, is not a sympathetic character.

The Usurper or Interloper. If a person takes up a position of power which they have not earned, particularly if they displace the rightful heir, they immediately attract resentment. They are seen as over-ambitious, self-asserting and self-appointed. If someone takes up a position which they weren't invited to fill and which no one wanted them to fill, they lose reader sympathy. This antipathy isn't permanent, it lasts only until the usurper proves that he deserves the position and wins the respect of others, and is accepted, receiving his 'invitation' after the fact. Heroes can begin as interlopers – outsiders who are resented because they take on the role of leader or problem-solver without being asked – but they always, eventually, win acceptance and approval. They are vindicated and prove themselves worthy of the position. It is a situation the reader can sympathise with – we have all gone into situations where we feel like interlopers, and tried to gain acceptance. The villain never wins the reader's acceptance.

Resentment. There are other ways to get the audience to dislike the villain. Things we dislike in people in real life work just as well with fictional characters. The well-educated and highly articulate Hannibal Lecter in *Silence of the Lambs* brings out in the reader and viewer all the resentment they have ever felt for sadistic school masters and others who have tried to convince us that they are our intellectual superiors. This probably accounts for the success of classically trained British actors as villains in American movies.

Insanity. The other quality we find disturbing in Hannibal Lecter is his warped world view. We are afraid of people who don't see reality the same way we do, whose behaviour we regard as irrational or socially unacceptable. It is impossible to reason with such a character, to persuade them that their 'reality' is incorrect. And if the villain manages to persuade others that his reality is the truth - as Hitler did, at least for a while - the reader's sense of fear and dislike grows. The kind of insanity portrayed in films and novels is usually psychotic or sociopathic in nature, though its accuracy in clinical terms is usually suspect. The danger here, of course, is that there is a fine line between creating an over-the-top movie psycho and perpetuating stereotypes about mental illnesses such as schizophrenia.

Attitude. The villain's attitude toward life, himself, and other people works in the opposite way to the hero's. The hero may be humourless and unable to laugh at his own mistakes; when things go wrong he will complain and blame others around him, never accepting responsibility himself. If things go right, he takes all the credit and boasts about 'his' success. He never worries about hurting other people's feelings, he never trusts anyone, he judges people harshly and never listens to their explanations or point of view. He favours the rich and powerful over the poor and powerless. He is a hypocrite. He treats other people as if they only exist to serve his purposes.

Empathy with the Devil: The Antagonist's Redeeming Features
If he is a fully-rounded character, the villain will almost certainly have some aspect which makes him sympathetic, or at the very least their motives will be understandable. Every person is the hero of his or her own life story, and so the villain must see himself in that light. He somehow justifies his actions to himself. Perhaps he believes that the ill-treatment he himself has suffered in the past justifies the way he treats people now. Maybe he thinks that everyone feels the same way he does, but most people don't have the courage to act on those feelings, or they simply pretend to be good guys. To depict the villain honestly, the writer must allow the reader to know the villain's side of the story.

Just as the hero can have flaws and weaknesses, the villain can have minor virtues - maybe his is a man of honour who keeps his word; maybe he is devoted to his family; maybe he has some quality which makes him vulnerable; or maybe he was very badly treated at some point in his life, making his hate and anger understandable to some extent. The idea is not to make the villain a sympathetic character, to persuade the reader to like him, but rather to give him some qualities which allow the villain to win some respect. A villain who is not a completely one-dimensional bad guy is a much worthier opponent for the hero.

But what the writer can't do is turn the sadistic, insane usurper into a sympathetic character, or the reader will feel confused and cheated: the problem won't have been solved, it will have been waved away by a magic wand. The only time a character can legitimately perform such an about-turn is if they have been pretending to be a sadistic, insane usurper in order to accomplish some greater noble purpose, or if the image of the character as a sadistic, insane usurper was a misconception, a reputation created by his enemies which was far from the truth.

12. The Challenge or Inciting Incident

This is also referred to as the exciting force, the point of attack, the catalyst, or 'call to adventure.' We refer to it as a challenge – or 'throwing down the gauntlet' – because it puts the hero on the spot and says 'here's your chance to do something about it.' The hero is aware of some problem in his world and/or feelings of unhappiness in his own life, and now he is being offered an opportunity to take action and – possibly – fix these problems. That is the challenge he is given. Put up, or shut up. This doesn't have to be the equivalent of someone challenging him to a duel. It could be the arrival of someone who just might be the person he could spend the rest of his life with. The challenge is a story's first major plot point and is an event that sets off a chain of action and reaction that continues throughout the rest of the story. Everything up to this point has been introduction and preparation. This event sets the story in motion. This means that the moment the challenge is issued is an important one, and needs to be of an appropriate emotional intensity and duration. It will probably unfold in a scene more than a single page long. A single line of dialogue wouldn't be sufficient.

There are three ways in which the challenge might be presented. In order of dramatic intensity they are: a specific action, which offers the strongest impact; the arrival of a message or piece of news; or a situation which builds over time until it reaches a head. Or it could be a combination of these things.

The challenge should be an event that *demands* a response from the hero. His initial response may be 'This is not my problem' or 'I can't do anything about it,' which is fine, but he cannot ignore or remain unaware of the challenge. The inciting incident upsets the balance of the hero's world and effectively makes his situation worse. He may decide that he'll do nothing and just live with it, but he has to make a decision. The challenge can be a positive event – a chance for a new romance; an offer of a new job; or an opportunity to do something he has always wanted to do. Even if the situation he is faced with is an unpleasant problem, it still offers him an opportunity to do something to change a life that he does not find entirely satisfactory. He doesn't know it yet, but it will also offer him a chance to face and overcome his own inner demons.

The challenge presents the hero with a dilemma – it provides him with an opportunity to change a frustrating situation, but accepting the challenge has risks attached to it. Challenges never offer a safe option – there is always some associated danger. The risk may be physical, emotional, or mental. Which of these you choose will be related to whatever the hero fears most, because the challenge – and the story – is designed to force him to face this fear. The challenge should also be such that accepting it will put the hero into conflict with someone, and perhaps even with himself. A policeman may have to commit a crime. A pacifist may have to fight. Choosing this romantic partner may put him at odds with his own family or social group. The dilemma the hero faces is that while the challenge offers him an opportunity to achieve something he *desires,* accepting it brings with it the danger of having to face something he fears.

The challenge is a crucial part of the set-up of a story. It provides the hero with a potential objective or *goal* and *motivation* – to achieve *this action* (whatever that is in the story) and achieve an improvement in his life circumstances. Do this and return your life to a new and better equilibrium. The challenging situation is usually brought about, either directly or indirectly, by the actions of the antagonist. It may be a stage in the plan he is currently putting into action, or it could be an accidental by-product of his plan. Obviously, the antagonist won't care that his actions are inconveniencing or even harming others.

Sometimes the challenge is actually issued by another character, a messenger or 'herald.' As well as issuing the challenge, this character serves to tell the hero – and the reader – that significant changes are coming. In *High Noon,* the herald is a telegraph clerk who brings Gary Cooper word that his enemies are out of jail and heading into town to kill him. The herald can be any character – major or minor – and may be a positive, negative, or neutral figure. The villain, or one of his men, might issue a direct challenge to the hero. Or they may act in such as way as to force the hero to make a decision. Or the herald can be a friend or mentor who urges the hero to accept the opportunity to improve his life.

The end of Sequence 1 provides the hero with an opportunity to do something to improve his present situation. The hero is aware of the challenge, but he doesn't actually respond to the challenge yet – that is the function of Sequence 2. The challenge can be quite disorienting for the hero, as it forces him to acknowledge that his world is unstable and that action will be required to restore its balance.

Yikes! That seems like a hell of a lot of stuff to include in just one-eighth of your story, doesn't it? The thing is, the first two sequences of your story have to include everything that your reader needs to understand what follows. And they have to include everything that you need to write a full-length story. One of the reasons that a lot of my old story ideas fizzled out after about 20,000 words was because I wasn't setting them up properly, so they had nowhere to go. In Act I, you're putting in place the things that you'll need to create that *looong* middle section, and also lighting the fuse for the major turning point that will be your *crisis* at the end of Act II, and also planting whatever information you're going to need to pull the surprise solution out of the bag at the *climax* in Act III, so that this doesn't look like a cheat when you get there.

I used to be writing 'middle stuff' when I should have been including all the Act I stuff. As you can see from the 12-point list, there's plenty to go at.

I mentioned previously that the quarters and eighths were only approximate measures, and that any one of them could be longer or shorter than the absolute numerical value of the fraction. Sequence 1 can be more or less than 15 pages of your 120-page screenplay, or 10,000 words of your 80,000-word novel. In a fast-paced adventure, you can often set-up your story elements in a lot shorter time. If you're introducing a lot of characters and/or a complex situation, you may need more. Do whatever feels appropriate for your story. But if you're coming up massively short, go back and check you've included everything. And if you're coming in way too long, check that you haven't started in on the middle stuff.

There's no reason why you can't put 'Section 2 stuff' in the first eighth of your story and tick things off early, but if you're starting to include 'Section 3 stuff,' you should probably ask yourself if you're doing it for the right reason.

Sequence 2: Responding to the Challenge

Previously on Plot Basics... We introduced the hero and saw him issued with a challenge. What will he decide to do? Once the challenge has been presented, the hero can no longer remain in the comfort of his ordinary world. He may hesitate to take up the challenge, but eventually he has got to act. There would be no story otherwise. The function of Sequence 2 is to show the hero's response to the challenge that has just been issued and to take him up to the point where he accepts the challenge and sets out on his quest to achieve his story objective. This sequence of the story is often referred to as the hero's 'refusal of the call.' It shows the protagonist's reaction to the inciting incident, and at the same completes the set-up stage of the story, taking us up to the turning point at the end of Act I. Blake Snyder refers to this part of the story as the 'debate,' as the hero and the audience are presented with both sides of the argument, for and against accepting the challenge. This sequence builds to the point where the hero accepts the challenge and chooses to go on a quest to achieve some objective that he believes will provide a solution to his external story problem. At the moment this happens, a question is posed in the reader's mind: Will the hero achieve his objective? This is sometimes called the 'major dramatic question,' and it is not answered until the climax of the story in Act III.

I've identified 16 headings for things to include in this sequence, though some of them are quite short, and some of them are plot functions that will occur simultaneously in the same scene – so again, this sequence is really only for ease of presentation.

1. Initial Reaction to the Challenge
2. The Hero's Greatest Fear
3. Refusal of the Call – The Reluctant Hero
4. Backstory
5. Subplots – The B-story & Other Secondary Plotlines
6. Consequences of Refusing the Challenge
7. Pressure to Accept the Challenge
8. Lock-in – Why Doesn't the Hero Run Away?
9. Introducing Other Major Characters: Ally, Romance, Mentor, Henchman
10. Stakes – What is the Worst Possible Thing That Could Happen?
11. Motivation
12. Decision: Accepting the Challenge
13. The Hero's Goal
14. Major Dramatic Question

15. Crossing the Threshold – Point of No Return
16. Turning Points

1. Initial Reaction to the Challenge

At the time the challenge was issued, the hero may have also been given a warning of some danger or tragedy that was associated with accepting the challenge. Or the nature of the challenge may have made it obvious that there was some risk involved in accepting it. The challenge should be such that it is not an easy thing for the hero to accept – there must be pros and cons in agreeing to take it on. The challenge having been issued, the first thing we will see is the hero's immediate *emotional* response. This will be instantaneous and *in character*. It will be typical of how the hero responds to difficult situations. Does the hero deny the challenge? Is he angry? Afraid? Amused? How does what he *says* about this situation compare to the actions he takes? After this first emotional reaction, the hero may return to his mundane life. He tries to go back to his life as it used to be. But the challenge has changed things. Perhaps he is now always looking over his shoulder. Perhaps he becomes distracted and unable to concentrate on anything except the nature of the challenge. Or perhaps his dissatisfaction with his normal life grows to a point where his present situation is no longer tolerable. The hero may or may not make some attempt to deal with the external problem at this point, depending on how much it affects him personally. He may see what he believes to be an easy solution – a quick fix or sticking-plaster job – and decide to use it. But this will be a temporary solution at best and is more likely to make the situation worse rather than better.

2. The Hero's Greatest Fear?

Heroes are not invincible. Even a superhero like Superman had weaknesses – Kryptonite and Lois Lane. I think the reason why the television show *Smallville* and the Christopher Reeve *Superman* movies appealed to audiences is that they got the Clark Kent part of the character right: he was warm and vulnerable and lacked self-confidence when it came to relationships. He was as 'human' as the rest of us. The more recent movies (as I write this) have somehow lost that, and concentrated on the superhuman side of the character, the 'man of steel,' making the movies seem cold, distant, and uninvolving.

James Bond gets all kinds of gadgets and supercars from Q, but he tends to lose these along the way so that in the final battle he's down to his own ingenuity and physical stamina – which has probably just been weakened by some cruel torture. The writers make him vulnerable, which makes us feel for him, and wonder whether he can succeed in the final battle.

What this means for your story is that you need to think about where your hero's vulnerability lies. This vulnerability is one of the things that makes a character likeable and helps a reader identify with them. A weakness engages the reader's empathy, sympathy, and/or curiosity. The hero's weakness is sometimes identified by another character, who challenges him after some demonstration of flawed behaviour: 'You know what your trouble is...?' The challenges that the hero faces in the story will bring his weakness into sharp relief – and the beliefs and behaviours associated with it will 'explode' at some point.

The hero's greatest fear is linked to some traumatic experience, a 'ghost from the past' or 'demon' that haunts him. The hero's greatest fear is having to face that traumatic situation again. This greatest fear has its roots in some – usually unstated – child hood trauma, which is symbolised by some more recent event in his backstory. This may have involved an emotional loss – the death of a loved one – or rejection, betrayal, abandonment, humiliation, or some past failure in life. It affects how the hero views the world, and it influences the actions he takes. This thing that he fears most is what he will have to face and hopefully overcome, during his 'darkest hour,' during the crisis at the end of Act II. In Sequence 2, the 'ghost' should be implied, but details should be withheld. This is not the time for masses of exposition or backstory. The full details are sometimes revealed in Sequence 5, in a scene that demonstrates how the hero has grown to trust his closest ally or his lover.

We have already mentioned the 'flawed hero' story. It features a story where the hero's inner conflict and fears lie at the heart of the story, and where a character development arc runs alongside the main plot line. For the moment, we will concentrate on stories without character development, and where the hero's fears impact on external plot development.

Secret Wish – Want versus Need

The fact that there is something lacking in the hero's life, some need that is unfulfilled, means that he has a secret wish or secret desire. He wants something that will resolve his need. He may not know what it is that he actually needs – and he may fixate on something that won't actually fulfil his need. In many movies, the hero believes wealth or some other form of 'winning' will fulfil his need; or that sex with a woman with big boobs will fulfil his need, when what he really needs is a proper relationship with another person. This means that the hero often chooses to go for the *wrong goal* at the end of Act I – he chooses something he *wants* rather than what he actually *needs*.

Want versus need is often highlighted by story theorists. In a romance, the hero often goes for the wrong girl, and mistakes lust for love, choosing 'want-girl' instead of 'need-girl.' The hero's lack tells us what he really needs in life – it is the source of his hopes and dreams. This dream or secret wish is something he rarely shares with others. He may even mock it as unrealistic himself. This dream will never come true for him until he overcomes his flaw. This dream foreshadows the ending – if the hero successfully meets the challenge and achieves his ultimate (correct) objective, his secret wish may come true with little additional effort on his part. He gets it as his reward for 'virtuous' behaviour.

The hero may share his secret wish with the co-protagonist in Sequence 5 in a scene that demonstrates the trust and respect that has developed between the two characters.

The Hero's Lack and the Challenge
The hero's feelings of unhappiness or lack of fulfilment existed before the story opens. He has not, until this point, been motivated to do anything about this. He has endured these circumstances, denied them, or ignored them. There should be some hint in the early pages of the story that this situation exists – and that the hero won't be able to live with things the way they are for much longer. As well as the external conflict that is brewing and threatening to destabilise the hero's world, there is an internal storm boiling up as well. The situation is building in such a way that an explosion of emotion and/or action cannot be too far away.

Readers do not identify with characters who sit and wallow in self-pity, enduring circumstances that are clearly making them unhappy. They like to see people who take action – who do something – to tackle their problems. That's because we all like to think we are – or would like to be – someone who *does something*. We don't want to think of ourselves as passive victims, and we don't want to see that in our heroes. As the story opens, the hero is already at a point where he needs to make an important decision about his future. He's been at this point for a while, but he keeps putting it off. He needs to make a choice: does he stay in his current, unfulfilling circumstances, or does he take some action in order to bring about a change? Up until now, he has been putting up with things, getting by, coping. He has tried to pretend to himself that everything is okay. His flawed thinking has kept him in this situation: he believes that he doesn't deserve happiness; or that he is incapable of changing, or has some other belief that holds him back.

The challenge – or 'call to adventure' – changes all that. It is an opportunity for change that he cannot ignore. He could decide not to accept the challenge, but if he did we wouldn't have much of a story. Or much of a hero. He may initially refuse the challenge, but ultimately he has to accept it, despite his fears. The hero doesn't actually know what he's getting himself into – if he did, he definitely would not accept the challenge! Up until the midpoint, he probably won't fully understand the nature of the problem he is facing or the importance of the opportunity he is being given. For the first half of Act II – Sequences 3 and 4 – as we shall see, he is typically 'acting in ignorance,' and may even be 'going for the wrong goal.'

3. Refusal of the Call – The Reluctant Hero

This is also sometimes referred to as 'resisting the call to adventure.' In many stories, after his initial emotional reaction to the challenge, the hero will make a decision to refuse the challenge he has been offered. He rejects the opportunity that the life-changing event offers him, or denies that there is a need to take action to respond to it. He may pretend to himself that there is no problem; or decide that it is not his problem, or just hope that the problem will go away of its own accord. He tries to hang on to things as they were – to the safety of the life he knows. Part of the reason for the hero's reluctance is that he recognises the danger inherent in accepting the challenge. He is aware, perhaps only subconsciously, that accepting the challenge will force him to face his greatest fear. Inherent in the challenge is the possibility of being faced with a situation similar to the 'trauma' that caused his psychological or emotional wounding. It could also be that the challenge itself is a dangerous proposition, offering risks that any normal person would be loath to accept.

Making the hero reluctant allows us to show that there is something important at stake for him – physically and emotionally. As we have said, this sequence can be presented as a sort of debate, as the two sides – taking action versus not taking action – are weighed up. The hero may question whether the adventure is necessary. He may be reluctant to accept the challenge based on past experience – cynical lovers and private detectives often do, referring to previous events that have left them sadder but wiser. This is an opportunity to weave in necessary parts of the character's backstory, or at least hint at it (see item 4 below). The hero's dilemma could be that he is being forced to choose between duty and desire, or between an opportunity to take action and a wish to run away. This is the point at which his difficulty in accepting the challenge is expressed, and it is the point at which we see the hero's original self-definition. If he wants to ignore the challenge or to run away, we see that he does not regard himself as capable of rising to the challenge. This also demonstrates the hero's primary emotional state, which could be fear, guilt, self-loathing, or whatever. The hero's reluctance is also part of the game. Readers like to see the hero's reluctance overcome – they enjoy seeing him try to avoid the challenge, see his excuses and attempts at avoidance, but ending up having to accept it anyway.

In some stories, the hero does make some sort of half-hearted attempt to deal with the problem. He attempts a quick-fix in the hope that this will do and allow him to get back to his everyday life. The choice he makes here will be a mistake, influenced by his inner flaw. He will underestimate the nature of the problem, or its seriousness, and so will do something that makes things worse rather than better.

Certain types of story do not have a reluctant hero. Adventure stories like the Indiana Jones or James Bond movies, for example, have a hero who leaps straight into action. Other stories feature a 'travelling angel' character who undertakes an adventure, but does not undergo any form of character development – he has no flaw to overcome or ends the story with his flaw still in place. *Shane* is an example of this. In a story like *Speed,* the hero is forced to take action, he has no choice. Sequence 2 in this type of story concentrates more on setting up the danger that the hero must face. And even the most willing hero may hesitate, as he assesses the implications of setting off into the unknown.

4. Backstory

A good story doesn't always begin at the beginning, at some convenient point when two characters first meet, or when some other initiating event takes place. It begins at a point where the action is well underway and already heading towards a climax. The villain's plan was probably put into action some time ago, and its impact on the ordinary world of the hero may have been increasing for some time. The hero's feelings of dissatisfaction began long ago, and have been building and building until he's like a pressure cooker about to blow. In other words, the reader enters at a point where things are just about to get *interesting*. To begin with, we introduce interesting people, places and situations in order to pique the interest of the reader. Only then do we need to worry about answering some of the questions the reader may have about who these people are, how they came to be in this particular place, and how they got themselves into the situation that they currently find themselves in.

The earlier events that took place, that brought about the present situation and set events in motion, are called backstory. Backstory is anything that happened to your hero – or anything that happened in the story world – in the hours, days, or years before the story opened, and which have a direct bearing on the present story. Backstory includes any past event that the reader must know in order to be able to understand the story you are telling now. Backstory is a form of exposition, and because it relates to past events rather than what is happening in the 'now' of the story, it is *telling* rather than *showing*.

In many stories, an event – or a series of events – occurs before the story opens that threatens to upset the balance of the hero's everyday life. The impact of this event does not become clear until the moment of the challenge or 'inciting incident' at the end of Sequence 1. In *Hamlet* – as in many whodunits – a murder has taken place before the story opens.

All major characters should enter the story with a past life. They will all have their own backstory – some of this will be relevant to the current story (so it should be included or hinted at) and some of it won't (and so it shouldn't be included). They will have memories of events in their lives, and a complex web of relationships with family, friends, lovers, enemies, co-workers, employers, and other people. Physical and social factors will have influenced them psychologically, making them into the people they are today, and causing them to behave in the way that they do. The writer needs to know where the character is coming from, as this will have a bearing on where he needs to go. Knowing the hero's current life situation and emotional state, along with what happened immediately before the opening scene, allows the writer to hit the ground running and create strong dramatic tension from the outset.

A writer should always know much more about the hero's backstory than will be included in the story. In order to know the character, the writer must know things like where the hero is coming from when the story opens and what happened immediately prior to the first scene in which the hero appears; why he has ended up in the place where his first scene occurs; and what his immediate and long-term plans are before the challenge is issued. How far back the backstory needs to go varies from story to story. Sometimes these events happened only an hour ago. Sometimes they happened in a character's childhood. These significant events may be known by only one character, or they may be known by everyone except one character. They may be used in the story itself as revelations that provide a dramatic jolt or plot-twist. Or they might serve as the cause of a complication or obstacle. Backstory events can also be used when a character comes to a point where he or she must make a decision. An event from their past can be used to influence or trigger a decision. Or these events may explain their attitude towards life and their typical reactions to situations – that is, they may be the cause of, or the result of, their character flaw.

While the scenes in this sequence will be of a more expository nature, there should still be some action and/or conflict in them. But it is important to vary the intensity of conflict from scene to scene. Every scene cannot feature car chases, gun fights, or characters yelling at each other. If your opening scene, or sequence of scenes, was action-packed or revealed an intriguing or puzzling situation, then you can safely have a slower-paced scene that provides some background material that will help the reader better understand the story situation. If your opening was more of a slow-build, then you may need to structure your exposition into some form of dramatic revelation: someone arrives dramatic news or reveals the details of a dramatic past event. Sometimes it is possible to present exposition within a conflict situation: someone trying to obtain information from a reluctant witness; an interrogation; or some other form of one-to-one confrontation. One of the best ways to make the reader pay attention to backstory is to make them want to discover what happened in the past. Refer to some past event, and then move on, leaving people to wonder what actually happened. Or have a character refuse to give the details of what happened. Of course, when the information is finally revealed, it has to have been worth waiting for.

The general rule of thumb is that exposition should be kept to a minimum. Give the reader only what is essential for them to understand what is going on. Dwight V. Swain puts it best in *Techniques of the Selling Writer* when he says: "Quit thinking your reader needs to know as much background to read your story as you need to know to write it." The reader of a story, he says, is interested in the future, "... not the past. He wants to know what will happen as desire struggles against danger; not what did happen that led to the present conflict."

The reader doesn't need to know the hero's whole life story, they only need those details that will help them understand why the character behaves the way he does. And those details should be revealed gradually, rather in a great expository lump. "Wherever possible," Swain says, "translate information into people doing things."

Generally speaking, we are only interested in the backstory of the hero in Act I – we may learn something of the backstory of the villain later in the story. We only really care about the backstory of other characters if it is relevant in some way to their relationship with the hero, and possibly to the thematic argument of the story.

5. Subplots – The B-story and Other Secondary Plotlines

Significant storylines that will run throughout the novel or screenplay – a romantic subplot, for example – should normally be introduced before the end of Act I. Lesser subplots may be introduced later, but all of them should be introduced by the midpoint of the story, as this is the point at which all of the elements should have been set-up and we start moving towards resolution. The A-story is the physical action of the story, usually hero versus villain. The B-story is usually a relationship story – either a romance between the hero and his lover, or a platonic relationship between the hero and his ally, co-worker, or 'buddy.' In the romance genre, the opposite is true: the A-story concerns the relationship between the hero and the heroine, and the physical action becomes the B-story – the external action is most significant when it impacts the main romantic plotline. There may also be lesser subplots which may, or may not, involve the hero. These will typically mirror or contrast with the relationship story involving the hero, or provide an additional variation or viewpoint on the thematic argument.

In *A Practical Manual of Screen Playwriting for Theatre and Television Films*, Lewis Herman writes that subplots are "foils for the main plot," providing an opportunity for contrast and comparison, and that "... they make excellent vehicles for comedy relief, crisis relief, and time-lapse cutaways. When the major story line becomes too tense, the action can always be cut away to the antics of the characters in the subplot." In order to be effective, Herman says, "a subplot must be integrated into the main story line. It must contribute to its development, influence its crises, or affect its climax."

Linda Seger, in *Making a Good Script Great*, agrees saying that the romantic subplot often causes major changes in the main plot. She also says that subplot typically carries the theme of the story. Seger also writes that where the main plot of a story is often fairly conventional, the subplot can offer something special and unique.

As well as the A- and B-plots, some story theorists refer to the C-plot as being the hero's developmental (or character growth) arc.

Good subplots will usually demonstrate variations on the main thematic argument of the story, showing characters in similar situations to the hero and the co-protagonist, but who make different choices or suffer different consequences to their actions. In this way, subplots can deepen a story. They can also add an additional level of complexity if the main plotline seems too straightforward. Subplots should always intersect with the main plot at various points, and should ideally serve as complications for the main plot. Alternatively, they can be used to set-up or plant things that will be needed in the main plot later. As we will see later, cutting between the action of the main plot and a subplot can also be used to vary the pace of a story, and to heighten suspense.

Significant subplots can be resolved before or at the crisis and climax of the main plot. Minor subplots will normally be tied up before this, so as not to distract from the main action. The final resolution of the main relationship subplot may not come until Sequence 8, when we see what the hero's future is likely to be, now that his adventure is ending.

How Many Subplots?

A straightforward genre novel or movie will probably have one or two subplots – a relationship subplot between the hero and the co-protagonist (his ally or lover), and a subplot featuring secondary characters that reflects or offers a variation on the main story in some way. Herman suggests it could be the romance of the heroine's girlfriend. If a subplot involves secondary characters, they should be introduced within the main plot first, otherwise the reader is likely to think: Who are these people? Why do I care what they are doing? Other types of plot may have more subplots. A film with an 'ensemble' cast could well have subplots relating to each of the heroes, and the same may be true for a novel which features multiple viewpoint characters.

The whodunit is unusual in that there is normally no relationship subplot – no B-story. But the structure of this type of story is also slightly unusual, in that the A-story consists – to all intents and purposes – of two intertwined plotlines: the detective's investigation, as he pieces together what really happened, and the version of events that the murderer has created to deflect suspicion from himself, i.e. what seems to have happened. Added to that, each suspect has their own story, and usually their own guilty secret, that is presented in one or more vignettes as the detective interviews them.

Subplot Structure

For the most part, a subplot is structured in the same way as the main plot, with a beginning, middle, and end – the main subplots will also have turning points, and may even have a mini-version of the eight sequence structure. It is usually advisable to work out the subplot as if it was a separate story, and then look at the best way to weave it together with the main plot. If the subplot features characters and locations in common with the main plot, you have less setting up to do. If your subplot doesn't include people and places from the main plot, then you need to make sure that it is connected to it in some other way, otherwise it risks looking like a pointless diversion. Subplots usually work best when they intersect with the main plot to cause unexpected obstacles or complications. The way to structure your subplot is to look at it separately and plot out its eight sequences. Some of these sequences may be short, sketchy, or simply implied, but a full subplot will be structured like a story in its own right. You also need to look at it in terms of its relationship to the theme of the main story – is the subplot a variation on the theme? Or does it serve the hero's development arc? Or is it related to the villain's plot? Or the ally or lover's story? If it does none of these things, you need to ask yourself whether it really belongs in the story. Minor subplots may not need the full three-act, eight-part structure – they may be more along the lines of a short story plot or a two-act or one-act structure. Plotting short stories and other act-structures is a separate thing that we don't have space to cover here – we just need to bear in mind that there are other story forms that we can adapt to use in subplots.

Usually, subplots will begin after the inciting incident and finish before the climax in Act III. The most important subplots will usually be the longest, starting earlier and finishing later. Less important subplots will be resolved before the end of Act II. Sometimes you may hold up the final resolution of a subplot until Sequence 8, where you will tie up all the loose ends, but you will want to get the bulk of the subplots out of the way so that the crisis and climax of the story concentrate on the A- and B-stories only.

6. Consequences of the Refusal – The Villain Gains an Advantage

The hero's refusal to take up the challenge will have consequences, one of which might be that the villain or rival gets the upper hand. By not opposing him, the hero has allowed the villain some degree of success, and the villain has moved closer to achieving his own objective, whatever that might be. The refusal will also have consequences for the hero himself, if only in a change in his emotional state or in his own opinion of himself, which will be reflected in his subsequent behaviour. If he feels guilty for refusing the call, for example, he may develop and exaggerated desire to please others in an attempt to make amends for his perceived failing. Or he might push people away, for fear of being 'found out.' He may feel unworthy of having happiness, love, or friendship. He may go into denial or lie about his own actions or feelings. This is an external expression of his internal emotional state and is probably linked directly to his character flaw. The hero's own feelings resulting from the refusal, and other people's reactions to his refusal of the challenge, will increase the pressure on the hero. The pressure will force him to re-evaluate his decision, and push him closer to accepting the challenge, or perhaps make him even more determined not to accept the challenge, depending on his character.

The ultimate consequence of the refusal is that the hero's external problem worsens. The effect of the external problem on the hero's world increases. In some cases, the hero may have attempted a quick-fix for the problem, rather than committing himself to finding a proper solution. In these cases, it will be the hero's half-hearted actions, rather than his refusal to act, that will have caused the worsening of the situation. Either way, things get worse. Pressure on the hero increases. The risk to the hero, and other people in his world, will increase.

The villain, or his people, may threaten or actually harm someone the hero cares about; or they may take this person away. In Mariner Software's *Contour* writing system, this person is referred to as the 'stakes character' and represents all of the people that the villain and his henchmen are victimising. It is usually someone the hero feels deeply about – his closest ally, perhaps even his lover or someone he wishes to be his lover. The antagonist harms this character in some way, taking something from him or her, or perhaps deceiving them tricking them into doing something to further the villain's plan, harming them or degrading the 'stakes character' in the process. Or this character may make some innocent mistake that ends up furthering the villain's cause. The antagonists' actions move the change from being something that is happening in the hero's world, to something that impacts him directly. They reach a point where they can no longer be ignored. This serves to reinforce or raise the stakes – the severity of the threat to the hero and his world is made much clearer, demanding that the hero make a response.

7. Pressure to Accept the Challenge

Having achieved some success unchallenged, the antagonist is likely to make another move towards his objective. He may become more openly daring in the absence of opposition, and the scale of his actions may increase. As such, the impact of these actions on the hero and his world increases. The ally or mentor character may also put pressure on the hero to accept the challenge. We are looking to develop a situation that will force the hero to accept the challenge. Something that will push him or pull him into the adventure. We need to get the hero to a point where not acting has worse consequences than he risks by taking action. A new act of villainy will probably prove to be the final straw as far as the hero is concerned. Its impact will be such that he cannot sit back any longer – he must act. In other words, the hero must change his mind and accept the challenge which has been issued, even though the stakes have now been raised by the villain's latest actions. As mentioned above, the last straw may have come about as a result of the failure of the hero's own half-hearted attempt to patch-up the situation: he may be directly responsible for the villain's recent success. Or the hero may make a shocking discovery. He may receive terrible news. Or there may be some sort of revelation that causes the hero to see that the situation is much worse than he originally thought. Someone may have a good reason – either a friend or a foe – for pushing the hero. Or an antagonist may pull the hero into the adventure. Or the ally or 'romantic interest' character may choose to accept the challenge in the hero's stead, and get themselves into trouble so that the hero – perhaps partially out of feelings of guilt – then has to go to their aid.

The final straw that causes the hero to make a decision can be either an external force – the villain pushes him, or an ally or mentor gives him an encouraging shove, or an internal force – he feels he must act to save himself from perceived danger, or to save someone else from danger. Eventually, the hero must find himself in a situation that is intolerable. This may be a combination of external and internal forces that bring about his decision to act. Where the inciting incident or challenge provides the hero with an opportunity to do something, the event we are talking about here is some specific incident that acts as the final catalyst that jolts the hero into taking action. It may come in the form of a specific action, such as a murder or a kidnap or someone holding a gun to the hero's head, or some other action that cannot be ignored. These are the strongest forms of catalyst. Or it may be a piece of information that the hero receives – the hero's house is going to be repossessed, his wife wants a divorce, or war has been declared. Or it could be a situational change of some kind: a series of minor events may build to a point where the hero runs out of options and has no choice but to accept the challenge of the situation. His comfortable everyday existence may just cease to be available. Or his everyday life may become so oppressive that he feels he has got to escape. The escalation of pressure on the hero gives the story a kick that moves it forward.

8. Lock-in – Why Doesn't the Hero Run Away?

There are a couple of logical questions that have to be dealt with early in a lot of stories: If the hero is troubled by a villain whose actions are criminal, why doesn't he just go to the police? And: If the hero doesn't want to have to face his worst fears, why doesn't he just run away? The obvious answer to both these questions is that if the hero did either of these things, we wouldn't have a story. But we need to answer them in some way that is logical within the context of the story. In the whodunit, we take away the option of calling for the police by having the murder take place in some isolated location. Or we make it clear that the official investigator isn't up to the task of solving the mystery. In a thriller, we typically have the hero unjustly accused of a crime, so that he has to hide from the police as well as the villains. Or the local police or national authorities may be part of the conspiracy. In other types of story, we rule out calling in the authorities for other reasons. Perhaps the villain is a friend or relative of the hero or the ally or the 'romantic interest.' Many families and organisations have an unwritten rule: we deal with our own problems, we don't bring in outsiders. Families don't want to wash their 'dirty laundry' in public, or they may not want a family member to go to prison, so decide to dispense their own form of justice. Companies and other public institutions may not want the bad publicity that would come from revealing their problem to outsiders. Some types of character just mistrust authority figures or the nature of their problem is such that they are not taken seriously by the police, or it is not the sort of thing a policeman could do anything about.

You also need to construct your story problem is such a way that the hero cannot simply run away or turn his back on it. Again, the whodunit's isolated location helps to keep everyone contained and forces the amateur detective to deal with the problem. In the man-on-the-run thriller, the hero does try to run away but discovers that there is no escape. And in other types of story, the setting is such that the hero cannot leave, or does not want to leave because he would lose too much by going away. Setting a story in an 'enclosed' environment such as a school, or a company, or a hospital provides a boundary within which the story has to take place. People face problems in the workplace every day – if they run away, they may lose their livelihood or any chance to further their career. You have to provide a reason that makes it seem reasonable for the hero to stay where he is. This is related to setting as well as to the hero's life circumstances. You need something that brings the characters of your story together and keeps them in this particular arena. Ideally it will be somewhere with physical boundaries, like the isolated country house of the whodunit; or emotional boundaries, like a family; or a hierarchical structure like a hospital or the military or politics, that not only keeps everyone together, but also allows you to treat it like a pressure cooker or crucible, turning up the heat under it to increase the difficulties of those inside.

9. Introduce Other Major Characters

Any character who is going to play a major part in the story should be introduced before the end of Act I. This doesn't mean that they have to appear on stage, but they should be introduced by the impact of their actions or in discussions between other characters. This is a book about plot, so here I will talk about characters in terms of the roles they play in the story. Other than the hero – the protagonist or main character – and the antagonist or villain, there are four other significant types of character:

- The Ally
- The Romance

- The Mentor
- The Villain's Henchman

The Ally

The ally may be the hero's 'love interest' (see *Romance* below) or the 'buddy' in a buddy movie; they could be a character's partner in work or in some other enterprise; they could be a 'rookie' the hero is training; they could be the other half of an 'odd couple' – someone the hero finds himself having to share living space with; or they could someone the hero finds himself forced to work with. Sometimes the hero seeks out or recruits his ally, who may then serve as both partner and mentor (see *Mentor* below). The ally may initially be reluctant to join the hero on his quest. In some stories, the hero may have a mentor and an ally, or an ally and a romantic interest, and sometimes he has all three. Usually only one of these will serve as the hero's co-protagonist throughout the story, and the relationship between the hero and the co-protagonist – whether it is a platonic friendship or a romance – makes up the B-story. As already mentioned, in the romance genre, the hero and the heroine usually serve as the main co-protagonist and antagonist for each other. Each may have a best friend with whom they discuss the tribulations of their romance, and each may have a 'love rival' who is seeking to replace them in the romantic relationship with their respective partner. Like the romance character, the ally is effectively a co-protagonist. The hero will, in all probability, spend most of Act II in the company of this character.

At the very simplest level, the ally is someone the hero can travel with and saves the hero having to talk to himself. He or she can be a sounding-board for the hero's ideas and can spur the hero on when the going gets tough. The ally usually supports the hero in his quest – he may have been instrumental getting the hero to accept the challenge, though he may not share the same motivation as the hero, or even agree with the hero's choice of goal.

Often the relationship between the hero and the ally begins antagonistically. They dislike each other on sight, have different viewpoints on life, and seem to have nothing in common. They are thrown together by circumstances and spend a fair amount of time bickering until each gradually comes to respect the other. *48HRS* teams a convict with the cop (Eddie Murphy and Nick Nolte) who are initially – and literally – at each other's throats, until they gradually bond and find a way to work together effectively. Like any friend, sometimes the ally will support the hero – even when he thinks the hero is wrong or doing something stupid; and sometimes the ally will actively oppose the hero. The hero will want the ally to help him avoid having to face the thing he fears most. But in actual fact, the ally will turn out to be someone who is ideally suited to help the hero face his demons and overcome them.

In some stories, such as the flawed hero story, it is through the relationship with the ally that we see the stages in the hero's character development. For this reason, the ally is sometimes referred to the hero's 'reflection' or 'mirror.' The ally typically mirrors the positive aspects of himself that the hero denies. While the villain mirrors the negative aspects. The ally may act as a role model, demonstrating positive qualities that the hero needs to develop. Or the ally could provide a negative role-model, being an exaggeration of the qualities and behaviours the hero needs to grow out of. Hero and ally may begin as opposites, or as virtual twins who come from the same situation and behave in the same ways. The hero will change – growing as a character – as the story proceeds, but the ally will not. This way we can see the hero's changes in starker contrast. The ally is like the 'control group' in an experiment – he remains the same so that the changes in the 'test subject' can be measured against him. The ally helps the hero recognise the impact of the hero's inner flaw by serving as either a positive or a negative example.

The ally is – or becomes – someone the hero can trust. His confidante. The hero will feel comfortable sharing his feelings, his hopes and fears, and his self-doubt with the ally. The hero feels safe showing his vulnerable side to the ally: they are able to laugh and to cry together. There is often a fairly intimate scene between the two in Sequence 5, immediately following the midpoint and the self-revelation that the hero has experienced. The hero usually explains his plan to the ally, setting up anticipation as the reader wonders whether things will work out as the hero believes they will. Especially if the reader knows something that the hero doesn't, that could derail the plan.

Create and develop the ally in the same way as the hero, but bear in mind that – even though the ally may have the same character flaw as the hero (or may have a different flaw, or no apparent flaw), he will not demonstrate character growth during the course of the story. The ally will be introduced in some situation that demonstrates his dominant character trait and attitude towards life, and these will remain constant.

The fact that the hero comes to depend on the presence of the ally can be used against him by the villain, who may seek to remove the ally in order to weaken the hero or to force him to give up his quest. Allies are sometimes taken hostage, and sometimes they are killed. And – perhaps most dramatically of all – allies sometimes turn out to be betrayers: they have been working for the villain all along.

The Romance

Sometimes referred to as the 'romantic interest,' lover, or – in days past – the 'love interest.' Years ago, the love interest served as a sort of 'prize' the hero won when he successfully completed his quest, and her only other role in the story was to get herself captured by the villain so the hero had to ride to her rescue. Today, the person in whom the hero has a romantic interest is better written as a co-protagonist and partner on the quest, combining the functions of lover and best-friend/confidante. Except in the romance genre, as mentioned above, where hero and heroine serve as both co-protagonist and antagonist for each other.

Everything that has been said above about the ally can be applied to the romance character. They may begin as reluctant and antagonistic partners, forced together as a result of circumstances. Or they may not initially trust one another, so they deny their attraction to each other. The hero may, as a result of his flawed beliefs and behaviour, seek to have a romantic relationship with the wrong person. He may, for example, mistake lust for love. In this case, there is usually a second character who is actually the right person for the hero – but the hero won't recognise her as such until he has overcome his own flaw.

If the writer wants the reader to approve of the hero's choice of partner, then the romance character must have qualities that make her seem lovable and allow the reader to feel sympathy for her. These qualities are created in exactly the same way as those for the hero. If we want the reader to see the hero's choice of lover as the wrong choice, we need to give her unsympathetic traits, in the same way as we did for the villain.

The Mentor

The mentor is usually a positive character who helps or teaches the hero, and who might also protect him and provide him with weapons, tools, or other 'gifts' to help him during his quest. The mentor is often a wise old man or a wise old woman. Merlin in Arthurian legend and Obi Wan Kenobi in *Star Wars* are mentors, as are the martial arts master Mr. Miyagi in *The Karate Kid,* Cinderella's Fairy Godmother, the Robert Shaw character Quint in *Jaws,* and the 'old cop' in the old cop – young cop teamings in such films as *Seven* and *Lethal Weapon*. Mentors are often people who were heroes when they were younger – they have survived the trials of life, and are now passing on the wisdom gained from experience. The mentor can be a wiser, more noble figure who the hero aspires to be like, a sort of role model. Mentors do not have to have been successful as heroes earlier in their lives – a failed hero can show the hero the pitfalls to avoid. Sometimes mentors teach in spite of themselves.

Some mentors may still be trying to complete their own heroic journey, but find themselves faced with a crisis of faith or a tragic flaw in their own character. Sometimes the mentor is suffering from the onset of age or approaching death; sometimes he may have fallen from the hero's path. The new, young hero needs the mentor to pull himself together one more time, and there may be serious doubt that the mentor can do it. Such a mentor may go through all the stages of his own 'hero's journey' in order to achieve redemption.

Mentors can be willing or unwilling. The mentor may seek out the hero and convince him of his destiny, or the hero may seek out the mentor to ask him to share his wisdom. A hero may learn from a series of mentors, each of whom teaches him a specific skill or provide him with one of the tools or weapons he will need for his adventure. Different functions of the mentor may be fulfilled by different characters. The mentor can also fill the role of a missing parent figure or may actually be one of the hero's parents.

In comedies – particularly romantic comedies – the hero has a friend or co-worker (usually of the same sex) who offers advice. This advice is well-meant but usually leads to a complication or disaster. The comic-mentor may suggest that the hero go out with someone else in order to make his/her true love jealous; or he may suggest that the hero pretends to be like someone his true love admires; or pretends to be interested in some subject or hobby which he believes his true love to be interested in. Following this advice leads the hero into deeper and deeper trouble. Sometimes a character may appear to the hero to be a mentor, but this character is, in fact, an agent of the villain whose aim is to lead the hero into danger and cause him to fail in his quest.

The mentor serves a number of functions:

Teaching or training the hero, helping him to learn skills or gain knowledge he will need to face the challenges ahead and to succeed in his quest. This may also, in the early part of Act II, include testing of the hero in order to see what skills the hero has, what he needs to develop, and whether he is proving himself a worthy pupil. The mentor will also begin the hero on the path of self-discovery, trying to assist the hero in identifying his own strengths and weaknesses. The mentor will not tell the hero what his flaw is, but he will help the hero to discover it.

Weapons or tools are often provided by the mentor – a magical sword such as Excalibur, or a magic potion, a spell, a medicine or talisman, or even an important piece of knowledge such as a clue or a life-saving bit of advice. The hero will usually have to earn the mentor's gifts of teaching and tools or weapons by passing some kind of test, proving himself worthy of the gifts. The hero earns the gifts through an act of learning, sacrifice or commitment.

Conscience. The mentor can also function as the hero's ethical guide, teaching him the moral code of the knight, and warning him of the dangers and seductive nature of evil.

Motivation. The mentor reassures the hero, helping him to overcome his reluctance and fear, and urging him to accept the challenge of the adventure. Sometimes the teaching and gifts are enough to encourage the unwilling hero to accept the challenge. At others, the mentor must arrange an incident which proves to the hero that he has what it takes to embark on the adventure, motivating him and giving him that final push which gets him to commit to the quest.

Planting. An important function of the mentor is to plant information or a prop that will become important later in the story. Plants are important facts or objects which the reader will forget about until they become important later. In James Bond movies, Q provides 007 with some new gadget which will help him escape from a tight spot later: planting the gadget early in the film stops its use later from seeming too improbable or too much of a cheat. Such plants also help to tie together the beginning and end of the film and show the importance of what the hero has learned from the mentor.

As previously mentioned, the mentor can only take the hero so far on his journey. At some point, the mentor must judge that the hero is ready to continue alone. A good mentor will not allow the hero to become dependent on him because he knows that he will not always be present to help the hero out in difficult times. The hero may feel he has been abandoned or betrayed by the mentor – until he realises that he no longer needs him. And, of course, a good villain will take away the hero's mentor before the hero is ready to continue the quest alone.

The Villain's Henchman

We have already said that in some stories, the identity of the villain – the mastermind behind the evil plot – often has to remain a secret, so that it can be subject of a dramatic revelation at the midpoint of the story or at the end of Act II. In the whodunit, the name of the murderer is not revealed until the 'drawing room scene' at the climax of Act III, though the killer will have been on stage throughout the story as one of the suspects. In a thriller, the person behind the conspiracy is typically a well-known and powerful individual in the story world, who will probably also have been on stage for at least some part of the story, but whose true nature does not become known until the crisis point of the story. Criminal masterminds of the Bond-villain variety often have a henchman to carry out their dirty work for them. These are usually highly-trained and ruthless individuals who serve to personify the force of antagonism. This is the person who will make several attempts on the hero's life during Act II, and who the hero will probably end up fighting at the end of Act II. A good henchman usually seems literally larger than life. They are bigger and more powerful than the hero; they are relentless in their pursuit of him; they are remorseless, not caring if innocent bystanders are injured as a result of his actions; incorruptible, they remain totally loyal to their master; impervious to pain; and often curiously attractive.

Jaws, Oddjob and Darth Vader have already been mentioned in this role. To them we can add Agent Smith in *The Matrix* movies; Luca Brasi in *The Godfather;* and – since some of the best henchmen are women – I'm going to nominate Pamela Swynford de Beaufort from *True Blood.* Sometimes henchmen are mute, but often they have some really great – and evil! – lines. If your story calls for a henchman, make him or her a memorable one, and don't allow the hero to kill him off too easily.

10. Stakes – A Potential Disaster

What is the worst possible thing that could happen to the hero? And what is the worst possible thing that could happen to the hero's world? The reader needs to know what is at stake for the hero. What does he stand to gain or lose by the adventure? What will be the consequences for the hero, and for his world, if he fails? What is the *potential disaster* that will be his fate if he doesn't achieve his objective? In most cases, the hero is risking his life or his future happiness, or possibly both. The reader must be convinced that something vitally important will be lost if the hero does not achieve his objective. In order for the reader to become emotionally involved in the story, the hero must be emotionally involved in the action. If the reader doesn't believe that it is *absolutely essential* for the hero to achieve his goal, they won't root for the hero. The stakes might be survival, the need to belong, self-esteem, or the survival of another person or of a whole community. But the reader must clearly understand why it is essential for the hero's physical or emotional or mental well-being to achieve his objective.

What does the hero fear most? How is that fear expressed in terms of his behaviours? He will need to face this fear at the climax of the story. You must match your hero to the story and your story to the hero. The climax will be most dramatic if you have a situation which your hero, based on his personal fears, is the least likely person to be able to face it successfully. By having your hero seem to be completely unprepared to tackle such a situation, you put the outcome in doubt –

and you keep the reader on the edge of their seat as they wait to see how things will turn out. The hero almost always succeeds – the trick is to make it seem that he won't, and also – if you can manage it – have him succeed in a manner that the reader isn't expecting. Who is the least likely person to be able to face the climax situation you have in mind? Make that person your hero. Or if you know your hero already, what sort of situation is the least likely to be able to face successfully? Put a coward in a situation that requires bravery. Put a greedy person in a situation where his wealth cannot help him. Put a strong man in a situation where physical strength is no use in solving the problem.

Stakes are important in storytelling, and they need to be raised at various points throughout the story.

11. Motivation – The Hero's Point of View

The hero's motivation at this point in the story is strongly influenced by whatever it is he fears most. Any decision he makes will involve trying to avoid having to face this fear. Even when he has been forced into a position where he has got to make a decision to accept the challenge or 'call to adventure,' his response will be in line with the typical, protective behaviours that arise from his character flaw. His choices will be based around the way he currently defines himself.

His motivation, along with the goal he chooses (see 13 below), tell us something about the hero. They tell us what he (currently) believes to be of value. He will not, at this point in the story, be ready to demonstrate his commitment to the 'virtue' side of the story's moral argument. He has not yet discovered what it is that he values most, or if he is aware of this, he is not yet ready to make a commitment to fight for this value. Again we are back to what the hero thinks he wants versus what he really needs.

12. Decision – Accepting the Challenge

This is the point at which the hero makes the decision to commit himself to the quest – he will take action to deal with the external problem. He will have been under pressure to accept the challenge, but he has to make the choice himself. He cannot be tricked, dragged, lured, or forced into making this particular choice. One of the heroic qualities we mentioned earlier was that of being a volunteer: we like people more when they choose to put themselves at risk in order to do what they believe is right. And we like people who are decisive and appear to be in control of their own lives, rather than appearing to be reactive victims of circumstance. In some stories, it appears that the hero doesn't have a choice to make, and is thrown into the adventure by circumstances. In a 'man-on-the-run' thriller, such as *The Thirty-Nine Steps* or *North by North-West*, the hero usually finds himself either kidnapped or unjustly accused of some crime, or in possession of something wanted by the villain, or in some other way is thrown into exile, and has no choice but to be a part of what is going on. He does make a choice – to try and escape and prove his innocence – but spends the first half of the story on the run, being reactive rather than proactive: he typically doesn't make a decision to try and defeat the villain until the midpoint of the story, when he decides he's not going to run anymore, he will take the fight to the villain.

The decision is a moment of change – the hero makes a commitment at this point. As we have already said, the hero's motivation for taking action may be confused at this point as a result of his fears. He may make a decision to act out of fairly selfish motives – to avoid being harmed himself or to try and fix things quickly so he can get back to his normal life. In other words, he may embark on the quest for the wrong reason – he may do it because he feels guilty or indebted to someone, rather than because resolving the problem is in the best interests of both himself and his world. Or he may choose to take action out of greed or some other selfish motive. Having made a decision to act, the hero will choose *how* he will act: he chooses a goal (see below) that he believes will provide a solution to the external problem. But, as we will see, he may choose the wrong goal. By committing himself to the 'quest,' the hero puts himself into a position where he will actively oppose the villain or rival.

13. The Hero's Goal

Having decided to accept the challenge, the hero now chooses some target to aim for. Having decided that he will do something, he chooses exactly what it is he will do. In this context, we are looking for a goal that is external and action-oriented. To kill the dragon. To find the man he believes killed his father. To win the heart of the person he believes he will spend the rest of his life with. These are tangible things that can represent intangible objectives, such as – perhaps – freedom from fear, justice, and to find love. 'To find love' is not a tangible objective, but 'to ask Mary-Lou to be my prom date' is.

The hero wants to succeed in something and chooses a goal which – to him – symbolises success. At this point in his life, the hero may choose the wrong goal. He defines success in terms of what his life experiences have led him to believe about the world. Or he may choose the wrong goal because of his lack of experience, or lack of understanding of the problem. Or – referring back to his motivation – he may choose the right goal, but for the wrong reasons. He is defining success in terms of his want rather than his true need. Whatever the goal he chooses, the hero will pursue it until the midpoint of the story. If he confuses wealth with fulfilment, for example, he will set off in search of wealth. Until, at the midpoint, he discovers that wealth doesn't automatically bring with it a sense of happiness and fulfilment. Or he may pursue someone he feels sexually attracted to, rather than seeking someone with whom he is genuinely compatible – confusing lust for love. Want for need.

At the midpoint of the story, the hero usually discovers something about himself and about the nature of his situation that makes him re-evaluate his beliefs and his priorities. Discovering that he has chosen the wrong goal and/or been acting from the wrong motivation, is an important stage in his growth as a character. The hero has an external problem – related to the actions of the villain – and an internal problem, relating to his flaw. As we have said, dealing with the external problem will force the hero to face and overcome his internal problem. But the hero doesn't know that. When he first chooses a goal, he goes for something that he believes will allow him to resolve the external problem without having to face his inner demon. That's why he chooses a wrong goal or a goal that is not sufficiently strong.

If you have ever worked in an organisation with any form of appraisal or performance management, you will probably have come across the concept of SMART goals or objectives when setting your priorities during your annual review. Although I have a strong aversion to corporate hierarchies and 'management speak,' I will include the idea of SMART goals here, as it is a tool you may find useful. A SMART objective is:

S – *Specific*. As we said above, it is something external and tangible. It should be something you can point to and say, yes, that has been achieved or no it hasn't. The hero's goal should be something the audience can see so that they know when he has achieved it. Or failed to. It could be to win a contest or battle; to escape from a dangerous situation, such as an earthquake; to reach a particular location; to obtain a specific object; to find or apprehend a particular individual; to gain a particular piece of knowledge or information; to protect a place or way of life from attack; to get a particular person to go out on a date...

M – *Measurable*. It must be possible to measure progress towards achieving the objective so that at any point you can stop and ask: is this activity bringing me closer to my goal or not? And also, how am I doing so far?

A – *Achievable*. Goals need to be realistic and attainable within any limitations that a person is acting within. A goal should stretch someone and ask the best from them, but it should not be impossibly difficult.

R – *Relevant*. This relates to context. Does the goal make sense, is it worthwhile within the overall strategic objectives or needs of our group, organisation, world or whatever.

T – *Time-limited*. There should be a target-date for achieving the goal. A goal with no finish date is likely to get put off and put off. Setting a target date for completion adds a sense of urgency, and also allows someone to prioritise this task in relation to other day-to-day tasks that may come up and potentially take precedence. Deadlines are an important part of a story, as they help increase tension: Time is running out, we have to get to X before Y!

14. The Major Dramatic Question

Once the hero has accepted the challenge and chosen a goal, we have effectively asked the major dramatic question of the story: Will the hero succeed? This is sometimes referred to as the overall story objective. We ask this question in Act I, and it is not answered until the climax of the story in Act III. A problem or an opportunity is presented at the beginning of the story, and the outcome is not revealed until the end. Part of the reason a reader keeps turning the pages is to find out the answer to this question. It is called the *major* dramatic question because there will be dozens of lesser dramatic questions throughout the story. Every scene will have at least one character who is trying to achieve a 'scene objective.' Other dramatic questions include things like: Has the hero chosen the correct goal to bring about the desired outcome? Will he overcome his flaw, or will his behaviour cause him to fail in his quest to achieve the goal?

The question is usually implied rather than stated directly. It provides the backbone of the story, and everything that follows – every action and line of dialogue – should be directly related to it, bringing us closer to knowing the final answer. In *Hamlet* the major dramatic question is: Will Hamlet convince himself of his uncle's guilt and avenge his father's murder?

As we know, the answer to the major dramatic question is not in much doubt: of course the hero will win. But it is *how* he wins, what obstacles he has to overcome along the way, and what he ultimately gains, that keep the reader's interest. The major dramatic question is hinted at throughout Act I but is usually 'asked' – implicitly rather than directly – at the end of the act, when the hero finally accepts the challenge and chooses his first goal.

15. Crossing the Threshold

I've taken the term 'crossing the threshold' from Christopher Vogler's *The Writer's Journey*. Other theorists have referred to it as the 'point of no return' and compared it to a one-way door – once the hero steps through it, he cannot go back to the life he had before. After this moment, things will never be the same again. At the end of Act I, as a visual demonstration that the hero has decided to leave the comfort of his everyday world, there is a physical or symbolic change of location. This could be an actual doorway or gateway that he passes through, a bridge he crosses, or a building he enters or leaves. There should be a sense of a door closing behind him, indicating that there is no going back. The hero may choose to pass through this portal after he has accepted the call to adventure; or he may be pushed or pulled through it before he makes the decision: it may be one of the final events that cause him to accept the challenge.

As the hero crosses the threshold into the 'new world' in which his quest will take place, Act I ends and Act II begins. The set-up of the story is complete, and the major dramatic question has been asked: Will the hero succeed? This moment is usually marked by a visible change of story location, a change in the tone of the story, or by some other incident that symbolises this change. The fact that the set-up is complete doesn't mean that the reader understands everything, only that they now have all of the information they need to make sense of the story as it unfolds.

16. Major Turning Point

The hero's acceptance of the challenge at the end of Act I is the story's first major turning point, so now is a good time to have a quick look at the concept of turning points and major turning points.

What is a Turning Point?

What makes a reader keep turning the pages, unable to put a story down? A story maintains reader interest when it is unpredictable, when there are intriguing twists and turns in the action as it heads towards the climax, posing new dramatic questions in the reader's mind. A story can have a variety of twists and turns – there will be a turning point at the end of each of the eight sequences that moves the story on into the following sequence – but there are two vital ones needed to keep the plot moving – these are the two major turning points, also referred to as major plot points. The first major turning point occurs at the end of Act I and sets up the situation for Act II. The second turning point occurs at the end of Act II and sets up the situation for Act III, the story's resolution. The major turning points are significant events which cause the story to change direction, dramatic twists which allow the story to develop in a new way. Decisions are made. As a result of these turning points, the story achieves momentum and stays on course.

Turning points always happen to the hero, they are character-related and are caused by the hero's actions. The hero will then respond to the turning point in some way, formulating a goal and a plan of action as a result. The turning point causes the hero to reassess his plan and possibly his chosen goal. It may also cause him to question his own motivation. And a turning point will usually raise the stakes in some way. The turning points are also dramatic incidents which grab the reader's attention and keep them intrigued. The purpose of the turning point is to propel the story onwards towards its major climax at the end of Act III.

Linda Seger lists the functions of major turning points:

- to turn the action onto a new direction
- to raise the major dramatic question and make the reader wonder about the answer
- to provide a decisive moment for the hero, a point at which a commitment or re-commitment is made
- to raise the stakes
- to push the story into the next stage – Act I into Act II, Act II into Act III
- to take the story into a new arena and provide a different focus for the action

Good turning points serve one or more of these functions, while the major turning points serve all of them. There is one more important turning point in the story, the midpoint, which we will cover when we get to it.

We have reached the end of Sequence 2, which is also the end of the first quarter of our story and the end of the traditional Act I. We seem to have covered a huge amount of material already, but that is because we have explored all of the things that need to go into setting up a story. Get this stuff right and you're much more likely to have a story that you will be able to write all the way to the end. Get it wrong and you could end up with another one of those unfinished projects – a beginning that never goes anywhere.

Act II: The Middle

The story so far... Act I has given us a hero who is strongly motivated to solve a problem or benefit from some opportunity; he has chosen a goal, an external objective, that he believes will allow him to solve the problem and/or bring an improvement in his life circumstances. The hero has accepted the challenge, leaving the comfort of the life he knew and crossed – either physically or metaphorically – a threshold into a 'strange new world' in which his quest for the goal will take place.

The Functions of Act II

The *middle* of the story, the second act, is effectively everything after the introduction of the main characters and conflict, and before the climax. It is the largest of the three acts, being fifty-percent (or more) of the total length of a screenplay or novel. In the eight sequence structure, we break this middle act down into four separate parts – Sequences 3,4,5 and 6 – so that we can construct something that is easier to write and more dramatic to read. In the middle of these comes the *midpoint,* which is the middle of Act II and the middle of the story as a whole: we will give the midpoint a short chapter of its own.

Act II is generally described as consisting of 'rising conflict' or 'rising tension,' as it continually builds and moves forward to the second major turning point, which sets up Act III and the climax of the story. This means that right from the start of Act II, you must be thinking about moving towards the crisis at the end of Act II and the climax in Act III. As Ansen Dibell writes in his book *Plot:* "The job of the middle is to build towards and deliver crisis." Nancy Kress and Blake Snyder both say that the purpose of the middle of the story is to deliver on the promise we make to the reader in Act I when we said: Read this and you'll see something exciting happen. According to Kress, the middle delivers on this promise by "... dramatising incidents that increase conflict, reveal character, and put in place all the various forces that will collide at the story's climax." The forces and conflicts developed in Act II must emerge naturally out of the characters and situation introduced in Act I. Snyder describes the first half of Act II as being 'fun and games' and says it answers the question: "Why did I come and see this movie?" It is the section that contains the exciting set-pieces that you see in the movie trailer. He says that it is less about raising the stakes – this will happen at the midpoint – and more about having fun with your characters, saying that it is "... where the buddies in all buddy movies do their most clashing." Michael Halperin, in *Writing the Second Act,* agrees that character revelation is an important part of Act II: "It helps us make the antagonist and protagonist believable within the context of the genre."

Although we may define Act II as consisting of 'rising action' or 'rising tension,' because this is an important overall effect to bear in mind, this part of our story does not actually consist of one headlong rush uphill towards our climax. This would be both monotonous and exhausting, and probably not terribly effective. There are highs and lows throughout Act II, whether you measure these in terms of 'action' or of 'emotion.' Ideally, you will have a combination of the two in any kind of story – dramatic events and dramatic emotional responses. And both of these will be constructed in a way that provides the reader with an emotional experience – because as we have said, we don't read a story in order to see someone else have an intense emotional experience, we want to feel it ourselves.

Act II will consist of a series of actions instigated by the hero – remember that readers like to see people who take responsibility for their own destinies, and who make decisions and do things. These actions will result in consequences – the villain or rival, or someone else, will react or respond to the hero's action, causing another change in the story situation. The consequences are usually such that the hero will find himself in a more desperate situation than when he started, raising the stakes and the tension. Each mini disaster or mini climax leaves the hero faced with a dilemma – should he carry on in the face of increased opposition and increased risk? Or should he rethink his plan and perhaps even his goal?

Each period of intense action or highly-charged emotion is followed by a quieter period of contemplation, where the hero recovers from what he has just experienced. Here we learn a little more of his life story so that we can gradually piece together the events that turned him into the person we first met in Act I. These reflective moments are usually interactions between the hero and the ally or co-protagonist. The hero may discuss his predicament with the ally, and – as he comes to trust this character – will reveal his hopes and fears for the future. He may use the ally as a sounding board as he considers what the next steps in his plan should be.

As Act II progresses, the obstacles faced by the hero will become bigger and more intense, and the choices he has to make will be more difficult. The effort he has to expend to make progress will become greater as we build towards the crisis at the end of Act II. Our definition says that the middle of a story delivers on the implicit promise by presenting dramatic incidents. Which specific incidents you dramatise depends, of course, on the story you want to tell. However, there are some guidelines that can be used to help you build on your beginning and propel the story towards the ending.

Let's move from *what* you need to achieve and look at *how* you can deliver it.

Sequence 3: Responding to the 'Strange New World'

Sequence 3 is the beginning of Act II, and it opens with the hero taking his first steps in the strange new world in which the story will take place. We see his initial reactions – in character – to his new environment. This is true whether the 'new world' is an actual physical place, or just a change in his emotional or psychological space, such as the beginning of a romantic relationship.

This sequence in a story is where the hero first learns that responding to the inciting incident isn't going to be quick and easy. He has accepted the challenge in the belief that he will need to perform one or two tasks that won't be too challenging, and then he'll be able to go back to his life as it was before. He will begin by doing the sorts of things that any of us might do faced with a situation – the obvious actions. We need him to do this for two reasons – firstly because if he doesn't do them, readers are going to think it odd. You don't want them to say "Why doesn't he just..." Linked to this is the fact that we want to begin narrowing the hero's options as soon as we can. Between now and the end of Act II, we will see the hero making choices and taking actions that he believes will bring him closer to his story goal – and as each of these attempts fails, his choices are reduced and the odds against him succeeding increase. Dara Marks, in *Inside Story,* calls this phase of the story 'exhaustion,' because the hero's possible solutions are gradually used up, and he himself is worn down as every step forward seems to result in him taking two steps back. One by one, outside sources of help should be cut off or proved useless. His options should be reduced, becoming progressively more difficult and less desirable, until the point – at the end of Act II – where he is forced to rely on his own efforts alone. And that all begins in Sequence 3.

The action in this sequence begins gradually: it consists of a series of small actions, whose cumulative function is to move the hero to a point where he realises that low-energy, half-hearted actions are not going to be enough and that he is going to have to come up with a proper plan of action. In other words, we drive him towards a decision, which is that he must make the First Attempt. The easy options and quick fixes having proved useless, and possibly (ideally) having made his situation worse and/or a solution more urgent, the hero decides that he must now make a properly considered major assault. Towards the end of Sequence 3, he makes plans and preparations for this, and the climax of the sequence is him committing himself by taking the first action.

All of the above fits pretty well with what Christopher Vogler writes about this part of the story in his *The Writer's Journey,* where he says it consists of tests, obstacles, learning, discovery, and preparation.

An important fact about the actions taken in both Sequence 3 and Sequence 4 is that they are *action taken in ignorance*. The hero does not yet know the full extent of the problem he is facing – he is only dealing with the first visible impacts of the antagonist's actions, and isn't aware of the full extent of what the antagonist is planning. Peter Dunne, in *Emotional Structure*, says that, at this point in the story, the hero is in a state of 'unconscious incompetence': he doesn't know the true nature of the problem he is up against and he is not yet prepared to be able to deal with it. He will not become aware of the full-scale of the problem until a moment of discovery or revelation at the midpoint of the story (the end of Sequence 4). At that point he will know what the problem is, and will discover that he does not have all of the necessary skills, knowledge, or experience that he will need to have in order to be able to deal with it – he enters a 'conscious incompetence' phase.

There are a number of things that can appear in the early part of Act II: they don't all belong in every story, but they are listed here as possibilities that you can consider for your own story.

1. First Test – the 'Threshold Guardian'
2. First Impressions of the New World
3. Initial (Emotional) Reaction
4. Hero as Outsider
5. Mistakes and Transgressions
6. Tests
7. Learning
8. Allies and Enemies
9. Recruiting
10. Beginning of the B-story Relationship
11. First (Minor) Actions Towards the Goal
12. Planning the First Attempt
13. Pinch Point I – 'Page 45'

The first three of these logically belong at the beginning of Section 3, and the last two belong at the end. The rest, if they occur in a story, can appear in any sequence, and some of them are functions that can occur more than once – there may be multiple tests for the hero, for example, and several learning opportunities.

We are still pretending that there are nice neat breaks between the acts and the sequences in a story, but this isn't really the case: some elements that were listed in Sequences 1 and 2 may occur as late as Sequence 3, and some from Sequence 2 may overlap into Section 3. Similarly, some of the items listed here can run on into Sequence 4. The only real 'rule' is that you should do what feels right for the particular story you are writing in terms of creating a dramatic story and an emotional experience for the reader.

1. First Test – The Threshold Guardian

Testing is a common feature in the early-middle part of many stories. We need to discover what skills and experience the hero has already got, and what is missing so that we know what he will need to gain. By this we mean physical skills – can he shoot a bow and arrow? – but also life skills – can he deal with failure and disappointment? We need a sort of baseline measurement of his skills, knowledge (including self-knowledge) and experience, so that we can see how much he needs to learn before he stands a chance of achieving his chosen goal. Testing will put him into pressurised situations which will allow the reader to see his typical behaviours and the extent of his various abilities.

'The Threshold Guardian' is a concept that comes from Christopher Vogler's *The Writer's Journey*, and refers to some small challenge that the hero must face to prove his commitment to, and 'worthiness' to attempt, the challenge. He comes to the 'doorway' that leads to the strange new world in which his goal-quest will take place, and he finds there is someone (or something) guarding the entrance. The hero must make it past this guardian before he can begin his quest. Facing the threshold guardian is a sort of initiation test. This first test serves to highlight the seriousness of the challenge and to demonstrate that something important is at stake. It is the first of several occasions in which the hero will be challenged to prove that he has got what it takes to proceed and that he is committed to the task.

The threshold guardian is not usually the villain or even the villain's main henchman, but it may be one of the villain's underlings. Or the guardian may be a completely neutral character who lives in the 'strange new world' and serves to protect it from undesirables who don't belong there. The function of threshold guardian can also be performed by one of the other characters: the mentor might test the hero to see if he is worthy of becoming his pupil. Or the ally may test the hero to see whether he has got what it takes to join him on an adventure in the strange world. Or a potential lover may test him to see if he is 'worthy' of her affection or to see if they genuinely have anything in common. In some stories the threshold guardian appears once and is then never seen again – sometimes to get past him, the hero has to destroy him. In other cases, the guardian may become an ally or mentor, joining the hero for all or part of his quest, or providing him with some learning experience that will help him later in the story. Other times the guardian will just wish him luck or encourage him to do his best. The threshold guardian may issue dire warnings: Go back, there is danger ahead. They may once have embarked on a similar quest themselves, and been defeated by it: scarred by experience, they try and persuade the hero not to make the same mistake they did. This is often the case with a reluctant mentor or a reluctant ally.

The skill or quality that the hero will need to demonstrate in order to get past the guardian will depend on the type of story you are writing. If the quest is going to require the hero to demonstrate intellectual abilities, he may be asked a riddle or asked to solve some other kind of puzzle. If the story is a romance, the hero may need to show that he is able to respond on an emotional or empathetic level. If it is to be a physical adventure, the hero may need to show that he can face a much bigger opponent and overcome him in some way other than a head-on attack. And sometimes the hero may simply have to show that he can handle defeat without crying and running away. The nature of this first test should be such that the hero learns something about himself, something about his opposition, or something about the strange new world he is entering, or perhaps all three. He may gain an understanding of this inhabitant of the strange world that will be of benefit to him later. He may 'fail' this first test, but this could tell him what not to do next time he is faced with the same sort of challenge.

The hero may need to learn that challengers are not necessarily negative forces. They offer learning experiences, may give advice or allow insights to be gained. In the best examples, the guardian enables the hero to learn something about himself. They may personify a negative quality (or a positive one) that the hero also has, but which he is afraid of or ashamed of. The correct solution is not for the hero to destroy the threshold guardian, but rather to gain an understanding of him, to avoid judging him as positive or negative, to feel compassion for him, and to accept him as a valid part of existence. The hero may not get this right first time: the mentor may advise the hero to befriend the guardian or to help him in some way, and the hero may instead destroy him – proving that he is not yet sufficiently enlightened to behave in an ideal manner. The hero may 'get past' the guardian in a way that demonstrates a weakness or flaw, rather than showing his worthiness as a hero. But this too is an opportunity for learning: the hero may not understand the mentor's disappointment right now, be he may grow to understand it later.

By some means or other, the hero gets past the threshold guardian. He may destroy him, trick him, bribe him, pay him a fitting tribute, seduce him, outwit him, outfight him, or simply run faster than him. Having done this, the hero steps over the threshold into the strange new world in which his quest will take place. This initial taste of success encourages the hero and makes him feel that his goal is attainable. But it may also cause him to be over-confident, such that he takes unnecessary risks or ignores sound advice – which will have consequences later. His success may turn out to have been 'too easy,' and to be a false success, having consequences that open up a whole new set of problems. Or the guardian may have been a decoy, guarding a false entrance, so that the hero sets off along the wrong road, a mistake that is not discovered until later. His 'false success' at the beginning of Act II may be a contrast with the 'false defeat' he experiences at the crisis point at the end of Act II.

2. First Impressions of the 'New World'

Having successfully completed an action that has allowed him entry to the new world of the story, the hero takes a moment to assess his situation. His initial landing here may have been a bumpy one, depending on the nature of the test he has just faced. Some of what he sees now may be beautiful and inspiring, other things may be terrifying. However he got there, this new world is strange and is not quite what he was expecting. By calling it a 'strange new world,' we make it sound like the hero has stepped onto an alien planet. What we really mean is that he has entered an arena that is not familiar to him. Someone who has just had a parent with Alzheimer's come to live with them has entered a new world, even though they have not left their own home. 'New world' simply means a change of situation or circumstances. Change means having to deal with something new – that is what stories are all about: how people deal with change in their lives.

What we are thinking about under this heading is not how the hero *reacts* to the new world (that comes next), but what he observes about it. How does it seem to him? What does he notice first about it? What are the things that seem *most* strange to him? These things will tell us something about the hero and about his life experiences to date. If you have travelled outside of your home town, try and remember what it felt like the first time you left the countryside and entered a big city or vice versa. Think about the first time you ever went to another country and experienced a different culture. The colours, the smells, and the sounds were all slightly different. The street signs and shop names were all in a different language. But some things were just the same – probably the cola and hamburger signs. Or remember the first time you went to a new job or a new school. Or the first time you had to go into hospital. You are trying to capture that initial sense of disorientation – of trying to get your bearings or your 'sea legs.' It's a period of adjustment.

3. Initial (Emotional) Reaction

Having caught his breath, how does the hero now react to the new world? What is the hero's initial *emotional* reaction to the strange new world? This reaction will be 'in character' in that he will respond to this in the same way we saw him respond to situations in Act I, which is to say, he will demonstrate his typical behaviours and outlook on life. He will probably be disoriented, but is he afraid? Annoyed? Shocked? Or does he have some other reaction altogether? Is he glad to be here, or does he regret having accepted the challenge? Does he miss home already, or is he enjoying his new-found freedom? Is he feeling nervous or overconfident? What action does he take? Again, his behaviour should be 'in character' as we understand him from Act I.

Two things have just happened to the hero: he has successfully passed a threshold guardian or small-scale test, and he has entered an environment that is not familiar to him. He reacts to these things in a way that is typical for him. We may also see the effect of these two things on other people around him. This includes any people he has brought will him across the threshold – his ally or mentor, perhaps – and anyone he encounters in the new world. How do they react to him being in the new world? How do they react to being in the new world themselves? How do they react to him having passed the threshold guardian and the methods he used to get past it? And we will see how the hero responds to the reactions of those people around him. Is he sympathetic to their feelings, or totally oblivious? Is he aware of the impact of this new situation on their lives, or doesn't he care? Does he acknowledge their help and support in getting into the new world, or does he take them for granted? Or take all the credit himself? Does he heed their advice to be cautious, or does he blunder on regardless? This will depend on the story you are telling and the kinds of people you are writing about. Whatever initial emotion the hero experiences, it will soon be joined by feelings of doubt as he wonders: What do I do now?

4. The Hero as an Outsider

No matter what his previous experience in life, the hero is now in a situation where he is an outsider. He doesn't know the geography of the place, doesn't know the rules or etiquette, and doesn't know anything about the social or power hierarchy. He is going to have to find these things out, and quickly, if he's going to survive in this strange environment. But this world and the people in it are not going to make any allowances for the fact that he's a new guy: they are going to throw everything at him and expect him to cope. It's like the first day in a new school or a new job – but much worse! People are going to notice that the hero doesn't belong here and they are going to be suspicious of him. He is going to have to learn how to fit in, and he's probably going to have to prove that he deserves to be allowed to stay. Being an outsider is something that we have all experienced at some point, which means that the reader can sympathise with the hero's present situation. We can intensify these feelings if we make the hero seem like an underdog, or if we subject him to undeserved misfortune just because he's a newbie here.

Eventually, the hero may attain the status of being an insider in this world. The knowledge, skills and experience he has gained qualify him for the status of 'belonging here.' He goes from being an apprentice to being a warrior (or some other form of master) in his own right, but that doesn't occur until the end of Act II or the beginning of Act III. For now, he is firmly in 'unconscious incompetence' mode.

5. Mistakes and Transgressions

Not knowing the rules might bring the hero into conflict if he accidentally commits some transgression and draws attention to himself, and this may put him in danger: the price for mistakes in this world will be higher than he is used to. The hero may struggle to tackle the problems he is faced with. His misjudgements will cause additional complications, hindrances, obstacles, and disasters – one after another, with each one being more difficult and more frightening than the one before, as each moves him closer and closer to a situation similar to the 'thing he fears most.'

The hero's actions to date are likely to have attracted the attention of the villain or rival. If this hasn't already happened as a result of the hero accepting the challenge and crossing the threshold, then it will happen when the hero starts blundering about in the strange new world. He may have triggered some sort of alarm or been spotted by some kind of sentry. The hero has effectively put his head above the parapet, and must now accept the consequences.

6. Tests

These early tests will reveal what skills, knowledge, and experience the hero already possesses, and they will highlight his deficiencies, showing areas where he has things to learn. By putting the hero under pressure, the tests will also reveal aspects of his character, especially his typical behaviours when faced with difficult situations. If the hero has been accompanied on his quest by a mentor, these initial tests may be part of the training he is receiving.

Some of the tests may be an intrinsic part of the landscape of this world: the hero will need to survive in the local environment, including how to face any natural disasters to which the landscape is prone. This world is also the villain's natural habitat, so there may well be traps, barricades, or checkpoints set by the antagonists, which the hero must learn to recognise, defuse, or avoid. Although he passed a challenge to enter this world, he now has to prove that he deserves to be allowed to stay. He may be called upon to make some sort of sacrifice or undergo some ordeal to prove himself. In Section 3, the hero may well fall into traps or set off traps which alert the antagonists of his presence. How the hero deals with these traps is part of the testing. Can he spot them? If not, can he survive them? Is he able to turn a bad situation to his advantage?

The purpose of these tests is to demonstrate where the hero currently stands in terms of readiness to face the challenge of the crisis at the end of Act II. And we should clearly see that he has a long way to go before he is ready. He will face other ordeals as the story goes on, which will allow the reader to see how much progress he has made, and how much further he still has to go. Any obstacle or ordeal the hero faces also helps to reinforce the importance of his objective, by showing how difficult it is to achieve. The challenges he encounters here may also sharpen his skills in certain areas, teaching him things he needs to know to survive in his new environment. Like everyone else, the hero will learn by making mistakes or by discovering what he doesn't know. Each challenge, ordeal, or setback is intended to be a lesson – a moral or psychological challenge – each of which gradually moves him closer to having to face his greatest fear in the end of Act II crisis, which will also provide him with an opportunity, finally, to overcome his fear.

The hero will probably find that the people in this new world do not behave in the same way as the people he is used to. He will need to be able to judge the character of the people he meets, to assess whether he can trust them. Heroes, especially younger ones, are often quite naive and find it difficult to recognise when someone is trying to deceive them. The hero may make a mistake and trust someone he shouldn't: he may choose an 'ally' who is actually working for the enemy, or who is prepared to betray him to the enemy for a fee. This increases the risk to the hero by giving the villain greater power in the form of an 'inside man' (or woman). The hero may not discover the truth about this 'traitor' until the end of Act II, or perhaps even the climax of Act III, though the audience is likely to know the truth earlier – possibly even right from the point of the 'fake' ally's introduction.

If the hero is travelling with a group, the tests may screen out unsuitable members, and reveal the abilities and personalities of those who remain. Some of the team members who leave – or perhaps are even killed – could be good people with vital skills, and the hero will need to decide how to compensate for their loss.

In a romance, the testing might be in the form of a first date or some shared experience which begins to build the relationship. And it might not go that well.

The tests provide the hero with small-scale, external opportunities to experiment with change. Initially, he will try and deal with problems using his old behaviours, but gradually he becomes confident enough, or desperate enough, to experiment with something different. The tests at the beginning of Act II are often difficult obstacles, but they aren't on the life-or-death scale of later ordeals. They are like 'training exercises' or 'dry runs' for the skills and insights the hero will need to demonstrate during his climactic confrontation with the antagonist. But at this point in the story, the hero is struggling to overcome even these basic challenges using his typical behaviours, and this doesn't bode well. And where the hero does successfully face an obstacle or opponent, there may be unforeseen consequences of his victory. The way that he has succeeded may be 'immoral,' and come back to haunt him in the second half of Act II.

7. Learning

Early in Act II, we must see that the hero has the potential to learn from experience and to change how he behaves as a result. This paves the way for a more significant change in the hero later in the story. The hero needs to learn the local rules or laws, the layout of the land, the social and power hierarchies, and local politics. How quickly he does this is a test of his ability to gather information and adapt to changing situations. Who is in charge? Who is responsible for law and order? Who is the local bully? One of the things the hero needs to discover is where he can find reliable information, and possibly recruit local people to join him on his quest. In fantasy novels, detective stories, and westerns, a bar or saloon is often the preferred location for meeting people or seeking people. *Star Wars* had the cantina scene. This may also be somewhere that he meets a character who becomes his main ally or romantic interest. Or he may encounter someone who becomes a 'victim' and who he feels the need to rescue and protect.

And the hero has to learn who his allies and enemies are...

8. Allies and Enemies

The hero will spend some time finding out, perhaps by trial and error, who he can truly trust and rely upon, and who will betray him or let him down. This is a test of the hero's ability to judge character and is something that can only be gained by experience. The hero may initially approach local people for information, and end up making friends and enemies as a result. Some local people the hero meets may not be villains, but they may fear the villain's retribution if they agree to help the hero, and so may act against the hero, exile him, or betray him. An important consideration is the fact that the hero is behaving in a way that is dictated by his fears or lack of knowledge. In order to protect himself from having to tackle his greatest fear, the hero may engage in behaviours that are – according to the thematic argument of the story – 'immoral.' He may not be aware that his behaviour is causing harm to himself and to others, but what he is doing is definitely on the negative side of the virtue-vice scale. A genuine ally or lover will understand that this behaviour is motivated by insecurity or fear, and will make allowances: people who genuinely care about us, love us despite our faults. But there may be some allies who side with the hero *because* of his faults. People who enjoy doing 'bad things' with the hero may turn against him when he comes to see the hero sees the error of his ways and tries to change. They will not support him when he adopts new 'moral' ways of behaving, and may even turn on him and oppose him.

Similarly, people who opposed the hero when he was behaving 'immorally,' may turn into allies when they see that he has changed, or is attempting to change. In a romance or 'buddy' story, the co-protagonist may initially oppose the hero because of his immoral behaviours, but will gradually grow to like and support him as the hero tries to change into a better person. They may be among the first to see his potential and support him through the difficult period of change. Early in Act II, the ally, lover, or buddy may support the hero's quest, but be mistrustful or antagonistic towards him because of his behaviour. They support what he is trying to do, but not the way he is trying to do it. If the hero has not already encountered these people, he may gain a mentor (perhaps in the form of a local 'guide'), an ally – his Robin, Tonto, or Watson – or a lover at this point.

In some types of story, it is necessary for the hero to put together a team of adventurers to join him on the quest...

9. Recruiting

The hero may need to put together a group of people with different skills (and personalities!) and try to bond them into a coherent unit. They may need training, they may need to gather equipment and supplies, and they will need to make plans and rehearse strategies. Their varied temperaments may cause issues, making it difficult to get them to trust one another and work together. Another test for the hero may come in the form of a power struggle, when another member of the group challenges him for leadership. The hero will then have to prove that he has what it takes to be the leader – or perhaps hand over control until some point when he can prove his suitability. The different skills, strengths and flaws of each team member will be explored at this point. Who can be trusted and who cannot? Who is reliable, and who is unpredictable or unstable? Who is committed to the quest, and who is interested only in the money? Who is loyal to the hero and who is a traitor? Who has a hidden weakness that will flare up and derail the quest at some crucial point? Which characters work well together, and which ones are in conflict? Who is the bully? Who is afraid? Which characters have past history that remains unresolved? Is one an impostor, lacking the skills he professes to have, or is one an agent of the enemy? Is someone tagging along on this quest with his own agenda, planning to use the skills and equipment of the team for his own purposes at some future point?

Having a traitor in the group, someone who is secretly working for the antagonist, adds suspense to the story. A traitor can also be a complex and interesting character, whose motivation can add depth to a story, and provide another viewpoint that is another variation on the thematic argument. A traitor who comes to side with the hero – to like him or to sympathise with his values – may then face a dilemma: does he betray the hero to the antagonist? Or does he betray his master/employer, and assist the hero in his quest? If he betrays the antagonist, will the hero and the rest of the team believe that the traitor has genuinely changed sides? And if he stays, will he put the group under greater threat of injury or death if the antagonist orders that the traitor be killed at all cost?

One crucial member of the team may be reluctant to join. He will take the role of the reluctant hero, for any of the reasons we discussed earlier under 'refusal of the call.' He may need to be bribed, cajoled, bullied or shamed into joining the group. He will usually be the last to be recruited.

If the hero has a group, the villain probably has at least a small army. We may see people being recruited to the villain's side – perhaps someone who refused to join the hero, and who may have been vital to the hero's plan. Or we may meet someone who defects from the villain's side to join the hero. Or we may just see members of each group standing on opposite sides of the street, sizing each other up, but making no move at this point.

10. Beginning of the B-story Relationship

The hero may have met the ally or the romance character in Act I, but their relationship doesn't really begin until the beginning of Act II. They may share the experience of exploring the strange new world together, or in the case of a romance, the romance itself has created a strange new environment that the two characters must learn about. The relationship between the hero and his co-protagonist is often a rocky one initially and may be openly antagonistic. The hero may need the ally's help, and the ally may want nothing to do with him or his quest. Or the hero may be forced into a close working relationship with the ally, even though he does not really want a partner of any kind. Whatever problem exists in the relationship between the hero and his co-protagonist may be rooted in the hero's personal weakness or flaw. In the film *Rocky,* the Sylvester Stallone character has to overcome his flaw – believing himself to be a loser – before he can feel worthy of Adrian's love.

The two may agree to work together for a limited time because it is mutually beneficial. They make no long-term commitment to one another, and the understanding is that they will go their separate ways and pursue their own goals when it no longer benefits them to work together. The two will probably be wary of each other, and neither will want to become emotionally involved with the other. Mistrust causes them to keep their distance. Often the first encounter, or first date, of two lovers is so disastrous that they part vowing never to have anything to do with each other again. It should seem impossible that they should ever want to see one another again, and then fate or circumstance will throw them back together in some situation that means they have to broker some kind of temporary truce.

The B-story relationship is where the theme of the story can be explored. The B-story also provides the writer with an opportunity to cut away from the A-story, to provide a break from the A-story action, or to build up the suspense by cutting away from the A-story action at a tense moment, keeping the audience on the edge of their seats for a while longer – suspense gets its own chapter too.

Once the hero has made a commitment to accept the challenge and has faced to threshold guardian, Act II enters a 'transition' phase where there may not be much happening in terms of action: the hero is finding his way around the new world. This can give the audience a chance to catch its breath after the climax at the end of Act I, and an opportunity to learn something of the hero's backstory (if this is necessary to the story). Starting a romantic subplot at this point helps to maintain interest in the story. Especially if the beginning of the relationship is a stormy one.

11. First Actions Towards the Goal

As I mentioned earlier, the first thing we need our hero to do is to get the obvious stuff out of the way first. If you're ever watching a movie and ask yourself: *Why didn't he just...?* it's because the writer forgot to do this. Look at your character's situation at the beginning of Act II and ask yourself: *What would a normal person do?* He'd phone for help – so you need to take away the hero's 'phone. He'd drive away as fast as he could – so you need to take away his car. He'd go to the cops – so you need to make it so he can't go to the authorities for help. Some of these things you can rule out by letting the audience know that the option isn't currently available. But some of them you need to show to be ineffective solutions. The hero tries these things and they fail.

Be careful how you do this. In some (bad) romantic comedies, the whole of the action relies on the fact that some misunderstanding occurred at the beginning of Act II, and the whole plot would crumble if that misunderstanding was cleared up between the two lovers. If you're twisting your plot like a pretzel to keep the heroine from finding out that the hero didn't really take a hooker as his prom date, then you've got a problem no amount of dick jokes and 'accidental' wet t-shirts are going to disguise. The audience *will* suspend its disbelief – they want to work with you and accept your premise, but if you insult their intelligence, you are just making an ass out of yourself.

Apart from helping with plausibility, exhausting the obvious has a couple of other advantages or functions. First of all, at this stage of the story, the hero's actions are influenced by his lack of awareness of the problem, and by the fact that his behaviour is designed to protect him from having to face his greatest fear. As a consequence, he is looking for a solution that won't cost him much either physically or emotionally. He wants to invest the minimum he can get away with. He wants to tackle the external problem without tackling the internal one. At this point, he doesn't really know what he is up against, so a half-hearted attempt doesn't seem unreasonable to him. At least he's doing *something.* His first minor attempt at a solution fails, so he has to try something else that is a little bit more challenging. This too fails. So he has to try something else. Zero for three. These failures have consequences and usually make his situation worse. And he is effectively failing tests, proving that he is not yet ready to be a 'hero.' But gradually he is coming to see that his typical behaviours, the things he usually does to tackle problem situations, are not working. How the hero reacts to these failures, and their consequences, also reveals something about his character.

Early in Act II, exhaust the obvious and quick-win solutions, get them out of the way and show that the hero really is some way along Poop River, and his canoe doesn't have one of those big spatula things. Once all the easy options have been discounted, we can get down to the business of coming up with something new.

12. Planning the First Attempt, or, How to Be A Success

What we need is a cunning plan! Blackadder and his sidekick Baldrick often had this conversation. I read on one of those dreadful motivational posters that: *A goal without a plan is just a wish.* I hope you could sense me typing that in a whiny sarcastic voice because I hate the triteness of those posters: they're loved by people who like to trot out things like 'If you assume, it makes an ass out of you and me.' No mate, you didn't need me to make you into an ass. As a writer, I am allergic to clichés and platitudes. Most forms of business communication make me mentally gag. Can you smell the vitriol melting my keyboard? Or maybe it's bile.

Where were we? Plans. Plans can be good things if done well. I believe that, and that's why I'm sitting here writing about plot structure while the sun is shining brightly outside my window. Why else would I be indoors doing this? Apart from hayfever, obviously.

If the hero sets out to achieve a story goal, then he is going to need a plan. The sort of steps he will need to take will be similar to those that we need to take when we try to achieve something in our own lives. There are any number of self-help books offering advice on goal-setting and planning for success, but the basic steps boil down to something like this:

1. Identify a desire or need
2. Set a specific goal that you believe will bring about your desired outcome
3. Create a plan containing the steps necessary to achieve your goal: stepping stones towards your ultimate destination
4. Consider what resources will be necessary to carry out your plan: do you have all of the knowledge, skills, experience, equipment, people, etc.?
5. Gain skills and equipment. Train your team. Obtain the resources identified as missing in step 4.
6. Create a schedule for the individual steps or activities that make up your plan.
7. Take the first step – do not procrastinate!

That, more or less, is the outline for success in any project, whether personal or work-related.

In an attempt to avoid having to confront his greatest fear, or in order to hide his lack of knowledge or experience, the hero may come up with a plan that is filled with escape routes and danger avoidance measures, to the extent that it is too convoluted to be workable. It is so constraining as to make successful action impossible. Or the plan may be naïvely optimistic, underestimating the time and resources that will be necessary. Either way, even at this early stage, it will have a whiff of potential failure about it.

13. Pinch Point I – 'Page 45'

In his book *The Screenwriter's Workbook*, Syd Field added the midpoint and two additional 'story progression points' to the paradigm he had presented in *Screenplay: The Foundations of Screenwriting*. These two additional points occurred around pages 45 and 75 in his 120-page model screenplay – the ends of Sequence 3 and Sequence 5 in the eight-sequence model. He called them Pinch I and Pinch II. Other writers sometimes refer to them as 'focus points.' These are turning points in the story, but they are not as major as the turning points at the ends of Act I and Act II. Field described them as "... just a little pinch in the story line that keeps the action on track, moving the story forward..." Pinch I moves the story on towards the midpoint, and Pinch II moves the story on towards the major turning point (the crisis) at the end of Act II. They are two more staging posts that help get us through the wilderness that is Act II.

Field also says that in some – but not all – stories, there is a link between Pinch I and Pinch II. He gives as an example the film *Thelma & Louise:* Pinch I occurs when Thelma and Louise pick up J.D. (Brad Pitt). At the midpoint, he steals their money. And Pinch II is when J.D. is picked up by the police and tells them where our two heroines are heading. This sort of symmetry can help make a story feel more like a unified whole.

The two pinch points serve other functions in the story as well. They can provide moments where we can 'compare and contrast' the hero and his situation – at Pinch I, we are still at a relatively early point in the story, the hero is perhaps a little naïve and over-optimistic, and he has just come up with the plan for his First Attempt. He believes it will succeed, but he is acting in ignorance and is in the 'unconscious incompetence' phase. At Pinch II, he has passed the midpoint 'revelation,' and so is now in the 'conscious ignorance' phase, he is now aware of the dangers he faces, but perhaps isn't yet aware of his lack of skills and experience. He has just come up with his plan for the Second Attempt – he is no longer naïvely over-confident, but he is still fairly confident of success. At both pinch points, the audience is probably aware that the hero's plan is likely to fail as a result of his lack of knowledge, or of particular skills or experience that are required for success. Pinch I sets him up for failure at the midpoint, and Pinch II sets him up for failure (and a major crisis) at the end of Act II.

Pinch I and Pinch II can also be used as key moments in the proving of the thematic argument. A key theme in *Thelma & Louise* is the idea of escaping from male oppression, and that men cannot be trusted: at Pinch I Thelma and Louise naïvely believe that the character of J.D. is one of those rare nice guys who won't try to exploit them; at the midpoint he proves otherwise, and at Pinch II, he betrays them to the policemen who are pursuing them. Pinch I suggests the possibility of freedom and fun with men; Pinch II shows the dark reality of men closing in on them to take away their freedom.

If you can come up with two points in your story like this, you can add depth and resonance, and give your story a feeling of being a well-thought-out and well-constructed whole. The idea of passing from a First Attempt optimistically planned in naïvety or unawareness, through a midpoint revelation or discovery, and on to a Second Attempt based on awareness and a more mature understanding, also helps give you some key moments that can be used to help plot Act II and keep your story on track.

14. First Action of the First Attempt

Having tried the obvious solutions, the hero puts into action a bigger, more elaborate plan to try and achieve his external goal. By default, this is an action taken *against* the antagonist, though the hero may not yet be aware of that. The hero has chosen a course of action that he believes will allow him to avoid having to face the thing he fears most. The climax of Sequence 3 is the hero starting the first action required by his plan. This is a new demonstration of his commitment to achieving the story goal. It is also quite possible at this point that the audience knows, or suspects, that the hero is going into battle without fully realising the size and strength of the enemy he is going up against. He's the man who is taking a knife to a gunfight. I lied about hating clichés.

Sequence 4: First Attempt, First Failure & Consequences

We've reached the fourth sequence of our story. It begins with the hero in action, as he makes his First Attempt to achieve the story goal, and it climaxes at the midpoint, which will feature a revelation or discovery of some kind that will turn the story around. The midpoint is where the hero discovers that he has been 'acting in ignorance' since accepting the challenge. For the first time, he discovers the full extent of what he is *really* up against. The midpoint is also where the hero has to admit his own internal conflict – whether this is related to a character flaw, or to some other form of 'lack' that is having an impact on his own life and the lives of the people around him. Before he is ready to admit his weaknesses at the midpoint, the hero will need to see proof – during Sequence 4 – that what he believes about both himself and the way that the world works is wrong or incomplete.

Sequence 4 is also important in the relationship between the hero and the co-protagonist – his ally or lover. During Sequence 3, they spent time together and their lives became more entwined, though these early stages of their relationship were mostly antagonistic. The action of the plot forced them together and made them have to work together. They did not want to be together, and so were probably pretty unpleasant to one another. Partly because they felt a spark of attraction and didn't want to admit it, even to themselves, never mind to each other. The audience could see that they were meant to be good friends or lovers, but the characters could not see this. As their feelings for each other develop, they might actually become more antagonistic for a while, as they may both be afraid of making a commitment to the relationship. They still find it difficult to trust each other. It could be that both characters have issues with trust and commitment, or this problem may exist only in one of the characters. If the co-protagonist has no trust or commitment issues, they may become frustrated by the hero's and be impatient for him to move on; or they may empathise with him and seek to guide or mentor him.

In Sequence 4, then, the *external* action of the plot has brought these two characters together, but some form of *internal* conflict – on the part of one or both of the characters – is keeping them apart. The reader will become aware of how important this B-story relationship is to the hero, and how his future success may depend on it, but the hero remains oblivious to the fact or denies it.

There are a number of things that can appear in Sequence 4. The first four listed below will probably occur in the order listed (though 3 and 4 can be switched around) – as there is a logical progression from one to the other. Item 5 is optional, though some sort of reaction to the failure of the First Attempt should probably be here. Item 6 is optional, but likely to be there.

1. The First Attempt
2. First Failure
3. Antagonist Counter-attacks
4. Consequences of the Failure
5. Co-protagonist and/or Team Confront Hero Over Failure
6. Hero Denies Problem

1. The First Attempt

At the end of Sequence 3, the hero undertook the first action of his plan, marking the beginning of his First Attempt to achieve the story goal. This is his first *major* attempt involving pre-thought and planning, in contrast to his earlier random actions to try and deal with the problem. The rest of the action of this First Attempt occurs in the first part of Sequence 4. If the hero described the steps of his plan in detail in Sequence 3, we will quickly see events veer away from the planned sequence, as unexpected obstacles and consequences arise. In a story, explaining a plan sets up anticipation of things to come, but we never see things turn out exactly as planned. In his book *Story,* Robert McKee talks about conflict arising out of the gap between an expected or hoped-for outcome, and what really happens. The hero is frustrated by his failure to achieve what he had planned to achieve.

The actions of the hero's First Attempt do not succeed, and the failure will have consequences that worsen the situation for the hero, his co-protagonist, and – if he has one – his team. If you remember our original description of the four quarters – bad, worse, worst, climax – then you will see that we are currently in the second quarter, the 'worse' phase. The action begun by the hero may fail purely as a result of his own actions – we'll look at this as item 2 below. Or it may fail because of action taken by the antagonist and/or his men, who are provoked into responding to the hero's actions – see 3 below.

2. First Failure

As a result of some miscalculation, lack of preparation, or some other mistake – or perhaps because of action taken by the antagonist (see below) – the hero's plan fails or at least does not go as anticipated. It fails because of something the hero doesn't know, or is unable to do, at this point in the story.

In *The Screenwriting Formula,* Rob Tobin writes about something called the hero's 'balk' (baulk in 'British English') by which he means some action (or inaction) by the hero, caused by his character flaw or weakness, that puts him and his ally or team in jeopardy, and results in their being trapped or injured, or simply causes their plan to fail. At a vital moment, the hero freezes, chickens out, or chooses a wrong path, and his choice of action is motivated by his desire to protect himself from having to face the thing he fears most or his lack of knowledge and/or experience. Imagine a horse racing up to a fence and then refusing to jump or a speaker standing on stage and discovering that the words won't come.

Whatever error or poor choice the hero makes should occur at a point where it has the most dramatic impact. Typically this means it will occur in the middle of the action or just before a vital action – at a crucial moment when the stakes are high. It may take place during the First Attempt (see above) or it may occur as the hero and his allies are trying to deal with the antagonist's counter-attack (see below) which was provoked by the First Attempt.

This failure will be the result of some weakness or lack on the part of the hero. There is some skill, knowledge, or experience that he needs but does not have. Or perhaps he has some deeply-rooted personal fear that prevents him from being able to to take the necessary action. An inner fear or 'tragic flaw' can cause someone to do things which effectively sabotage their own efforts – without them being aware that they are doing so.

The hero's failure at this moment in the story will have consequences – both for himself and for the people around him (see below).

It is possible for this failure to *appear* to be a moment of success for the hero. But if so, this will be a false success. He may achieve something that he *wants*, but he will not have gained the thing that he *needs*. He has successfully managed to avoid having to face his fear, but as a result, he has not actually attained anything meaningful. At this point in the story, the hero's definition of 'success' is wrong, because it is based on flawed beliefs about himself and about the way the world works. In terms of our major dramatic question – Will the hero succeed in achieving his objective? – the answer at this point will be no. He cannot possibly succeed until he is prepared to face and overcome his fears. He doesn't know it at this point, but the failure of the First Attempt has brought him a step closer to having to face the thing he fears most.

The action the hero takes at this point is still taken in ignorance. He pursues something that he believes is the right thing to resolve the problem. But he may be going for the wrong goal because he doesn't have all of the facts yet. During the course of his actions in Sections 3 and 4, the hero will gain insight into what is really needed to resolve the external problem – and what is needed to resolve his inner problem – but he is not yet ready to accept this insight and act upon it. For now, he may remain oblivious to some of the lessons he is learning, or he may deny the validity or the necessity of the changes that he is being told are necessary.

3. The Antagonist Counter-Attacks

The rival, opponent, or villain takes action to prevent the hero and his ally or team from achieving their objective or acts in retaliation. This action could be what places the hero and the antagonist(s) in active opposition to one another for the first time. The counter-attack may begin during the hero's 'first attempt' (see above), with victory being handed to the antagonist as a result of the hero's failure. The antagonist has his own objective and his own plan for achieving it. He also has his own value-system and his own point of view. His viewpoint will present the negative side of the moral argument of the story. His values will be opposition to the hero's. The battle between hero and antagonist then symbolises the battle between two moral viewpoints. The fact that the antagonist has now taken direct action against the hero means that our hero has now lost control of his life: someone else is now directing the shots. Whatever else he wants to do, the hero is going to have to deal with whatever the antagonist throws at him. This is an important turning point in the story: events have been set in motion that the hero cannot stop or slow down. These events will escalate and speed-up as the story approaches the end of Act II. What will the hero do now? Surrender? Run away? Or stand and fight? This will depend on what sort of person the hero is, and on his typical behaviour in response to difficult situations.

4. Consequences of the Failure

The main consequence of the failure of the First Attempt is that the hero and the person or people with him will find themselves in a worse situation than before the attempt. The failure may have been caused by action taken by the antagonist, or it may have occurred as a result of some mistake or failing on the part of the hero. In either case, it is likely that something is lost or someone is hurt as a result of the failed attempt – the hero and/or his team suffer a loss. If the failure was all the hero's own work, then a consequence of it may be that he has attracted the attention of the antagonist, who takes some action harmful or obstructive to the hero and his people – that is, the failed action provoked the antagonist into retaliating (see above).

5. Co-protagonist and/or Team Confront Hero Over Failure

Another consequence of the failure comes in the form of the reaction to it by the co-protagonist and – if he has a team – the other members of the hero's group. They may be aware that the hero's actions caused the failure, and so may challenge him on this – especially if the hero failed to take action at a critical moment. Or they may blame the hero for the failure simply because he was the leader and it was his plan.

Although the co-protagonist may challenge him, he or she will normally continue to be supportive and encouraging, even if they are disappointed, and have possibly even been harmed as a result of the failure/antagonist's counter-attack. Other team members may be less forgiving, particularly if one or more of them has been injured or even killed. They express their anger and disappointment. One or more team members may abandon the hero, or one of them may challenge him for leadership of the group, arguing that he is not up to the task. Anyone who does stay with him may give him an ultimatum – he has one more chance to prove himself, or else.

6. The Hero Denies There is a Problem

The hero's response to the failure may be to deny that there is a problem. He refuses to admit that his actions (or lack of action) at a key moment caused the failure. He may blame fate or circumstances – 'bad luck.' Or he may blame poor preparation or execution on the part of other team members. In short, he will blame anyone or anything, refusing to take responsibility himself. This is more likely to happen if he has a weakness that he is trying to hide. If the hero froze at a key moment, the reader and the people around him may be aware that he has a problem – that he is being held back by his own fears. But he may be unaware of the connection or may be denying it to himself.

All of this sets us up for a significant story point that marks the middle of the story – the midpoint revelation.

The Midpoint

The first half of Act II, which we have characterised as 'acting in ignorance' and 'unconscious incompetence,' builds up to a dramatic revelation or discovery at the midpoint. The second half of Act II then deals with the consequences of the midpoint reversal. At the midpoint the hero becomes aware of whatever it was he didn't know – he learns something that the reader has known, or at least suspected, for some time. The full nature and extent of his situation becomes apparent to the hero for the first time – and it is much bigger, worse, or life-changing than he ever suspected. From this point on, he is no longer 'acting in ignorance,' that phase of the story is now over. The hero moves on from being in a state of 'unconscious incompetence,' because he is now aware of what he is up against. But as he sees the scale of the situation – whether it is a problem or an opportunity – he also becomes aware that he is not yet ready to be able to deal with it. In other words, he is entering the phase of 'conscious incompetence.'

The midpoint is where the hero is forced to acknowledge that he has been 'acting in ignorance' since accepting the challenge. He has been unaware of the full-scale of the situation he is facing, and he has underestimated both the danger involved and the resources – both physical and mental/emotional – that will be required to resolve the situation. The midpoint provides a major revelation, discovery, or reversal of fortune. As a result of the midpoint, the hero's situation will change dramatically.

The midpoint often provides a point of no return. Whatever happens at the midpoint causes the hero to reassess his quest for the story goal and consider whether or not to continue: once this decision is made, he will have gone too far to be able to turn back. In a romance, the point of no return occurs when the couple say 'I love you for the first time,' and mean it. This may be symbolised by a first kiss or the first time they go to bed together. Having reached a point of no return, the hero obviously has fewer choices open to him.

In other types of story which have a romantic B-story, the first moment of intimacy may not come until Sequence 5, after the midpoint revelation relating to the A-story.

If the hero has a lack or a flaw, the midpoint forces him to face it and admit to it.

The midpoint is often an *emotional* highpoint (or extreme low point) in the story, but may be relatively quiet in terms of the external action of the story. Usually, there will be some form of external action that symbolises the emotional impact. The hero may seem to be overwhelmed and may do something that indicates an admission of defeat. Or he may give up on the story objective completely, and say that he'll live with the consequences of the antagonist now gaining victory unopposed. This is another example of the hero refusing to deal with his own fears. He knows that if he continues with the quest, he will end up in a situation where he will have to face the thing that he fears most. He would sooner abandon the quest than do that.

The midpoint occurs immediately after the failure of the First Attempt, and so marks a low point for the hero. The midpoint revelation or reversal makes a bad situation even worse. Not only has he failed, but the hero now discovers that the situation is much worse than he ever imagined it could be. His self-confidence has been badly dented, and he feels particularly vulnerable. He seriously considers giving up the story-goal quest and accepting whatever consequences this may bring.

The midpoint revelation or discovery can be presented in a number of ways:

- the failure of the First Attempt may have dramatic consequences, resulting in injury to, or perhaps even the death of, someone in the hero's team;
- the co-protagonist may confront the hero and question him about his part in the failure of the first attempt; he or she may threaten to abandon the hero if he doesn't admit and explain his failure;
- the co-protagonist or another character may act as a positive role-model, taking charge of the aftermath of the failure and getting the team back to safety;
- the co-protagonist or another character may act as a negative role-model, 'going to pieces' in the aftermath of the failure in some dramatic fashion;
- someone in the hero's team may, as a result of the failure, decide to betray the hero and change sides; or someone may prove to have been working for the antagonist all along;
- the First Attempt may have drawn the attention of the antagonist, or his henchman, and the hero may find himself in a face-to-face confrontation with them, or they may just mock him in the aftermath of the failure;
- the hero, still in a state of denial, may express his frustration and anger at the failure, and seek to blame external circumstances or members of his own team; this may, in turn, provoke someone in his team, perhaps even the co-protagonist, to speak their mind about the hero's part in the failure;
- the hero may come to the realisation on his own, and feel ashamed of his part in the failure; he may hand over leadership of the team to a 'better man,' or he may try to sneak away and hide – but find himself instead cornered by the co-protagonist

The midpoint can serve a number of functions:

i. It makes the hero realise that he has misunderstood the nature of the situation;
ii. It causes the hero to re-evaluate his story goal and his motive for trying to achieve it. He reassesses his priorities and his viewpoint in terms of what constitutes 'moral' behaviour;
iii. It focuses the conflict between the hero and the antagonist: the hero finally discovers what he is really up against; and it raises the stakes, setting the hero on a collision course with the antagonist, as their respective goals are now very much mutually exclusive; and it clarifies the thematic argument of the

story, as the hero and antagonist choose sides, demonstrate their motivations, and the types of behaviour – the actions – that they consider acceptable in pursuit of their respective goals;
iv. It (possibly) marks an important point in the hero's growth as a person;
v. It marks a significant point in the B-story – the relationship between the hero and the co-protagonist

(i) What the Hero Learns About the Story Situation

The midpoint revelation or discovery causes the hero to look at things in a new way. He may discover that he has been looking at things in the wrong way, and his new perspective means that things suddenly begin to make sense. This applies to both external events and internal emotions, and it causes him to reassess everything that has gone before, and (possibly) to re-evaluate the relationships he has with various people. He may discover that past events had very different meanings – causes and effects – than he previously thought. Or he might have misunderstood someone's actions – their feelings, intentions, and motivations.

What the hero learns at the midpoint, and the way he learns it, may not require a big action set piece. It may not be a dramatic climax in the way that the major turning points at the ends of Act I and Act II are. It will be dramatic because it turns the hero's situation and the story around, and it could be a highly emotional moment. But there may not be significant physical action. It could be as simple as a door closing or a first kiss. It may be a piece of information that the hero receives. It may be a significant piece of backstory – something that happened in the distant past or just before our story opened, and that has the effect of turning the story around and changing its meaning. It causes the hero to re-evaluate everything that has happened in the story up to this point.

In many stories, the midpoint is where the hero learns the full extent of the villain's plans. Previously he may only have been aware of one small part of them – a single battle in the villain's war, or the first action in a series that will culminate in something drastic. In *Star Wars* Luke Skywalker learns the significance of the stolen Death Star plans. He reassesses his goal – and expands it from 'rescue the princess' to 'rescue the princess in order to save the rebellion.' In thrillers, the hero is often trying to escape from the villain and spends the first half of Act II running away. But at the midpoint, he decides or discovers that escape is impossible, so he will turn and fight the villain: he changes from being the pursued and instead becomes the pursuer. This change is often motivated by his discovery of the true nature of the villain's plan – the microfilm actually contains the plans for a secret weapon that the villain will use to attack Russia and provoke a nuclear war.

In other stories too, the hero may have seemed to be a victim during the first half of Act II, reacting to circumstances thrown at him, rather than actively instigating actions himself. He may have been trying to avoid taking responsibility for dealing with his situation and was not totally committed to resolving it. Hius failure during the First Attempt was a subconscious act of self-sabotage that demonstrated this. After the midpoint, all this changes. He can no longer avoid the responsibility: he must choose between total commitment or total surrender.

A consequence of this new knowledge is that the hero becomes aware that there is much more at stake than he previously thought. It isn't just his own happiness or safety that is at stake – he is now aware that other people are at risk.

(ii) The Wrong Goal or a Change of Goal

At the midpoint, the hero may discover that he has been trying to achieve the wrong goal. The specific object or destination he has been aiming for, he learns, will not bring him the outcome that he desires or needs.

In the example of *Star Wars*, we saw how Luke Skywalker's story objective was expanded by what he learned at the midpoint of the story. Some might argue that Luke achieved his initial goal (save the princess) and that this was replaced by a new goal (save the rebellion), but the two are so closely tied that it doesn't really matter. In *E.T.: The Extra-Terrestrial*, Elliott does change his goal at the midpoint – initially, he wants to hide E.T. and keep him as a friend; after the midpoint, he wants to help E.T. get home. David Siegel believes that the best films have a change of goal at the midpoint, and he uses it as the basis for his two-goal, nine-act structure. The first goal may be achieved at the midpoint, and a new one may take its place. Achieving the first goal may, as a consequence, cause a new problem that creates the need for the second goal. An apparent victory may prove to be a false victory, calling for a whole new goal-quest. Or the original goal may be expanded or adapted as a result of the midpoint revelation.

Or the hero may discover that he has pursued the right goal, but for the wrong reason. In the first half of Act II, his motive may have been a selfish one, but at the midpoint he discovers an unselfish reason for pursuing the same goal. He stops thinking about only himself and his own desires or wants, and instead starts thinking about someone else, or perhaps a benefit to his whole 'society' or group. A clichéd example of this occurs in teen comedies where the hero pursues the new girl because he and his friends have made a bet to see who can 'get her in the sack' first – but as he tries to woo her, the hero finds himself genuinely falling in love with her. He still wants to 'be intimate' with her, but his motive has changed as her happiness and needs become more important to him than his own (isn't that what love means?).

(iii) Conflict with the Antagonist and the Thematic Argument

As we have said, the midpoint often reveals the full extent of the antagonist's plan. Even if he doesn't appear in person yet, we learn what it is he is trying to achieve, and have a much better idea of the lengths he is prepared to go to achieve it. We will discover the antagonist's point of view, in terms of the 'virtue and vice' sides of the thematic argument. And we may also learn something of his motivation – about *why* he is trying to achieve his nefarious ends.

The midpoint may be the moment when the hero defines his position as being in opposition to the antagonist. Previously he was acting against the antagonist by default – the actions towards the hero's goal co-incidentally acted as obstacles to the antagonist achieving his objective. But at the midpoint, having discovered what the antagonist's plan is, the hero declares himself to be in opposition to it. He officially enters the battle against the antagonist. This too has the effect of raising the stakes, as this may be the first time that the antagonist becomes aware of the hero as an active threat to his own plans.

In some stories, the midpoint is where the hero and the antagonist meet for the first time, or where the hero discovers the nature and/or identity of the villain. Or discovers that there actually *is* an antagonist.

(iv) The Hero's Personal Growth
The midpoint revelation often changes the hero in some way and marks a significant stage in his growth as a person. It is a moment of 'recognition' for him. He sees the error of his ways and becomes a less selfish person. Or he is made wise by experience, realising that he has been deceived or exploited as a result of his own idealism or naiveté. He learns the value of something he previously took for granted. Or he learns that he has to take responsibility for his own actions. Or he may discover that it is time for him to grow up and put away 'childish things.' Between the inciting incident and the midpoint, we have seen the hero in a variety of situations and seen that, on the positive side, he is resourceful and adaptable, and is capable of changing in order to deal with unstable circumstances. On the negative side, we have been made aware of his major shortcomings – whether that is in terms of important skills or abilities, emotional maturity, or just the number of soldiers in his army. Although the midpoint changes the hero's outlook, it doesn't fix these deficiencies – so he becomes aware that he doesn't have everything he needs in order to face the challenge he has just learned about.

(v) The Relationship or B-Story
The midpoint also marks a turning point in the relationship between the hero and his co-protagonist, whether that character is an ally or a lover. As we will see in Sequence 5, in the immediate aftermath of the failure of the First Attempt and the midpoint reversal, the relationship between these two characters – the B-story – will take centre stage for a little while. The midpoint is where the hero and the co-protagonist change from being antagonistic towards one another, to being supportive, trusting, and respectful. This doesn't happen all at once, but the midpoint is where this change begins. The working relationship they have established develops into something stronger – either a genuine friendship or a romance, depending on the needs of the story and the characters you have created. After the failure of the First Attempt, the co-protagonist may want to confront the hero about his refusal to act or whatever else caused the failure, but at the same time, the failure has caused the hero to be much more honest – in admitting his culpability and expressing his fear that he isn't up to tackling the situation as he now understands it, the hero displays a vulnerability he's never demonstrated before, and the co-protagonist responds to this.

It has been said that in many stories, the midpoint marks a change such that where the first half of the plot was dominated by events and action, the second half is dominated by relationships: an action-adventure story becomes a romance, for example. The hero is no longer acting in his own interests alone: he has a lover or a friend whose fate is also at stake. In a genre romance or romantic comedy, the reverse is often true – the first half of the story concentrated on the relationship, bringing the two lovers together, and the second half of the story is filled with events and action that serve to drive them apart, at least until the climax of the story.

By making the relationship important to the hero, and then threatening it, we can raise the stakes in our story, whatever its genre. At the midpoint, the hero makes a new commitment to his story goal-quest and also to his relationship with the co-protagonist. In the second half of the story, relationships and emotions become much more central to the story, serving to provide both motivation, increased stakes, and added obstacles.

Sequence 5: Reacting to the Midpoint & Raising the Stakes

At the midpoint, the hero discovered something important and had to admit that *things can't go on like this – it isn't working*. The hero has realised he has been looking at the situation wrongly, or has denied it's true nature, or has completely misunderstood it. Following this realisation, he has to change the way he does things. His external goal may change or his motivation for achieving it may change. Something changes that sets the story off in a new way, And at the same time, the stakes are raised: the hero now has more to lose. Often the new stakes include a relationship – a friendship or romance – that has become important to him. Or he goes from being a passive character who reacts to events, to an active one who decides to make things happen, therefore putting himself in a riskier position. In a romance, the main characters found that they could no longer deny their attraction. In a thriller, the hero learns that he cannot run away from the problem, he must turn and confront it.

Sequence 5 exists as a reaction to the midpoint realisation or revelation. It is the hero's response – emotional, physical, and intellectual – to what he has learned. For this reason, it tends to be more of a transition sequence rather than a major action sequence.

In many stories, Sequence 5 will focus on the relationship between the hero and the co-protagonist – the hero's ally/buddy or his lover. The midpoint marked a change in this relationship, with the hero effectively saying, 'I can't do this without you – I need your help.' Or 'I don't want to be alone anymore.' As a result, trust develops between these two characters and they become closer. The relationship is now important to both of them. This is most obvious in a romance story or a story with a romantic subplot, because at the midpoint the couple come together romantically for the first time. Sequence 5 then becomes a sort of honeymoon period where they spend time together, the relationship develops, and their bond strengthens. The couple have gone from denying their feels to trusting and acting upon them. A similar thing happens in the platonic relationship in a 'buddy movie.'

Spoiler alert: One of the reasons why we give the hero an important relationship at this point in the story is so that we can whip it away from him at the end of Act II.

In stories that do not have such a significant relationship, we have to find another way to deepen reader interest and raise the stakes for the hero. In a Hitchcock-style thriller, for example, the hero moves from being a passive victim to an active combatant: he will try and resolve his problem situation by taking the fight to the villain. Sequence 5 then shows us the hero being active on a small scale and achieving some kind of success that boosts his confidence, encouraging him towards the Second Attempt that will be the focus of Act II.

Dara Marks, in *Inside Story*, refers to this part of a screenplay as a 'period of grace.' The midpoint has provided some sort of epiphany or enlightenment allowing the hero to move from a state of ignorance or unknowing, to a state of awareness. Marks notes that during this period the hero tends to thrive, as the tension is relieved for a while. This period of grace also offers "... a glimpse of what life might be like for the protagonist if he or she can reach the goal." We see a glimpse of the prize that the hero could claim if he succeeds in his present adventure.

In most stories, this moment is intended to lure both hero and audience into a false sense of security, causing them to lower their defences. Creating this lull makes the resumption of action all the more dramatic. This brighter moment also contrasts nicely with the 'darkest hour' that the hero will suffer at the end of Sequence 6.

The events that occur in Sequence 5 may differ depending on whether a hero/co-protagonist relationship is important in your story or not. Below I've listed a dozen things that can be included in this sequence – the first nine are common to all stories, the last three will only occur where the hero has a significant relationship with an ally, lover, or team. The sequence below is for ease of presentation only – the three relationship-related actions will need to be mixed in with the others if you use them in your story. 1 and 2 in this list will appear near the beginning of Sequence 5; 8 and 9 will occur near the end – everything else can be shifted around to suit the needs of your story.

1. Emotional Reaction to the Midpoint
2. Reluctance to Go On
3. Decision and New Commitment
4. Hero Tries to Prove Himself
5. Hero Redeems Himself
6. Active Hero
7. Active Antagonist
8. Planning the Second Attempt
9. Pinch Point II – 'Page 75'
10. Hero Tries to Convince Ally, Lover or Team to Give Him Another Chance
11. Hero and Co-protagonist Bonding and Increased Intimacy
12. Hero and Co-protagonist Unite Against the Villain

1. Emotional Reaction to the Midpoint

Just before the midpoint of the story, the hero suffered a defeat: his First Attempt to achieve the external story goal failed. He may even have discovered that he had chosen the wrong goal as a way of solving his external problem. The hero has also discovered that the world does not work the way he believed it did, or that the situation he is currently facing is not as straightforward as he thought. Or both.

He may also have learned something important about himself as a person. The hero's immediate response to all of this will be an emotional one.

Initially, he will be shaken by these realisations and revelations, because they require him to reassess his understanding and beliefs. He may become depressed as he realises the scale of what he faces, believing the problems to be insurmountable. Up until this point, the hero thought he knew what was expected of him, and believed he had the necessary knowledge, skills, and experience to succeed. But his confidence has been shaken by what occurred at the midpoint. He is troubled by self-doubt. He is afraid. These feelings of fear and uncertainty may be the result of the fact that the villain has just tried to kill him. Or they may have been caused by the fact that he has just fallen in love with someone.

If there is an ally or lover, they will also have an emotional reaction at this point – both to the failure of the First Attempt and to the perceived changed in their relationship to the hero.

2. Reluctance to Go On

Given the failure of the First Attempt, the hero may initially feel that he does not want to go on with his quest. He wants to abandon his goal and live with whatever consequences this may bring. His failure has shown him that resolving his situation will require more effort than he thought. It will require some sort of sacrifice on his part, and he doesn't know whether he is prepared – or even able – to make that sacrifice. He may express reluctance to continue, telling people that he doesn't think he's the right person for the job. He probably won't say publicly that he's afraid, instead he'll say that he made a mistake or misjudged the situation, and that he feels he should step aside and let someone else take over – someone who is better qualified or more committed to the cause. His fear may be such that he denies that he ever wanted to resolve his problem and that he was happy with things as they were. Better this than to have to face his fears head-on, or so he thinks.

The co-protagonist – whether they are a lover or an ally – may be confused by this reluctance. Why is he backing out now? They may feel that the hero is exactly the right person to be undertaking this goal-quest. They may share some of the hero's nervousness about continuing, but they do not have the same deep-seated fears as him.

3. Decision and New Commitment

Someone or something prompts the hero to make a decision. The co-protagonist or other members of his team may decide to continue with the quest, with or without him, and he must decide whether to go after them. Or the antagonist may take some action that the hero has to respond to – making him choose whether to give up or go on. Having had an emotional response to the events before the midpoint, the decision marks the hero's intellectual response. He thinks rationally about the situation he now finds himself in. The failure he has experienced causes him to re-examine both his objective and his motivation. He may also have to give some thought to what it is he is afraid of and why it paralyses him.

If the hero is involved in a relationship with an ally or lover, it may be this that swings the balance and makes him choose to continue: he wants to save the relationship. If the hero of your story has no such relationship, you will need some other incident to prompt him to reach his decision. The decision will need to be brought about by some combination of external event – another action taken by the villain, perhaps – and some inner pressure relating to what the hero wants or needs in life.

Part of his decision may include choosing a new, more appropriate, goal – something different that he believes will allow him to achieve his overall story objective. Or he may choose to make another attempt for the same goal, if he believes it is still the correct goal. There may be a change in his motivation – *why* he wants to achieve the story objective, and there will almost certainly need to be a change in the method he employs to achieve his goal. He will need a new plan for the Second Attempt.

The hero renews his determination to achieve his external objective – to deal with the problem situation or opportunity – and makes a new commitment to achieving his goal.

4. Hero Tries to Prove Himself

His failure before the midpoint, and his decision to continue his quest in spite of this, mean that the hero has now got something to prove – to himself, to the reader, and to his ally, lover or team. It is not enough for him to just *say* that he's recommitting himself to the adventure, he must *demonstrate* it. This will require him undertaking some concrete action that shows he means what he says.

The exact nature of this action will depend in part on who the hero of your story is, the type of story you are telling, and the nature of the thing that the hero fears most. In some stories, asking for help – saying 'I can't do this on my own' – is the right action: the hero may ask for a mentor or ally or lover or team's support. In other instances, the opposite may be true – the hero may need to prove that he can take responsibility for acting on his own without back-up. It may be necessary for the hero to admit he is vulnerable, and admit that he made a mistake before the midpoint. Or he may need to prove that he is strong – perhaps even having to defeat someone who challenges him for leadership of the team.

This action is not easy for the hero to perform because in some way it reminds him of, and perhaps bring him closer to, the thing he fears most. The stakes were raised at the midpoint and he is acutely aware of the added risk.

A lover may be keen to encourage and support the hero in taking these actions, seeing them as evidence of his new commitment. An ally or team may be more sceptical and less supportive: they have seen him fail once and are wondering how strong this new commitment really is.

5. Hero Redeems Himself

The hero successfully completes an action that proves his new commitment or suitability to himself, the reader, the co-protagonist and/or his team. This may involve him putting himself at risk of physical or emotional risk to protect others. Or it may be performing some action that he failed at, or was afraid to attempt, during the First Attempt. Whatever it is, it earns him a chance to undertake a Second Attempt.

6. Active Hero

Related to 4 and 5 above is the need for the hero to take action. During the first half of Act II, he tended to be reactive rather than proactive. He may have regarded himself as a victim of circumstances, responding to events as they arose, and trying to escape from the problem. He was also a novice and a wanderer in the 'strange new world' in which his quest was taking place. He made mistakes because he didn't know what the rules were or how to behave in this place, and he didn't really understand the nature of the problem he was trying to deal with. He was a bumbling amateur acting in ignorance. The revelations and/or realisations at the midpoint changed this. As he moves into the second half of Act II, he has gained experience and learned from his mistakes. He's starting to find his way around in this world and knows what is expected of him. The things he learned at the midpoint mean he is no longer in the dark about what he is up against: he has a better understanding of the forces that oppose him. The hero may not yet have all the skills, knowledge and experience that he will need, but is no longer in a position of 'unconscious incompetence' but has moved to what Peter Dunne calls 'conscious incompetence' – he now knows what he is lacking and can take action to achieve something closer to the competence that success will require. Sequence 5 is where he begins to try and close that gap.

After the midpoint there is often an obvious change in the hero's behaviour. In a romance, the main character no longer denies their feelings, instead they accept them and act on them. In a thriller, the hero has been chased by the villain but now turns the tables and becomes the pursuer, setting out to stop the villain's evil plan. The hero becomes more active in this part of the story and actually instigates his own actions rather than just reacting to things done by the antagonist. This new proactivity is one of the things that helps to redeem the hero in the eyes of other characters and of the reader.

7. Active Antagonist

We've said that Sequence 5 is more of a transitional period than an action sequence, because it provides the hero time to reflect and readjust to what happened at the midpoint. The relationship – the B-story – often takes precedence over the A-story here. But that does not mean that the main action of the plot stands still while this happens.

Blake Snyder calls this part of a screenplay 'the bad guys close in.' The villain or opponent carries on with his own plans regardless of what is going on in the hero's life.

One of the things the hero often discovers at the midpoint is information about the antagonist's wicked plan. As well as showing the hero what he is really up against, possession of this knowledge makes the hero a threat to the antagonist. As a result, the antagonist will increase his efforts to capture or destroy the hero, so he cannot reveal what he has learned or put it to use. Having obtained this knowledge – which may be a 'Macguffin' such as secret plans or a person he has rescued – the hero now has to keep hold of it and get it to someone or to somewhere that it can be used. The hero may not yet fully understand the value of what he has discovered, and the antagonist may want to silence him before he discovers the importance of the information he has gained.

The hero's actions during the First Attempt have gained the attention of the antagonist: if the villain wasn't gunning for the hero before, he is now. While the hero is recovering from his defeat, the antagonist may attack, taking advantage of his vulnerability. It may be the response to this attack that allows the hero to redeem himself.

Given that the hero has just discovered the nature of the antagonist's plan, we can now introduce a deadline or countdown, increasing both suspense for the reader and pressure on the hero. If the hero knows the villain plans to do 'X' on a specific date, this limits the amount of time the hero has to put a stop to the plan. The clock is ticking.

There are other sources of antagonism that may be active during Sequence 5. The hero and the co-protagonist may find themselves at loggerheads. Or there may be infighting within the hero's team – problems of dissent, doubt, jealousy, or a challenge for the leadership position.

8. Planning the Second Attempt

Having made a decision to continue with his quest, the hero makes a plan for the Second Attempt to achieve the story objective. This takes place in a very similar way to that detailed for the First Attempt in Sequence 3. Do not duplicate things the reader or viewer has already seen, instead concentrate on showing things that are different between than planning session and this one – what has changed?

9. Pinch Point II – 'Page 75'

In Syd Field's 120-page screenplay plot 'paradigm,' there is a second Pinch Point at page 75. This turning point is related to the climax at the end of Sequence 3, page 45 in the screenplay. These two 'pinches' – along with the midpoint – are staging posts on the hero's journey, each one providing a test so that we can see how far he has progressed since the challenge was issued. It can also be that something set-up on page 45 finally pays off at page 75; or page 75 could act as a reminder that this thing was set-up, paving the way for it to pay off later in the story.

10. Hero Tries to Convince Ally, Lover or Team to Give Him a Second Chance

In a story with a significant relationship subplot involving a co-protagonist or a team, the hero may find himself having to apologise for his failure during the First

Attempt. His actions let them down and may have put them at risk, or even caused them actual harm. An ally or a team might want to continue the story quest without the hero. Or someone – possibly the lover or ally – may challenge the hero for leadership of the team. The hero may have to fight to prove himself a worthy leader. Or he may have to step down and allow someone to take his place – at least until he can redeem himself (see above) in the eyes of the people around him.

11. Hero and Co-protagonist Bonding and Increased Intimacy

Following the hero's new demonstration of commitment (see above), and aware how difficult the action has been for the hero, the co-protagonist – the ally or lover – may grow closer to him. A greater bond of trust and respect grows between them. They may have had a falling-out at the midpoint, in part because of the co-protagonist's disappointment in the hero, but now they are reconciled. It may be a little while before they feel able to fully trust each other, but the bond is repaired.

As a result of the things they have been through together, they have formed a strong working relationship – the initial antagonism has faded, and they have come to respect each other. Trust is developing, but the hero – and possibly the co-protagonist as well – does not have the emotional experience to be able to deal with his feelings: particularly if their relationship is developing into a romance.

Eventually, their trust may develop into a more intimate relationship – either platonic or romantic. There are several things that can occur during this part of the story:

Co-protagonist Makes a Commitment to the Hero. Having accepted he hero's apology and seen him redeem himself through concrete action, the co-protagonist makes some gesture of commitment. They say to the hero I trust you, I believe in you, and I am going to support you through the remainder of your quest.

Co-protagonist Requires Commitment from the Hero. Having committed themselves to supporting the hero, the co-protagonist wants a promise from the hero in return. This is typically along the lines of 'no more secrets' – they are in this together and they have to trust each other. Completely.

Sharing of Hopes and Fears. As the hero and co-protagonist spend more time together and become more open with each other, we may learn more about the backstory of each of them, usually in the form of some sort of memory or anecdote that gives us an insight into how their life experiences to date have shaped their view of the world, and influenced the way that they behave, and the way that they form relationships. Each may tell the other something about the thing they fear most in life, and may perhaps reveal the circumstances that gave rise to this fear. They may also share details of their dreams – the ideal life that they hope to find some day.

This period of bonding and increased intimacy is part of the 'moment of grace' that Dara Marks talks about. It is a taste of the happiness that the hero could have if he manages to complete his goal-quest successfully.

12. Hero and Co-protagonist Unite Against the Villain

The hero and the co-protagonist have made a commitment to work together from this point on. 'We're in this together, no matter what.' They are both aware that this is going to mean that, at some point very soon, they are going to come face-to-face with the antagonist and there's going to be a fight. They have now agreed that they will fight side by side.

The key outcome of Sequence 5 is that we have raised the stakes for the hero. One of the most effective ways of doing that is through his relationship with an ally or lover. By making the hero care deeply about someone else, we make him more vulnerable. We give him more to worry about. He is no longer responsible for just his own physical, emotional and mental well-being – he feels a duty to protect this other person as well. And the feeling is mutual.

Going into Sequence 6, we should feel that the hero is now willing to fight to preserve and protect his relationship with the co-protagonist. Being together has become more important to him than surviving alone. He is also approaching a point where he is prepared to risk his own safety and happiness to save the co-protagonist. By the end of Act II, we need the hero to have reached a position where he is prepared to make the ultimate sacrifice to protect the people and the principles that he cares most strongly about. We need him to be at a point where he will face and conquer his greatest fear. This point at the end of Act II is when the A-story and the B-story converge. At the end of Sequence 5, he is not quite there yet – but he is a good way along the road.

At the end of Sequence 3 (page 45), circumstances had forced the hero and the protagonist together, but their personalities kept them apart – they mistrusted each other and were antagonistic. At the end of Sequence 5 (page 75), a close relationship has now developed so that they want to be together, but external circumstances – the continued actions of the antagonist – mean that they cannot concentrate all of their efforts on their relationship: they have to get the business of the quest out of the way first.

After their brief respite and moment of reflection, the two characters are forced to respond to the continuing actions of the antagonist. As well as demonstrating a commitment to each other, they must also show a renewed commitment to achieving the external goal. The revelations or discoveries made at the midpoint have provided a new perspective on the external problem, which informs the new plan that the hero determines to implement. This may or may not include a change in the nature of the external goal, and/or a change in motivation. The midpoint revelation may have shown the hero the nature of the forces of antagonism. He will have learned how dangerous the opposition is, even if he may not yet have discovered the actual identity of the main antagonist. Similarly, the failed attempt made by the hero before the midpoint will have revealed his identity to the antagonist. Now that he is known to the antagonist, the danger for the hero has increased. There may also be an element of time pressure added – a deadline or a sense of time running out – as the antagonist races to complete his evil plan before the hero can stop him.

The climax at the end of Sequence 5 is the hero being ready to take the first action of the Second Attempt to achieve the external story goal. The major part of the action of this attempt will be carried out in Sequence 6, and that will develop into the crisis at the end of Act II (page 90 in our screenplay) when the Second Attempt fails.

Sequence 6: The Second Attempt, The Fall, & The Crisis

The final quarter of Act II has been referred to as the 'fall' or the 'unravelling,' because this is where everything falls apart for the hero. At the end of this sequence he ends up at the major crisis point in the story, sometimes called the hero's 'darkest hour' or the 'dark night of the soul.' This is a major turning point in the story that marks the end of Act II and sets up the climax in Act III. Sequence 6 builds to this crisis point. The hero made a major discovery at the midpoint of the story, and in the scenes that followed this, he seemed to be on top of the situation. Sequence 5 was a period of positive relationship building and of planning the Second Attempt. But, there is still some problem that the hero hasn't tackled yet – he may be denying it, or ignoring it and hoping it will go away, but it is waiting in the wings to trip him up. He is doomed to failure because of some action – or inaction – on his own part.

Sequence 6 presents the second major test for the hero. He puts a new or revised plan into action and expects it to succeed because he believes that the midpoint revelation, and his improved relationship with his co-protagonist, gives him everything he needs for success. The hero may not suspect that tragedy is looming, but the audience will know – either because the danger has been made obvious to them, or because they just feel that, on a subconscious level, something is not quite right. Often there is something that the hero has 'conveniently' forgotten or ignored – something that is going to come back and bite him in the bum. This may be an unforeseen consequence of an action he took earlier or a delayed reaction. In a teen comedy, the hero usually does something stupid in the first half of the story – in either Sequence 2 or 3 – and then his life changes as a result of a new relationship with the co-protagonist, but then this stupid thing comes back to ruin everything in Sequence 6. To take our clichéd example, a new girl moves into the area and a bunch of guys make a bet on who can get her into bed first – it's the sort of stupid, misogynistic thing guys in movies typically do. The hero gets to know the girl, he and she really do fall in love, and the stupid bet is forgotten. Until the moment when its revelation can do the most harm. She learns of the bet, believes he's only stringing her along so that he can win the bet, and so she tells him to get lost: she never wants to see him again. Boy loses girl. End of Act II.

Sequence 5 offered the hero a glimpse of what his ideal life could be like. It dealt mainly with relationship issues, and everything seemed to be going pretty well. The external threat from the antagonist may have been forgotten for a while – though, of course, the audience knows that he hasn't gone away. The midpoint has given the hero a new outlook on life. He learned something important about himself, or about the way the world works, and possibly both. His relationship with the co-protagonist helps him begin to adjust to this change. But whatever new insight he has gained needs to be integrated into his life – or it may overwhelm the hero and upset the balance of his life, like a pendulum that has swung too far in the other direction. This integration requires patience and prudence – but he may not have these qualities in place yet. He may become drunk on his new-found feelings of freedom and power and, in an attempt to 'seize the day,' he may suffer poor judgment and an inflated ego, and so engage in reckless and irresponsible behaviour. Sequence 5 shows the hero the prize that could be his – but in order to take it, he is going to have to give something up. Some part of his old existence has got to be sacrificed. But he doesn't have the wisdom to recognise this yet. He believes that he can have everything he had before as well as this new thing: he can have this new life without having to make any commitment to it by giving up his old life. This sort of thinking isn't going to end well.

The hero may end up in a kind of ambivalent fantasy world, where he is not fully connected to either his old life or his new one, and the danger then is that he could lose both of them and finish up with nothing. Sequence 6 is a test: is the hero ready to sacrifice his old life and fully embrace his new one, accepting all of the responsibilities that it brings with it? And the hero is going to fail this test. He will lose everything – at the crisis point of the story – and then he will have to decide what he is going to fight to recover and rebuild from the wreckage. The beginning of Sequence 6 is where things begin to slip. The hero's inability to fully commit means that the idyllic situation in Sequence 5 cannot possibly last. It is built on a poor foundation. The co-protagonist believes that the hero should move on from his old life and fully embrace his new one, which includes the relationship with the co-protagonist. But the hero is clinging to his old life, and perhaps trying to keep this secret from the co-protagonist, perhaps even denying it to himself. This level of dishonesty is not sustainable. His ambivalent attitude – literally trying to maintain the old life and the new – means that the hero begins to engage in half-truths and lies. Misjudgements and miscommunications occur.

The hero may have someone from his old life trying to encourage him to come back to it. They will give the hero poor advice, perhaps deliberately, perhaps not. They may try to sabotage the hero's relationship with the co-protagonist. They may push the hero into situations that will prove that he hasn't moved on from his old life – forcing the co-protagonist to see that the hero isn't ready to commit to a new life. Sequence 6 is a place where unfaithfulness or betrayal, duplicity or treachery, take place or are imagined to be taking place. The co-protagonist may come to feel that they cannot trust the hero. The hero may feel that the co-protagonist is trying to manipulate him and force him to give up a way of life that he doesn't need to move on from. The sacrifice that the hero needs to make – giving up the old and proving himself ready and 'worthy' of having the new – is something that he is afraid to face. He may not know this consciously, but he certainly feels it. Major life changes are scary, and we may avoid committing ourselves to making them. We may try and deny that the change is even necessary. Remember the Kubler-Ross change-curve?

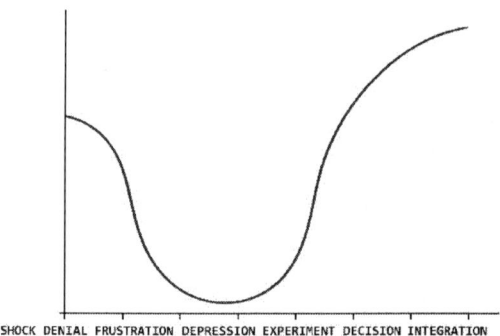

SHOCK DENIAL FRUSTRATION DEPRESSION EXPERIMENT DECISION INTEGRATION

The thing about change is that it often causes life to get worse before it gets better. What prompts change is often an uncomfortable experience that prompts us to risk trying something new. And often the hardest part about change is that it means we have to let go and ride with it – we can't control the journey or the outcome. The desire for control belongs to the old way of life that we need to move away from. Change means letting go. And we often have to be forced into doing that. Things have to get worse before we are ready to let them get better. Sequence 6 is going to take the hero from the happiness of Sequence 5 to the deepest trough of depression, the darkest hour, that is the crisis at the end of Act II.

His fear of change makes the hero indecisive, and his commitment to the external quest is all but forgotten. While he is distracted, the antagonist has a clear road and can make progress unhindered. And the antagonist's success is effectively handed to him by the hero. Feeling that he is no longer in control of his own life, and feeling that he is being pushed towards the kind of situation that he fears most, the hero is likely to become angry and defensive. He will push the co-protagonist away – either deliberately or inadvertently – because he sees them as the cause of his present discomfort. He may unconsciously sabotage their relationship. He may engage in the worst excesses of his old kinds of behaviour, as he tries to regain the familiar feelings of comfort his old life gave him. He may do things in an attempt to 'punish' the co-protagonist – effectively 'cutting off his nose to spite his face.' And all this means that things begin to fall apart for the hero. The unravelling occurs at the point when the hero has the most to lose. When he is most vulnerable. And it drives him towards the kind of situation that he is most afraid of. The 'worst thing that could possibly happen' actually happens at the end of Act II. And it's even worse than he feared it would be.

What we are describing here is the psychological, the inner experience of change. In a novel or screenplay, we need to translate this into external actions. The hero's journey, as described in Chris Vogler's book *The Writer's Journey,* tries to do this using the metaphor of the heroic quest. I should note here that although I am lifting stages from the hero's journey, I am placing them in a different place in my 'model plot' than Vogler does. In his circular plot diagram, the supreme ordeal occurs at the midpoint of the story: that doesn't work for me, so I have the supreme ordeal occurring as the 'crisis point' of the story at the end of Act II.

Sequence 6

The Experience of Change in the Hero's Quest
In the hero's journey, the midpoint has the hero seizing a prize – which equates to the midpoint discovery or revelation that we described in our midpoint chapter earlier. The hero learns something about himself and/or the way that the world works, and this discovery is going to be something that is vital in achieving his external and internal objectives. But having gained this prize, what is the hero going to do with it? In Sequence 5 we saw him effectively taking a breather and coming to terms with what happened at the midpoint. He celebrated the positive side of gaining the prize – while, for the most part, ignoring the consequences and responsibilities that came with seizing it. Sequence 6 is where those consequences and responsibilities have to be dealt with. But is the hero ready for them? Hint: No, he's not.

The hero's journey model gives us a number of possible stages that we can include in this part of the story:

   i. Preparation for the Ordeal
   ii. Opposition
   iii. The 'Underworld' or Villain's Lair
   iv. The Supreme Ordeal

Using the terminology of the hero's journey model, Sequence 6 becomes the *approach to the inner-most cave* or *approaching the villain's lair*. This dark place is the thing the hero fears most – his inner fears externalised as a terrible place. This action is the equivalent of James Bond making his way into the villain's secret base in order to confront him and stop his evil plan. Or it can be seen as the hero leading his team onto the battlefield where they will face the biggest battle of the war. In other words, the hero may make the approach alone, or as part of a group. Whichever works best for your story. When it comes to the crisis at the end of Act II, the hero will be physically or figuratively standing alone, and having to face the villain without a back-up or a safety net, but for now he may still have people working with him.

(i) Preparation for the Ordeal

What we are seeing in this sequence of the story is the hero's Second Attempt to achieve the external story objective. The exact nature of this objective may have changed as a result of what was learned at the midpoint so that the hero is no longer going for the 'wrong goal.' Knowing his goal, the hero must formulate a new plan. The steps involved in this will be similar to those that were required for the First Attempt. Here they are as a reminder:

1. Identify the desired outcome
2. Set a goal that will bring about the desired outcome
3. Create a plan to achieve the goal
4. Identify resources to carry out the plan: knowledge, skills, equipment, people, etc.
5. Conduct a review of available resources

6. Obtain resources identified as missing in the previous step, including recruiting team members and/or carrying out training
7. Create a schedule for the individual actions in the plan
8. Perform the first action

I'm not going to go over these in detail again. In your story you should avoid showing the reader anything that they've seen before – don't make this 'planning and preparation' sequence the same as the earlier one. Highlight things that are different, highlight new conflicts, and gloss over anything that is identical, mentioning it only in passing.

If the hero is leading a team, things will have changed between the first abortive attempt and this second one. There may have been changes to the personnel that make up the team. Some may have been wounded or killed in the first attempt, or may have left the team for other reasons. Team members may be promoted to new roles, having proved themselves in the earlier battle. Others may have to take on roles that they are not trained or comfortable to assume as a result of the original incumbents having been lost. The hero's mentor may have been lost in the first major attempt, leaving the hero to lead without his most valued advisor. Preparation for the new battle may involve cleaning and testing weapons, and repairing and putting on armour – or equivalent tasks. Team members may enjoy a meal together or share a joke, knowing that dawn will see them taking to the battlefield.

(ii) Opposition

An individual hero or a team may face a variety of internal and external obstacles. There could be a leadership challenge in a team. One or more team members may abandon or betray the hero. Others may seek to escape their responsibilities or may express misgivings. All of these things can affect and undermine morale in the team as a whole. The hero will need to promote calm and confidence. The approach to the villain's lair is likely to be well-defended, making the journey towards it challenging. These physical defences are also symbolic of the internal obstacles that the hero and members of his team face. Overcoming these barriers provides new information, experience and confidence, that can be used in the final confrontation to come. Skirmishes fought during this part of the journey may rob the hero of valuable resources, and even members of his team. These losses increase the odds against success and dent the confidence of the team members remaining.

(iii) The 'Underworld' or Villain's Lair

Depicted in mythology as a dark cave or the 'land of the dead,' the villain's lair represents the thing that the hero fears most. It is a situation that resembles whatever traumatic incident in his past made the hero fearful of change. For Humphrey Bogart in *Casablanca*, it is recognising that he is still deeply in love with Ilsa and faces losing her all over again. For James Bond, it is entering the upside-down world of the super-villain, whose ambitions and moral values are the opposite of everything that Bond is licenced to defend. The 'villain's lair' is something that threatens the hero's physical well-being, his mental health, and/or his emotional stability. It is an insane, mixed-up, and confusing place where the normal rules do not apply. It is a place that will take your deepest, darkest fears and use them against you. It's Disneyland for psychos. Possibly.

The 'underworld' doesn't have to be an actual dark place or even involve a change of location. Though there is often some sort of symbolic crossing of a threshold, perhaps even a challenge from a threshold guardian. What we really see is the hero entering a situation that he is afraid to face. The situation that the hero finds himself in now will usually be almost identical to a situation he faced earlier in the story – or earlier in his life – and failed to deal with. This is a second chance, an opportunity for the hero to redeem himself. But this time the stakes are much higher.

The hero may have to pass a threshold guardian in order to enter the underworld, he will typically be required to demonstrate different skills than were required to pass the guardian at the end of Act I / beginning of Act II. Back then he used force or trickery or charm – anything that worked to get across that threshold. What he was doing then was proving a commitment to accept the challenge. At this new threshold, he will need to demonstrate that he has learned as a result of his experiences in the story so far. Crossing the threshold cannot be achieved by force or a face-to-face encounter. Rather, it will require a more empathic approach. The hero will need to demonstrate an understanding of the villain's world – as with the first threshold, he is trying to prove that he is 'worthy' of entering this dark world, which requires an understanding of the qualities of the 'demons' who inhabit this world. In action stories, the hero often gains entry to the villain's lair by disguising himself as one of the villain's men. He has to be able to look like, and behave like, a minor demon in order to enter. This requires an understanding of the people who inhabit it. Christopher Vogler identifies another way that the hero can pass this empathy test: he can demonstrate an understanding of the threshold guardian's position, and make an emotional appeal such that the guardian will allow him to pass. Rather than trying to kill the guardian, the hero puts himself into the mind of the guardian and asks himself: what would I be feeling in his situation? What would persuade me to allow someone to pass? He has to prove himself to the guardian in a non-violent way. Crossing this threshold, whether it is physical or psychological, is a big step for the hero, as it is the first step in facing and conquering the thing he fears most. Once he crosses this border, he is trapped in the underworld and cannot go back – he must face whatever danger lies ahead.

A feature of this stage of his quest is that the hero usually finds himself isolated and facing his fears alone. His mentor will be gone – having bowed out because he has nothing more to offer the hero or having been killed by the villain or having proved himself no longer suitable as a guide. Members of his team will have abandoned him or been taken from him. And now, like Gary Cooper in *High Noon,* he stands alone, about to face the ultimate test. Having entered the underworld, the hero now stands at the heart of the problem, he is in the centre of the spider's web, the treasure room of the dragon's lair, the deepest, darkest cave of the demonlord's realm. Which may only be the home of his lover's parents, but it is the most frightening situation he has ever faced. As the hero progresses deeper and deeper into this shadowy realm, the spaces he encounters often get smaller, and the passages he goes through gets narrower. This symbolic narrowing is like a noose tightening: the forces of antagonism – both internal and external – are closing in on him, and his options for action and gradually being reduced. He is being funnelled towards an encounter with the thing he fears most.

Has the hero got what it takes to face this ultimate ordeal? Stay tuned to find out...

(iv) The Supreme Ordeal

The hero squares his shoulders and steps forward, prepared – or so he believes – to face the ordeal. He has done as much preparation as he can, he has all the information he needs – he thinks he knows what it is he is about to face – and that he knows what will be expected of him. All he has to do is take the correct 'moral' approach, and his success is more or less guaranteed. It's going to be a tough few hours, but it isn't nearly as bad as he had always feared it would be.

Or so he thinks. The ordeal is the final part of the unravelling and is where things really fall apart for the hero.

There are a number of stages that this part of the story can include – these have been pulled together, for the most part, from the plot models of Christopher Vogler, Dan Decker, and Rob Tobin.

1. The Hero Takes Action
2. The Antagonist Strikes Back
3. An Act of Desperation
4. A False Solution
5. Attack by the Co-protagonist
6. The Fall
7. Second Major Failure
8. Crisis – the Hero's Darkest Hour
9. Meltdown – the Hero Reaches Breaking Point
10. The Antagonist Prevails

1. The Hero Takes Action. The hero puts his plan into effect, carrying out the first action. At this point, he feels fairly confident because he knows that he is doing 'the right thing.'

2. The Antagonist Strikes Back. The antagonist, or his henchman, responds to the hero's first action, causing it to fail or weakening its impact. The result of this action is usually that the antagonist increases his area of threat, and the hero increases his area of concern. That is, the stakes are raised. Typically, the antagonist retaliates and someone other than – or as well as – the hero is threatened and/or suffers. As a result of the hero's actions, someone else is put at risk. This means that the hero must now accept responsibility for the fate of this person or group.

3. An Act of Desperation. Responding to the increasing pressure, the hero breaks his own rules of conduct and/or morality – trying to fight fire with fire and beat the antagonist at his own game using the antagonist's own methods. This is the moment when the hero and the antagonist are most alike – with the only difference between them being that the hero is breaking his own rules, doing what he knows is wrong, while the antagonist is acting in accordance with his rules and doing what he believes is correct and acceptable. Same actions, but different points of view. This 'immoral' act by the hero fails. It may initially appear to succeed, providing a false solution (see below), but if it does, this action will have unforeseen consequences that will quickly make the hero's situation much worse than it was. The hero's immoral act may result in harm to the co-protagonist or may result in the co-protagonist being captured by the antagonist. The hero may be captured at the same time or may attempt to rescue the co-protagonist and then be captured.

Breaking his own rules was a last resort for the hero – he now has nothing else left. What can he do? He has run out of options. Except that he hasn't. Abandoning his principles was a desperate act, motivated in part by the fact that the hero doesn't want to face the 'thing he fears most.' But that is exactly what is required of him at this point. He's not yet ready to face this – things will have to get even worse before he is prepared to accept this final challenge. Up until this moment, the hero has been trying to destroy the antagonist – but what is really required is for him to get inside the head of the antagonist and understand him. But to do this requires the hero to accept the dark side of his own character – which the antagonist symbolises – and that is too terrifying for him to contemplate. He despises this aspect of his own character and refuses to acknowledge it exists.

4. A False Solution. It may appear that the hero's 'immoral' action has succeeded and that he has put an end to the antagonist's plan. This will only be a temporary success, and the antagonist will soon be back stronger than ever and twice as angry. Another form of false solution occurs if the hero's 'immoral' action does not succeed in 'defeating' the antagonist, but does cause the antagonist to come to the hero and make him an offer. Having seen the hero act immorally, the antagonist will say 'we are not so different, you and I' and then offer the hero a partnership. They will rule together. Depending on his current state of mind, the hero may seriously consider this offer. Perhaps for a brief moment, he enjoyed behaving immorally. The freedom from his own self-imposed rules may have been intoxicating. This is a moment of temptation, and one of the final tests the hero has got to face. The hero may even be tempted to try and depose the antagonist in order to seize the throne for himself – he will become the new crime lord or super-villain. Overthrowing the antagonist is the right goal, but doing this simply to take his place would be doing the right thing for the wrong reason.

The hero may join the antagonist for a while, until the real implications of the immoral actions of the antagonist are brought home to him in a very real way. Or he may pretend to join the antagonist, in an attempt to get stay close to him and hope to find a moment when he can finally defeat him. Or he may say to the antagonist 'I'd rather die!' In which case, the antagonist will agree to grant him that wish.

5. Attack by the Co-protagonist. Whatever happens in 4 above, the hero is likely to be confronted by an angry co-protagonist. His immoral action has caused him to lose the respect of the co-protagonist, and possibly of other people around him. The co-protagonist – his ally or lover – will challenge him over his 'immoral' actions. Here the co-protagonist is acting as the hero's conscience, like Jiminy Cricket. The hero knows what he has done is wrong. He may deny this, even to himself. But he knows. As a result, he may become extremely defensive and refuse to accept the co-protagonist's criticism. This response by the co-protagonist increases the pressure on the hero, forcing him to question his values and behaviours. This additional strain may be the final straw that damages the relationship between the hero and the co-protagonist. The co-protagonist may give the hero an ultimatum. Or the co-protagonist may decide that the hero is incapable of doing what must be done, and so abandons him and sets off to try and defeat the villain without the hero. This may result in the co-protagonist being captured, injured or even killed. This further increases the pressure on the hero. Or the co-protagonist may say 'to hell with you,' and end the relationship, leaving the hero standing alone and stunned.

6. The Fall. With the co-protagonist abandoning him or having been taken from him by the antagonist, the hero has in the final stages of his unravelling. The unravelling has been caused in part by the fact that the hero remains uncommitted – he is trying to hold on to his old, comfortable way of life, while at the same time wanting to seize the opportunity that his new life offers. But these two are incompatible – to have the new, he must sacrifice the old. In his heart, he knows this, but he is terrified by the prospect. He needs one final push – the fall – to force him to make this choice. The hero is close to giving up his quest for good, because his story objective seems impossible to reach. Everything that he used to depend on – the people; the places; the behaviours; the skills, knowledge and experience – have all been taken from him or been proved inadequate to the task. He feels the earth crumbling beneath his feet and has nothing left to hold on to.

Things can't possibly get any worse, can they? Of course they can! And they will.

7. The Second Failure. The hero's Second Attempt at achieving his external objective fails, even after he has made a last-ditch attempt to succeed by using 'immoral' actions. These actions either fail immediately, or they appear to have no effect or even to have succeeded, and then have a delayed consequence that results in failure. It appeared that the hero would finally achieve his external objective, and it may even have appeared that he had done so. But victory is snatched from him, and instead he suffers a disastrous failure. This is worse than the hero ever feared, because not only is his own fate (or happiness) in the balance, but also that of the people he cares about. And it is his fault. His choices and actions have resulted in innocent people being put at risk. And he has lost not only what he had in Act I, his old life, but also any chance of the amazing new life that he was offered a glimpse of in Sequence 5, following the midpoint revelation.

8. Crisis – The Hero's Darkest Hour. This failure – which is the thing the hero has feared most right from Act I – has come to pass. And it is worse than he ever feared.

The hero feels lost, clueless, hopeless, and foolish. This is the lowest moment of his life – he is devastated and believes that he has lost everything. In an action movie, this is the point where the hero has been captured and is at the mercy of the villain, with death only a heartbeat away. In a romance it is the moment when 'boy loses girl,' and there seems no possible way that the two could ever be reconciled. Both the hero and the reader should be convinced that there is no possible hope of turning this situation around. This is part of the game – the situation at the end of Act II must appear hopeless. We need the reader to be willing us on, hoping that we will be able to get the hero out of this deep, dark hole.

The hero has failed, and he must be aware that he has failed. He has to be brought to this worst possible moment in order to (a) learn humility – that he cannot control events and people by force of will; and (b) be forced to re-evaluate his priorities in life. Only when he has lost everything is he able to see the one thing that matters to him more than anything else. Only now can he possibly be ready to make the sacrifice that needs to be made that will prove the thematic argument of the story, and prove him worthy of having whatever has been lacking in his life, his greatest need, finally fulfilled.

Note that the crisis is the opposite of the outcome at the climax of the story in Act III. There will be a major reversal of the hero's fortune in Act III. If you are planning a happy (or an ironic) ending, the crisis at the end of Act II must be a tragedy. If, however, you are planning a tragic end for your character at the climax of the story, then this situation at the end of Act II will be the opposite – it will appear to be a victory.

9. Meltdown – The Hero Reaches Breaking Point. Things have gotten so bad that the hero loses control. And this loss of control frightens him. This is his emotional response to the crisis. High emotion – laughing or crying or screaming in anger – are a demonstration of his frustration and vulnerability. The hero experiences extreme disappointment, and feelings of loss. He will feel disillusionment and anger, and may feel that he has been betrayed or let down people the people and situations around him. He will feel that the moment of happiness he experienced in Sequence 5 was a cruel trick, because now any chance of achieving that happiness in the long-term has been snatched away from him. He may want to blame others, but deep down, the hero believes that this terrible situation is all his fault – it is the result of his own actions, or his failure to act. He has allowed the antagonist to win. He will believe that he has to fix the problem himself. Alone. This is the last sign of him trying to dominate and control the situation by force of will, rather than opening himself up to live in the moment and gain a real understanding of what is required of him. He may push others away, refusing any offers of help, saying 'no, this is my problem.' He is also so vulnerable and afraid, that he feels unable to trust anyone else. He needs the support and understanding of the co-protagonist at this point but will push them away if he hasn't already lost them. At this moment, he is overcome by self-destructive feelings. His situation is hopeless, he believes, and nothing can be done about it. And this is true, unless he can overcome this moment of self-doubt.

Note that the 'meltdown' can occur *before* the 'act of desperation' – losing his grip could be what prompts the hero to undertake an 'immoral' action.

10. The Antagonist Prevails. The antagonist appears to have won. Everyone the hero cares about is now in danger. The antagonist begins his final actions towards his own (villainous) objective, seemingly assured of achieving it. The antagonist does something that the hero must respond to. It is a new stimulus. But to respond to this stimulus successfully, the hero will have to make an important decision.

I believe that Sequence 6, and Act II, ends with this cliff-hanger – the hero defeated and faced with deciding what to do next. This may be regarded as melodramatic, but subtlety isn't really my thing. You may have noticed that. Other theorists believe that Act II ends with the hero making his decision and ready to take the next action. To be honest, it doesn't really matter where you draw the line that says end of Act II / beginning of Act III since the act breaks aren't real – they're just something we use to help us plot out our stories. Since other sequences begin with a 'transition' scene in which the hero reacts to the previous sequence climax and makes a decision about how to respond, I reckon that means that Sequence 6 ends with the crisis, and Sequence 7 begins with the hero's decision. I suppose, to some extent, it depends on how dramatic you can make the decision – is it worthy of being a sequence and act climax? That is for you to decide. I'm putting it in Act III.

The end of Act II is the Second Major Turning Point in the story. It sets up Act III. This turning point must be something that is caused by the actions of the hero and should be something that involves him directly. And it must lead logically into Act III and the final climax of the story.

In case you blinked and missed it, this is the end of Act II. We made it through the long haul. That's the tough part over. All we have to do now is create the climax – the highest point of the drama and emotion in our story – and we're about done.

Act III: The End – Climax & Resolution

"When the end of the movie is the most exciting or emotionally involving part, then the audience troops happily out of the darkness and that's how word-of-mouth is born."
– William Goldman

In Act I you promised conflict, a clash of opposing forces, fireworks both physical and emotional. The climax of the story is where you finally have to deliver on that promise. The last thing you want to happen is for your reader to feel let down or cheated by your ending. We also learned what the hero was most afraid of, and what terrible fate awaited him if he failed to achieve his story goal.

Act II left the hero in a hole, effectively defeated – his whole world in tatters and everything he cared for and hoped for apparently lost to him. His worst fears have come true and the terrible fate has befallen him – or something even worse! And now he faces the last and biggest decision of the whole story and possibly of his whole life. As the smoke clears and the debris settles, whether physical or metaphorical, he has to make a choice: will he make one more desperate, do-or-die attempt to achieve his story objective? Everything you have written so far has been leading up to this decisive moment. Are you feeling the pressure?

Act III is the *end* and is made up of Sequences 7 and 8. Sequence 7 is the *climax* of the story, where the Major Dramatic Question is finally answered. Sequence 8 is the aftermath of this climax, where any loose ends are tied up, and we return the hero to the equilibrium of a new sort of everyday life. Assuming he survives the climax.

Your reader should be eager to read on and discover how the hero is going to get himself out of the end of Act II hole. And you as the writer should be eager to write it, so that you can discover how it finally turns out. If you see creating this final clash as the last chore to get out of the way so that you can finish this damned book, then you are not in the right place to write an effective climax. Either you haven't done the necessary preparation to get yourself into a position to be able to write it, and write it quickly and well. Or something has gone wrong earlier in your story, and your subconscious is telling you that you're going to need to fix it before you can properly write the big finish. If you're bored with the idea of the climax because you know what's going to happen, then there's every chance that your ending is too obvious and the reader will see this ending coming from a mile off. We will look at some different ways you can rethink your ending and come up with something that will seem both inevitable and yet unexpected.

Act III needs to do four things:

i. Provide a strong, emotional climax that lives up to the promise of conflict that was made in Act I and the anticipation that has built up during Act II;
ii. Resolve the relationships established in Act I and developed in Act II;
iii. Provide an emotionally satisfying resolution;
iv. Answer the Major Dramatic Question and 'prove' the Thematic Argument.

In the final confrontation with the antagonist, at the climax of the story, the hero must face and defeat the antagonist. This will require the hero to face some near-impossible challenge, and he will have to make a sacrifice of some kind to prove that he is prepared to pay any price in order to protect the thing – the person and/or value – that he cares about most.

Don't include anything new in the ending. No new characters, no new settings. There is no time for setting up or for exposition during this part of the story. The ending of a story must arise logically from what has gone before, but at the same time should still be surprising: readers like to try and guess how a story might end, but they do not want to be able to predict exactly how it will end. The reader must find the ending emotionally fulfilling. This does not mean that an ending needs to be happy, but it does need to be satisfying. A satisfying ending delivers on the promises made in Act I. In Act I, forces were introduced and set in motion, heading for a collision. During Act II, those forces were brought closer and closer to collision – and now in Act III, we see the impact that everything has been building towards. A satisfying ending must feature the same characters, situations and conflicts that were introduced in Act I. There should be no new element appearing at the eleventh hour – no cavalry riding over the hill to save the day. This would just feel like a cheat. The situation must be resolved by the hero's own actions.

The ending builds on what has gone before. Robert J. Ray and Bret Norris, in *The Weekend Novelist,* say that Act III should "... focus on echoes that resound – echoing images, echoing lines, echoing incidents – repetitions that replay themselves in your novel as you move, in the end, towards an effect not unlike a symphony."

And the ending must show the collision that has been advertised: it cannot evade the collision by having the two opposing sides reach a mutually beneficial compromise. You cannot have the final clash occur offstage and then cut to the aftermath. Your reader bought front row tickets for a clash of the titans, and that is what you must deliver. This does not mean that there has to be a physical battle as such – but the climax must be filled with tension and powerful emotions. A satisfying ending is also one in which the characters each get the ending they have earned by their actions during the course of the story. James Frey, in *How to Write a Damned Good Novel,* calls this issuing a verdict in the Court of Poetic Justice, with punishments that fit the crime. And the ending should be decisive – we should know who wins and who loses; we should see whether or not the hero achieves his objective. We should see the major dramatic question answered. And as we shall see later, it can be answered with one of four types of ending – one of which will be most appropriate for the story you are telling.

To create a satisfying ending, one that delivers everything the reader is expecting, you need to look back at what you promised to deliver back in Act I. The choice of genre promises certain things – you will need to deliver a genre-appropriate climax. Your choice of main character, with their particular hopes and fears, promises certain aspects of the ending. The mood and style of storytelling you began with should influence the ending – if you began with gritty realism, a slapstick ending is unlikely to feel right to your reader. Did you promise the reader a cold and harsh story or a warm and cosy one? The beginning also promises an emotional experience, which the ending must deliver. Did you promise the reader a love story? Terror? A fight for justice? The exposure of corruption? Exploration of a fantastic other world?

If your story has turned out to be something other than you originally intended, but this new ending is better, then you will need to go back and fix the beginning – replacing your original promises with a new set that your ending can deliver on. That's one of the great things about being a writer: time travel.

Sequence 7: The Climax

Act II ended with the hero at crisis point, facing his 'darkest hour.' Sequence 7 begins with him having to make a decision: should he give up, or make one last ditch attempt at his story goal? This decision scene is one of the most important in the whole story – everything has been building to this moment. But it is also a relatively short scene: we are close to the end of the story, and things need to move more quickly – it's downhill all the way now. Once the hero decides on a course of action, effectively choosing to make a Third Attempt, his preparation time will also be relatively brief. Time is almost always ticking away in Sequence 7 of a story, as the hero has to race into action to try and prevent the antagonist from finally achieving his ultimate objective. From here on in, there will be no pauses, no moments for reflection or relaxation. For this reason, the climax of many stories consists of a single scene or closely-related sequence of scenes.

Things that can be included in this Sequence are:

1. Reaction to the Crisis – A Decision or Dilemma
2. Action by the Antagonist Forcing a Response from the Hero
3. A Discovery or Revelation
4. Highest Stakes
5. Reader Learns of an Increased Threat
6. Thematic Argument – Points of View Restated
7. The Final Battle
8. The Battle Begins Badly for the Hero
9. Hero Learns of Increased Threat
10. Hero Discovers a Way to Fight Back – Act of Self-Sacrifice
11. Outcome of the Battle

(1) Reacting to the Crisis – A Decision or Dilemma

> *"Crisis: a state of things in which a decisive change one way or another is impending."* – Lajos Egri

At the beginning of Sequence 7, the hero stands battered and confused: he has lost everything that is important to him – everything he had in Act I, before the inciting incident, and everything that he has gained since. Even the co-protagonist is gone – having been taken from him by the antagonist, or having abandoned him as a result of his actions during the Second Attempt. He is in a state of shock and this may quickly become depression – it is the Kübler-Ross change curve all over again, but this time he must move through the stages pretty rapidly, as time is running out. He must now make a decision about what he will do next. The crisis decision is the moment that the whole story has been leading up to. It is our scène à faire, our 'obligatory scene.' Everything – plot, character, and theme – converges here. It is the final decision that the hero makes in the story, and whatever choice he makes will determine the answer to the major dramatic, the proof of the thematic argument, and the direction of the hero's life going forward.

This turning point at the end of Act II is similar in nature to the inciting incident in Act I. The hero is faced with a difficult choice – a dilemma. The hero as we met him in Act I would not have been able to make the correct choice here. He would not even have been able to recognise the opportunity. He must choose to give up his old life and his old way of behaving – completely – and make a total commitment to his new life. Now that everything else has been stripped away, he is in a position – for the first time in his life – to be able to judge what is genuinely important to him. His judgment is no longer clouded by trivial worries and shallow concerns. The crisis has brought him so low that he is able to experience and demonstrate humility. During the second half of Act II, the hero's life has been torn apart. His self-image – who he believed he was – has been proved false. Friends have betrayed him. He has found love and lost it. Behaviours and skills that he has trusted and relied upon have backfired. And his beliefs about the way the world works have been proved wrong. Only when he reaches this place, with his old self torn down, is he ready to rebuild a new, true version of himself. Only now is he in a position where he could, if he makes the right decision, fully embrace his new life. This point in the story is sometimes referred to as a 'death' experience, in which the hero's old self must die to allow him to be 'reborn' as his new self. His old beliefs and ways of behaving have outlived their usefulness, and he needs to let go of them. This is the moment the story has been building to. The hero is being offered an opportunity to change his life forever. Everything depends on the choice he makes at this moment. The stakes are the highest they have ever been – both in terms of his internal conflict and the conflict in the external world. He stands naked and alone, filled with self-doubt. And he is invited to make the biggest sacrifice he has ever made in his life. His physical and emotional survival will depend on the outcome of this decision, and the action he takes as a result. He must make a final leap of faith. But is he strong enough to go through with it?

Borrowing from a list in F. A. Rockwell's *How to Write Plots that Sell*, here is a list of qualities that the main story crisis must have:

i. a dilemma, offering two choices of action where the hero is forced to make a decision
ii. two choices that each offer the hero something that he wants, but at the same time they must each require him to sacrifice something that he also wants
iii. high stakes – there must be something significant at risk for the hero – and it must provide a highly charged, emotional experience for the reader
iv. a decision that reveals the true nature of the hero, and profoundly alter his life going forward
v. a decision that is related to the thematic argument
vi. a situation that is the culmination of a series of crises that have risen in intensity as the story has progressed

The nature of the choice the hero is faced with depends on the type of story you are telling. In the most straightforward plot-centered story that depends solely on external action, the hero's first two attempts to deal with his story situation have failed, and he must decide whether to make a third attempt, and if he does, he will have to choose what action to take. In the whodunit, for example, the detective typically discovers one final clue that appears – to the reader – to make the whole investigation more confusing than ever (the 'crisis'), but the hero takes the clue and announces that he now knows the identity and motive of the murderer. His decision is a fairly simple one – how to reveal the truth to the suspects and to the reader. This could be the classic 'drawing room scene' or it could require a plan to trap the murderer and trick him into revealing his own guilt. The theme in this type of story is a fairly obvious one – justice prevails, innocence is rewarded and guilt is punished – and the detective proves himself a hero by demonstrating his skills as an investigator and his doggedness in ensuring that justice triumphs.

In a story that features both external and internal conflict, the hero must make a moral choice, and is usually faced with choosing between a selfish course of action, where he gets what he wants, or a selfless course of action, where he sacrifices what he wants in order to achieve something that benefits 'society' as a whole.

Finally, in the flawed hero story, the hero is faced with the same moral dilemma, but his decision is made all the more difficult because he is also battling to overcome his own internal flaw – and this flaw will make him tend towards the selfish decision, rather than the selfless one.

For the time being, let's concentrate on the features of the story that features both internal and external conflict, as this is the most common type found in genre and popular stories today. The two together add depth to a story and work together to prove the thematic argument.

The crisis point in the story is the moment of greatest opportunity, and of greatest danger: there is everything to play for, and everything to lose. The decision will be between two courses of action, both of which promise the hero an element of loss as well as whatever he will gain. Each will require him to make some kind of sacrifice, giving up one thing in order to achieve another. The choice may be between the greater of two mutually exclusive goods – if he chooses one, the other is automatically lost. Or he may have to choose between the lesser of two evils, where eliminating one automatically enables the other. Once the crisis decision point is reached, there can be no going back: the hero must make a choice, there is no room for compromise, and he cannot say *none of the above*.

The two things that the hero has to choose between at the crisis are introduced, or the choice is at least implied, in Act I. In a love triangle, the hero meets the two people who will become his or her lovers in Act I. If the crisis choice is between his relationship and his job, both of these will be introduced before the end of Act I. If his final choice is between saving the life of his lover and saving the lives of the people of a whole city, Act I will introduce us to the lover and the importance that the hero places on helping his community. During Act II we can explore and demonstrate the importance of these two things in the hero's life. The hero may spend time with each of the two lovers, taking part in fun and enjoyable activities (and possibly sex) with each, and discovering that he or she has much in common with each of them. Our hero may try and divide his time between his partner and his job, sometimes giving his partner priority and sometimes his work. Or we may see our hero engaged in a job or a voluntary activity where he can help large groups of people, and we also see him falling deeply in love with that one special person. Both 'sides' should be set up and shown to be equally important to the hero so that when he is faced with having to choose between them, he is genuinely faced with a difficult choice. The crisis choice should be the most difficult test that he has faced in the story, and the reader should believe that the hero's decision really could go either way.

In *Story*, Robert McKee says that the scene in which the crisis decision is made should be a 'deliberately static moment.' We should be there, suffering with the hero as he wrestles with his decision. McKee likens it to a dam that holds back the emotion, allowing the pressure to build before it is finally released in the action of the climax. I like that image. As an example, McKee mentions *Thelma & Louise*, where the two protagonists are sitting in their car on the edge of the cliff, about to make their climactic choice.

Although both options should seem equally desirable (or undesirable) from the hero's subjective point of view, the story events should have been structured so that the reader knows which one the hero should choose. An objective viewpoint shows us that one of the choices is the selfless moral choice, and the other is a selfish immoral choice. One choice benefits only the hero, giving him what he wants; the other choice benefits his community or mankind as a whole, protecting some value that is vital to human society. The reader should be willing him to make the right moral choice, while at the same time worrying that he might choose the selfish option. Often in a story, we will try and make it appear that the immoral choice is much more likely to prevail and that the moral choice is highly unlikely. This helps raise the suspense and emotional involvement of the reader. The decision that the hero makes here tells us what sort of person he really is because we reveal our true selves in the decisions that we make. Dara Marks calls it the transformational moment because it is where the hero decides his own fate. Other people may try to influence his decision one way or the other, but ultimately it is a personal choice. The decision – his intention – is actually more important than the outcome of the action he takes as a result of his decision. Whether he succeeds or fails, he has taken the action for the right reasons. Or not, depending on what you are trying to prove in your story.

In *Narrative Technique*, Thomas H. Uzzell provides a diagram to help us visualise the two conflicting desires affecting the hero:

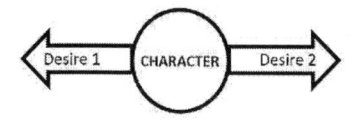

⇐ Desire 1 — CHARACTER — Desire 2 ⇒

If that doesn't help, try imagining your hero tied between two horses (or two trucks) that are pulling in opposite directions.

When we reach the main crisis point of the story, something has got to give, and it does. The hero could give up and admit defeat at this point – but he won't because our story wouldn't have a climax if he did. Instead, he makes his final decision and chooses a course of action that sets up the confrontation – the big showdown – that constitutes the climax of the story. The hero's situation is so bleak that it forces him to re-evaluate his priorities. Having lost everything, he is finally able to see the one thing – the person and/or value – that he cares about more than anything else. His losses have provided him with a new clarity of understanding, and – perhaps for the first time in his life – he actually has an understanding of what he needs to do. His experiences at the end of Act II have effectively stripped away everything that was unimportant, leaving him with a stark choice – and he makes it. He performs an act of self-sacrifice that proves, once and for all, that he is a hero who is committed to preserving and promoting the value that lies at the heart of the story's thematic argument. His actions say: This thing is so important to me that I am willing to die to defend it. Or, I am willing to live alone for the rest of my life to achieve it. Or, I am willing to give up everything from my old life, in order to have this new life.

Following this decision, there may be a brief period of preparation as the hero readies himself to make the Third Attempt – his final attempt. This time he is likely to be acting alone, having lost any supporting characters that may have been with him during the two previous attempts. Even the co-protagonist is no longer there to offer support. As he takes his first action to put this plan into action, the major dramatic question is raised one final time: Can the hero succeed?

(2) Action by the Antagonist Forcing a Response from the Hero

At the beginning of Sequence 7, the antagonist probably believes that the hero has been defeated, and may even be celebrating his own success. If he is a rival or opponent, rather than a villain, he may be presenting himself as the legitimate victor and coming forward to claim his 'prize' – whether that be a valuable trophy, a position of power, or the hand of the king's daughter. If his diabolical plan has not yet been completed, the antagonist will move forward thinking that he can do so without opposition. Some action by the antagonist or his men will jolt the hero into action, forcing his hand and causing him to make his final decision and take action. The antagonist's action is also likely to start the clock ticking on the final countdown – the hero now only has hours (or perhaps only minutes) to stop the antagonist succeeding and gaining his objective.

(3) A Discovery or Revelation

The hero discovers or is told something important. It is an important clue. In action movies, this clue is often revealed while the antagonist is holding the hero at gunpoint and delivering his backstory: 'Do you want to know why I became the most powerful supervillain on the planet, Mr. Bond? I will tell you.' Believing that the hero is no longer a threat, the villain may gloat and reveal details about his plan. Though post-modern villains tend to be aware of the risk involved in this, and so give nothing away. But the hero is able to gain the information some other way – perhaps from a henchman who is bragging on behalf of his boss; or perhaps from someone working for the antagonist who has begun suffering pangs of conscience and wants to betray him. Sometimes this informant is the 'threshold guardian' whom the hero treated sympathetically when he crossed the threshold into the villain's lair. However it happens, the hero finally understands the antagonist's motive. And because the antagonist is a dark reflection of himself, the hero is able to empathise with the antagonist and understand his point of view. This is a moment where the hero discovers that he and the villain have certain things in common – aspects of their past lives that have caused them to adopt a certain outlook on life. The antagonist is an extreme version of the hero's shadow side. This allows the hero to have an insight into the antagonist's plan, and seeing it from the 'inside,' perhaps he is able to see a weakness or flaw in it that can be exploited.

This discovery or revelation may explain the mystery of the inciting incident: this incident, which is what drew the hero into conflict with the antagonist, may turn out to have been a mistake made by the antagonist. It accidentally drew attention to what he was doing. If the inciting incident was a mistake, the cause of the mistake may reveal to the hero another weakness that he might be able to use in his final battle with the antagonist.

One area where the hero and the antagonist are very different is in the fact that the hero is prepared to sacrifice his own happiness, or even his own life, for someone that he cares about, and for a value that is important to mankind in general. The villain would never sacrifice himself for another person or for a cause or belief. All he cares about is achieving his own plan and gaining power or wealth or whatever else it is that he is personally seeking. The antagonist, unlike the hero, is not able to empathise with other people. He cannot put himself in their shoes and imagine what they are feeling. This means that he cannot see how the hero could be willing to sacrifice himself for others. And this blind side gives the hero another weakness he might be able to exploit.

The hero should demonstrate that he has learned from his experiences during the first two acts – that he has taken on board everything he has learned from his mentor, the co-protagonist, threshold guardians, and the antagonist.

With this new information, the hero moves forward with his actions for the Third Attempt.

(4) Highest Stakes

What is at stake at this point in the story? The answer is *everything!* The reader must be clear about what 'terrible thing' will happen if the hero fails in the Third Attempt. In some stories it is the life of the hero, and probably the life of the co-protagonist, and possibly even the 'fate of the free world.' In other stories, it is a relationship at stake, or a career, or a person's self-respect. It depends on the situation that has developed throughout the story. Usually, the stakes have increased so that by the climax of the story it is not only the hero's fate that is in the balance, but also that of someone – or a group of people – who are more important to him than his own health and happiness. The climax is the point when the hero demonstrates that he is willing to pay any price to prove his commitment to the person or people or to the value he feels strongly about. We should also be made aware of what terrible fate awaits the antagonist if he fails – we should see that he will stop at nothing to make sure that his own plan succeeds. And we should see a demonstration of the lengths the antagonist is prepared to go too – an example of his complete disregard for human life, for decency, and a complete lack of mercy.

(5) The Reader Learns of an Increased Threat

The reader – but *not* the hero – learns of a new and greater threat that will drastically reduce the hero's chances of success in the coming battle. We apply Alfred Hitchcock's favourite method of creating suspense – dramatic irony – by giving the reader information that the hero needs, and making the reader lean forward hoping the hero will discover the new or increased threat before it is too late; fearing the consequences if he doesn't; and feeling frustration that they can't warn him. The climax of the story needs to be emotional as well as physical, and this increased tension is one way that we deliver that.

The audience may learn that something that is important to the hero's planned Third Attempt has been in some way damaged, compromised, or removed. A vital piece of equipment may be damaged or sabotaged. Someone the hero is relying upon may have been killed or captured, or they may have betrayed the hero and be working for the antagonist. A couple of additional possibilities: a character thought dead is really still alive; and, two characters thought unrelated are in fact related in some way (this includes the idea of one of the hero's friends being a traitor who is working for the antagonist).

(6) Thematic Argument – Points of View Restated

Just before the final battle begins, or during the early stages of this final confrontation, the reader should be reminded of the two sides of the thematic argument. We can do this by making it clear from the hero's actions that he will behave only in accordance with the positive 'virtue': we should see that he believes that this value is important and is worth fighting for. There is a line that the hero will not cross, and there are things that he will not do. From the antagonist's actions, we should see that he is prepared to act in a way that demonstrates the 'vice,' and that there is no line for him: he is ruthless and will do whatever it takes to prevail. The antagonist may mock the hero for his moral values, pointing to them as a sign of weakness or a lack of free-will: he is allowing other people to dictate his beliefs and behaviours. The villain will believe that only ruthless self-reliance can bring success, and that namby-pamby liberal values, rules, and conscience are a handicap that ties the hero's hands and will prevent him from succeeding.

(7) The Final Battle

Showdown. The hero and the antagonist go head to head, each committed to defeating the other. At this point in the story, the hero knows the full extent of what he is up against – or so he thinks: there is still the new or increased threat that he doesn't know about. This climactic action will decide who – if anyone – wins, and its outcome will prove the thematic argument. This is the other half of the 'obligatory scene' that includes the hero's crisis decision and his climactic act of self-sacrifice. This will be an all-or-nothing, winner-take-all fight. There should be the feeling of a headlong rush towards the final outcome, as well as a send of intense pressure, and a concentration of forces – it should take place somewhere where there is no way out, and no alternative routes: it is two opposing forces, moving at high speed, heading for a collision in a space that is getting narrower and narrower. It is like a funnel – everything has been squeezed down to this one final confrontation.

(8) The Battle Begins Badly for the Hero

The antagonist is in a strong position, he is well-resourced, well-prepared, and ruthless. In comparison, our hero looks small, weak, and poorly equipped. We want the hero to seem hopelessly outclassed – because our readers will feel sympathy for an underdog. We should also see that the antagonist is prepared to lie and cheat, and do anything that will give him the slightest advantage and eventual victory, while the hero is restrained by his own moral code. Almost from the start, the hero will suffer physical and emotional attack from the antagonist's men, and the damage will have a cumulative effect.

The antagonist may engage in psychological warfare, denigrating the hero's efforts to date: if the hero had been a better opponent, the antagonist would not be in the commanding position that he is now in. The antagonist's success is thanks to the hero's mistakes, fear of taking action, or ignorance, and people have been put at risk, harmed, or perhaps even killed, as a result of the hero's actions, or his failure to take action. The antagonist may also criticise the hero because of the 'immoral action' he took – his 'act of desperation' – during the Second Attempt: where were the hero's high moral values then? Who could take him seriously when he abandons his 'deeply held beliefs' so easily? And if a member of the hero's own team has betrayed him, the antagonist has another stick to beat him with – offering up the betrayal as proof that the hero's beliefs can be easily cast aside; or as proof that people leave his side because he can't be trusted. If the co-protagonist walked away from the hero because of his immoral behaviour during the Second Attempt, the antagonist may use that too. Any possible weakness he can find, the antagonist will exploit: no blow is too low for him.

The only response that the hero can make to this is to admit his culpability. He admits his past mistakes – he has nothing to gain by lying or denial, and so is quite prepared to be honest with himself and others. He will try to make amends for past mistakes if he can, and one way he can do that is to try and uphold the values he believes in. He restates his point of view and promises to stand by his principles from now on.

(9) The Hero Learns of the Increased Threat

Just as his destruction seems inevitable, the hero learns of the increased threat that the reader has been aware of for some time. Knowing about it, he can now attempt some form of countermeasure. Whether the antagonist knows that the hero knows at this point is a choice for you to make as the writer.

(10) Hero Discovers a Way to Fight Back – An Act of Self-Sacrifice

Just as the situation seems hopeless, the hero will discover or learn something that could give him a chance to beat the antagonist. It is only a slim chance, but it is the only chance he has. This should be something that demonstrates what the hero has learned throughout the story, and it should be something that enables him to demonstrate his moral behaviour. While it offers an opportunity, this potential solution also requires that the hero perform an act of self-sacrifice.

In *Plot and Structure,* James Scott Bell says that at the climax of a story, the hero can be called on to demonstrate either physical courage or moral courage. Or perhaps both. Physical courage is necessary if the hero is prepared to sacrifice his safety, possibly his life, in a final battle. Whereas moral courage is necessary where the hero is faced with a final choice: he is on the horns of a dilemma – he could choose to pursue his personal objective, but at a moral cost. Or he can give up his personal goal, his want, and 'do the right thing' for the greater good.

Self-sacrifice or selflessness – being prepared to suffer, or give up one's own needs or desires, so that others may survive or benefit – is regarded as a heroic quality. British philosopher Jeremy Bentham said: "It is the greatest good to the greatest number of people which is the measure of right and wrong." Mr. Spock said something similar: "The needs of the many outweigh the needs of the few. Or the one." This is a quality or value that the hero is able to demonstrate that the antagonist is not. The antagonist is completely self-centered, ego-driven, and would never dream of giving his own life for another person's. Sometimes this concept is so alien to an antagonist that he cannot foresee that someone else might be prepared to risk everything in order to save someone else: this gives the self-sacrificing hero a brief advantage – he can take advantage of the villain's moral blindness.

Of course, you have to set up your story situation so that all of the hero's other options have been removed, to the point where he is prepared to make this final noble act. And you have to have established that there is something – some human value or some human being – that he cares about more than he cares about himself. It may be true that it is more heroic for a man to give up his life for a principle and to die to save a stranger, than it is to give up one's life for someone we love – which still has an element of self-interest associated with it – but in terms of drama, it doesn't get much better than being prepared to die for a friend or a loved one.

(11) Outcome of the Battle

The hero defeats (or is defeated by) the antagonist. The decisive action that brings this about must be performed by the hero: he must not be passive, and he must not be rescued by someone or something else (that just smacks of *deus ex machina*). And we can't have the villain defeating himself because of some mistake or action that backfires – though *Raiders of the Lost Ark* sort of got away with that one. The outcome must show whether the hero or the antagonist wins. And it must show whether the hero succeeds in achieving his external story objective. As we will see below, under Types of Ending, there are different ways in which the components of the outcome can be combined in order to create a happy, tragic, or ironic ending. The outcome of the final battle should also prove the thematic argument – virtue is rewarded, vice is punished. William Goldman says that the outcome should give the audience what it wants (usually meaning that the hero succeeds), but not in the way that it expects it. We will look at some techniques for doing this later in the chapter.

Types of Ending

Two questions have to be answered at the end of a story: Did the hero succeed in achieving his external story goal? And: Did he manage to fulfil his need and overcome the 'lack' in his life? In other words, did he resolve both his external situation and his internal one?

This gives us four possible types of ending:

i. *Happy Ending.* The hero resolves both his internal and external situations. He achieves his external objective and achieves personal happiness and fulfilment at the same time.

ii. *Tragic Ending.* The hero fails to resolve both his internal and external situations.

iii. *Personal Tragedy.* The hero achieves his external objective but fails to resolve his inner problem. He wins the prize, but it brings him no personal fulfilment, or he has had to sacrifice so much to achieve it that his success is a pyrrhic victory at best. The whole experience may leave him bitter, or sadder but wiser.

iv. *Personal Triumph.* The hero fails to achieve his outer objective, or abandons the quest for it, but achieves something that is more important to him. He may have discovered that he was going for a wrong or unworthy goal, or been going after the goal for the wrong reason. He discovers the error of his ways and achieves a more meaningful kind of personal fulfilment instead.

(iii) and (iv) above are both *ironic* endings, in that the outcome isn't what the hero expected it to be. Ironic endings tend to occur in stories with a strong character development arc. In *Rocky*, the hero realises that he cannot win the climactic fight, but discovers that he can achieve something that is more personally fulfilling. And in *Casablanca*, the Humphrey Bogart character sacrifices an opportunity to be with the woman he loves in order that a more important victory might be attempted. These ironic endings prove the thematic arguments of their respective stories.

Tragic endings usually occur when the hero fails to learn an important lesson: he doesn't complete the journey of self-discovery which would allow him to 'earn' a non-tragic ending.

Linear and Circular Endings

A linear story is a journey that takes the hero from point A to point B. A circular story takes the hero away on an adventure but then brings him home again. A linear story ends virtually at the point that the final destination is reached, with only a brief resolution scene following it. Adventure stories and whodunits are examples. Once the climax is reached, the main situation of the story is resolved and there is little more to add. With this type of ending, subplots will tend to be resolved before the climax, and there are usually few loose ends to tie up.

A circular story will usually have a longer resolution after the climax, as the hero 'brings home' whatever knowledge, experience, objects, or 'healing elixir' he has gained as a result of his quest. The place that a character returns to may not be a literal homecoming, it may be a return to an emotional equilibrium he had previously. Circular stories usually have an element of 'before and after' in their resolution, as we see how the world has changed; or we see how the world has stayed the same and the hero has changed. Where a hero has been battling to preserve a world, or return it to health, this coming back is a way of demonstrating his success. A birth or a marriage may be seen as symbolising the fact that the disruptive elements have been taken care of, and normal life can be resumed.

Building a Climax

An effective climax should be the biggest scene in the story, where the final battle is waged between virtue and vice. It should be dramatised – that is, *shown* through action, rather than being talked about or happening offstage. The hero faces the greatest obstacles he has faced so far, and when the scene is complete, the major dramatic questions will have been answered. The climax will involve some kind of dramatic reversal, from positive to negative or negative to positive – a value swing at the maximum possible level, and one that will be irreversible. The action by the hero that brings about this change is what proves the thematic argument of the story. It effectively says: In a situation such as this, a hero will behave in this manner. Conversely, the antagonist or villain will be shown behaving in a contrary fashion, demonstrating an immoral value. These actions on each side should be unambiguous and require no explanation. You want the reader to be able to form their own judgment, and at the same time feel things emotionally: this is right-minded behaviour, and this is wrong. The climax should be a scene in its own right, in which the hero faces the greatest obstacles he has ever faced. And these obstacles will come in the form of a direct, face-to-face confrontation with the antagonist. The outcome of this climactic confrontation will be that one of them wins and the other loses. There are no half measures.

The outcome of the climactic action should be brought about by the actions of the hero. This means that the climax needs to be appropriate for this particular hero. Just as the crisis was a crisis for this particular character, so too is the climax.

Nancy Kress, in *Beginnings, Middles and Ends,* asks: If the hero had been a very different person, would this story still ended with the same sort of climax. The answer, she says, should be *no.* The ending should grow naturally out of who the character is. We choose our hero because of his 'climax potential.' The hero will solve the problem at the climax using his own skills, knowledge and life experience, including anything that he has learned during the course of his adventures in Act II. At the climax of the climax, the antagonist is defeated and the conflict ends. The hero's external objective, the story goal, is achieved. Or he fails to achieve it, depending on what type of ending you are creating.

The hero's choice of action at the climax of the story – whether he acts in accordance with virtue or vice – determines whether or not he deserves to be rewarded. His reward will be success in achieving the overall story objective, and/or success in fulfilling the 'lack' that he has experienced in his life up to this point. The ending of the story reaffirms our belief that if we make the 'right' choices, and if we are prepared to sacrifice our own needs and desires, perhaps even our own lives, then we are worthy of recognition. The climax itself dramatises the action that the hero chooses to take, and its immediate consequences. It is the final example of cause-and-effect that gives our story meaning, and – by implication – reassures the reader that the choices we make in our own lives have meaning.

The climax, as we have said, begins with a *choice* of actions. The hero is asked to choose between two specific, concrete courses of action. The crisis of the story at the end of Act II was a pivotal, life-changing event that has effectively used up all of the hero's reserves of strength, intelligence, and courage. All that he has left to rely on at this point are his emotions. He must make his choice on what he *feels* to be right. He responds on a much deeper level than thought, a subconscious level where his true self resides – he is trusting to gut instinct and emotion. This is the self that jumps into the water to save a drowning child or makes us speak out when keeping our heads down would be safer. Or in a lesser man, it is the part that allows us to take the treasure for ourselves, and to hell with everyone else.

The crisis has removed all other options and all possible sources of strength, so that the hero has only his true self to rely on. The whole of Act II was designed to get him to this point so that he can prove what sort of person he *really* is. His façade is gone, there is no room left for pretence, it's just him and his conscience. But it must be a *choice.* He must have an alternative. He must choose between self-interest and principle. Between virtue and vice. It is making the right choice that defines him. And it should not be an easy choice. There should be obvious risks involved in making the right choice.

The film *Casablanca* has the hero, Rick Blaine (Humphrey Bogart), faced with just such a decision. What he wants to do is get back together with Ilsa, the only woman he has ever truly loved. And she offers him the opportunity to do just this. But Ilsa's husband, Lazlo, is a key figure in the resistance effort against the Nazis, and he needs Rick's help if he is to evade capture and continue with his vital work. The right thing to do is to sacrifice his relationship with Ilsa and help Lazlo escape, but to do so would be to put his own life at risk if the Nazis discover he has helped the resistance fighters, and Rick has stated several times during the story that he 'sticks his neck out for no one.' This choice at the heart of the story is one of the things that makes *Casablanca* a classic piece of storytelling.

The pressure was building throughout Act II, and the climax in Act III is where all of that pressure is finally released. The moment that the hero makes his decision to take action is the trigger for the release of built up tension, and the action itself is the discharge. The reader must see that this is a difficult choice, so we cannot make it something he can decide quickly or with a flip of a coin. We must prolong the agony – for the hero and the reader.

Eventually, he must decide, which means we must do two things:

a) *Force* the hero to make a decision
b) Make the reader *believe* that the hero would make the right decision

We can force the decision by setting up the circumstances such that the hero must make a decision and make it now. Someone holds a gun to his head. His ally is hanging over a cliff and his fingers are slipping. The woman he loves is opening the door to walk out on him. These are obvious and melodramatic examples, but they show the kind of situation we need to set up here. You make the hero's decision believable by preparing for it much earlier in the story. You foreshadow or plant something that will be echoed or used at this decision-making moment. Dwight V. Swain suggests using a 'gimmick' or talisman: some object planted earlier in the story which spurs the hero into making his choice. He gives the example of a St. Christopher medal given to the hero by his mother: the sight of this medal encourages him to make a decision that would make her proud of him. The audience has been made aware of the significance of the medal, and so believes that it would prompt him to do the right thing.

Less 'gimmicky' might be a line of dialogue that recalls an earlier scene in which the hero was faced with a similar decision, though a less dramatic one. Or his present situation may exactly mirror a situation earlier in the story. Perhaps in the earlier situation, he made the right decision, and so we are not surprised when he does so now. Or, better still, perhaps in the earlier situation he made the wrong decision, and the consequences are something he feels guilty about. At the climax we see him waiver – will he make the same mistake again? When he makes the right choice – the choice we as readers want him to make this time – we believe it because we see that he has learned his lesson and become a better person. This is what we require of our heroes.

Once he was made his decision, we have to make the hero translate his choice into an 'irrevocable act.' The climax has to be caused by the actions that the hero takes. It cannot happen by accident or through the choices and actions of someone else. The antagonist should believe that he has already won – that the crisis has seen off the hero. At this point in the story, the antagonist's actions only serve to provide a ticking clock that increases the pressure on the hero to make his decision now. The antagonist's actions at the climax are a *response* to the stimulus that is the hero's action. If the hero did not act, there would be no climax.

The climax of a screenplay or novel must always be an external action. The action may only be symbolic, but we need to see something happen. This climactic action focuses everything that has gone before onto a single, decisive point. And the action must be irrevocable. There can be no going back. This is a do-or-die moment. A last desperate effort. A moment of ultimate commitment. For the final time, we ask the major dramatic question: Will the hero succeed? And the answer to this question will be provided by the action he chooses to take at this climactic moment in the story. The outcome of the story is teetering on a knife-edge. This is a moment of high tension in the story, as we hold our breath and wait to discover how things will turn out. Will or hero prove himself a hero, or will he be crushed by the antagonist?

Technically, the action taken by the hero does not have to be successful. He may try to do the right thing and fail. It is his *motivation* at this point that is the key thing. A heroic failure is still heroic. But we do need to see the hero take action. And nobody really wants to see the hero fail – though an ironic, partial failure can provide a satisfying end to a story (see *Types of Ending* above). The outcome of a story doesn't have to be a happy ending, but – as Christopher Keane writes – there should be some kind of hope for the future. As someone once said, readers don't mind being told that life is difficult, but they don't want to be told that life is shit. You can use the idea 'heroic failure' to create a twist in your story. You can have the hero's action appear to have failed. Then he can snatch victory from the jaws of defeat – or employ some other cliché – that brings about the kind of euphoric ending that the reader craves.

The 'action' of the climactic action does not have to be noisy and violent, Robert McKee says, but it must be full of *meaning*. It is meaning that provides the emotional experience that we are seeking to create here. We create an ending that turns from negative to positive, or positive to negative – with or without an ironic element. It is a final, definitive and irreversible swing. This is the end.

William Foster-Harris, in *The Basic Patterns of Plot,* says that the answer to the major dramatic question is a "diametric reversal of the question." He gives as examples the coward who finds courage; the reluctant lover who agrees to marry; and the sinner who is redeemed. "It's a reversal: things are somehow turned upside down." This relates back to what we said about the crisis and the climax being specific to the hero involved. You make the decision that begins the climax a difficult one by selecting a hero that would have difficulty making it. You make the climactic action difficult by having a hero who would find the most difficulty in completing this kind of action.

Robert McKee, in *Story,* says that if you know your climax, you can write your story backwards from that point. Real life flows forwards from cause to effect, but when we are plotting a story, we can work backwards from effect to cause; response to stimulus. Knowing the climax – knowing what will happen, even if we as writers aren't yet sure exactly how – is the way we ensure that what we set up in Act I, and everything in Act II, builds towards this single event. The reader wants a story climax that fulfils their expectations – which means that we need to shape their expectations so they are not disappointed by our climax.

Aristotle wrote in *The Poetics* that the ending of a story should be inevitable and yet unexpected. William Goldman has said that the ending of a story should give the reader what they want, but not in the way that they expect. As we have already said, the ending of a Hollywood movie or a genre novel is usually not in much doubt. The hero will win, there will be a happy ending. People prefer happy endings – they are inevitable. The trick then is in how you deliver the happy ending so that it occurs in a way that the audience did not expect. We will look at ways to surprise the audience below.

The outcome of the climactic action demonstrates what the hero and the antagonist deserve. They will be rewarded or punished in accordance with poetic justice. The outcome also releases virtually all of the tension that was built up during Act II. The meaning of this outcome should be visible and obvious, requiring no dialogue or exposition from the author to explain it. It is left to the resolution of the story to show the consequences of this action – what fate do the hero and antagonist gain as a result of the outcome of this action? And there may still be the B-story relationship to resolve.

How Big Should the Climax Be?

We have already said that the climax should be the biggest scene in a novel or screenplay and that it provides a peak in terms of emotion. It should deliver action and emotion at a level that is appropriate for the story that you are telling. For a story about a family in crisis, it would be inappropriate to bring in car crashes and explosions for the climax. There might be violence, even death, but it will be handled at a level that is in keeping with what has been developed during Act II of the story. The climax should be of a length that is in proportion for the story. In a novel, it will occupy at least one chapter, and possibly several. In a screenplay, it will occupy perhaps ten pages or so. We spent the whole of act two setting up this moment – if it flashes by too quickly, the audience is likely to feel cheated. You don't want people to feel that if they'd blinked, they would have missed it. In a screenplay, the importance of something is denoted by the amount of screen time given to it: the climax is the most important scene in the story, so needs to be of appropriate duration. Less than ten minutes is likely to feel rushed, and if the film is two hours or more, you will be looking at fifteen to twenty minutes.

How Do You Surprise the Reader?

In popular and genre stories, the ending will probably turn out to be the one the reader has been hoping for all along. Yes, the hero will win. Yes, the hero and heroine will get together at the end and live happily ever after. What will happen is usually in little doubt, so the surprise must come in the *how* this ending is brought about. But at the same time, this unexpected delivery must still be plausible given what has gone before. Just because an event is surprising doesn't mean that it is dramatic. To succeed dramatically, an event must be emotionally fulfilling for the reader. And to do that it must arise naturally from the actions and personalities of the people involved in the story. The hero's problem cannot be solved by the equivalent of the cavalry riding over the hill, and they cannot be solved by some coincidence or accident. These things all reek of *deus ex machina,* which is a Latin translation of an Ancient Greek term describing a plot contrivance whereby an actor dressed as a god was lowered on a rope – 'by machine' – into the middle of a play to solve everyone's problems. Stuart Griffiths, in *How Plays are Made*, has this to say on the subject of endings: "The final reaction of an audience to a dramatic action, perfectly rounded out and complete, is not really one of surprise, however stunned they may be. In Arthur Miller's phrase, it is: 'Oh, God, of course!'"

Twist Endings

Dwight V. Swain suggests a way of creating a twist ending in *Techniques of the Selling Writer*. Instead of showing the hero 'winning' the final battle, despite having made a moral decision and taken a self-sacrificing action, show him failing and then apply the following technique to 'twist' the outcome:

a) The hero suffers an anguished 'black moment' after the climax
b) You reverse his situation with an unanticipated development
c) The hero receives his just reward

The Hero's Black Moment. In the moment immediately following the action of the climax, the hero stands dazed – and convinced that he has failed. He feels that everything he cares about has been lost and that he is about to be destroyed himself as a consequence of his failure. Let the reader share this moment with him – let them worry for a little while longer. The stronger you can make this feeling of loss, the greater the release when the reversal finally comes.

Reverse the Hero's situation with an Unanticipated Development. Something unanticipated happens that upsets the balance of the situation. According to Swain, this reversal must meet the following criteria:

i. It must be desired. The reader must desperately want to see the hero saved. We must care about his ultimate fate.
ii. It must be unanticipated. The reversal will lose its impact if the reader can guess what is about to happen.
iii. It must be logical. The reversal must be believable, and the way to achieve that is to make sure it has been properly prepared – the seeds for it must have been planted during Act II. An effect without a legitimate cause will not be believable.

The Hero Receives His Reward. In Section 5, the hero often reveals to the co-protagonist his hopes or dreams for the future. His reward is to achieve this dream, or at least to have moved closer to achieving it. Or to have had it replaced by a reality that is better than he had hoped or dreamed of. Whether you deliver your hero a full, happy ending, or one of the two types of ironic ending – personal triumph or person tragedy – depends on the type of story you are telling, and on the moral argument you want to prove.

Subplots

If you can resolve one or more subplots with the climax of your main story, then this is a good thing. With the exception of the B-story, the relationship subplot, all other subplots should be resolved either at or before the climax. You can tie up any loose ends in a brief denouement, but you don't want to spend too much time after the climax on anything that is going to detract from the impact of the climax.

How to Get Endings Wrong

A successful ending has to be appropriate to the story that is being told, it needs to be believable; there should be an element of surprise, and it must deliver an emotionally satisfying experience to the reader. You can get this wrong if you ignore reader expectations and try to deliver the wrong sort of ending, and you can get it wrong if you don't turn the emotional dials up high enough. In an article titled 'The Big Finish' on www.wordplayer.com, Terry Rossio writes about two films which he believes have unfulfilling endings because they failed to give the sort of ending that the audience had been led to expect. *Young Sherlock Holmes* tells of the early life of the great detective, whose greatest skills are problem-solving – intellectually, he is a remarkable character. But the ending of this film involved a physical battle that made no use of the hero's abilities as a detective. It was the wrong kind of ending. Similarly, *The Witches of Eastwick* set up the Jack Nicholson character as smart, witty and cunning. But the climax consisted of a bunch of pointless special effects. Again, it failed to live up to the promise of the story that was set up in Act I and built up in Act II.

As we've seen, the ending of a story can make effective use of surprising twists to provide an unexpected way of delivering the outcome. But tossing aside the characters and situations you have developed in order to create some empty big screen spectacle is a major mistake. Especially in a novel. Some stories deliver the right kind of ending but fail because they do not deliver emotion at an appropriately high level. The climax is meant to be the emotional peak of the story, so we need to pull out all of the stops – a phrase that relates to the way pipe organs work: pulling out the stops increases the airflow so that the instrument can make the loudest possible sound. That's what the climax needs to do. But with emotion rather than noise.

There are a number of ways that you can screw up the ending of your story; the four at the end I first saw defined in Ansen Dibell's *Plot:*

i. Failure to ensure that the hero is faced with only two possible courses of action at the end, and forced to choose one of them. There must be no compromise and no third alternative: if any suggest themselves, you have to go back to an earlier point in the story and somehow eliminate them. Too many teenage romantic comedies are ruined if you ask an obvious question such as: Why doesn't he just tell her he lost the car in a stupid bet?

ii. Failure to make choosing the 'moral' option sufficiently risky. Making the right decision should not be an easy thing to do. It must involve self-sacrifice – the hero must have to give up something that is important to him.

iii. Failure to make the hero's story goal important enough to him. The hero must be strongly motivated to achieve this goal, right up to the end of the story. If he could just give up his quest with nothing more than a shrug,

there's a problem with the external goal and the character's reason for needing to achieve it. If achieving it is not of vital importance to him, you need to go back in your story and fix things so that it is.
iv. The build up to the climax is not sufficiently dramatic. The climax is supposed to be the emotional peak of the story – Act II should build up to it, and the climax should then deliver on that promise. Failing to focus the action toward this one final decisive moment because of a lack of clear direction in the plot is going to blunt the effect of the ending.
v. Shifting the focus from the hero. The climax should be caused by, and completed by, the actions of the hero. If the hero is not centre-stage for this key moment of the story, the ending will not be as strong as it needs to be.
vi. Trick endings. Unexpected endings only work if they are prepared for, and if they are appropriate to the story being told. Just pulling the rug out from under the hero and the reader for shock effect is unlikely to be effective. Trick, or 'O. Henry-style,' endings can work for a short story, but using a full-length screenplay or novel to set up a joke on the reader is a very risky thing to do. Even if you did pull it off, it would not create the sort of novel that someone would want to re-read – or the sort of novel someone would pick up in the first place the ending has already been leaked to them as a 'spoiler.'
vii. *Deus ex Machina.* We have already mentioned this, but it is worth repeating the warning. The ending should be set-up during Act II, and it should be performed by the hero. Anything that happens without proper motivation and foreshadowing is cheating and will feel unsatisfactory.
viii. No ending. The climax should be a dramatised scene and should end conclusively. If you fail to answer the major dramatic question, the reader is going to feel that they have wasted a good few hours of their life on your so-called story. We read because we want to know what happens. So something has to happen. Inconclusive endings and stories that just fizzle out aren't worth anyone's time. Leaving things ambiguous and saying 'I want to let the reader decide' is a cop-out – you are failing in your job as a writer by not delivering on the promise you made to the reader in Act I.

There are probably dozens of other ways to ruin the ending of your story, but you don't need to worry about them because you already have the tools necessary to create a successful ending. It would be a mistake not to use them.

Sequence 8: Resolution and Denouement

This part of the story is anything that happens after the climax. Its function is to demonstrate the consequences of the climax, reveal the fates of any characters that were not decided by the climax, and to resolve any subplots and other loose ends.

It has been said that the beginning of a story should be designed to sell your screenplay or novel and that its ending should be designed to sell your next screenplay or novel. This isn't to say, necessarily, that you should pave the way for a sequel – though that may be an appropriate way to end your story – rather it means that you need to craft a *satisfactory* ending to your story that delivers on the promises you made back in Act I. You want to make the reader feel that he or she got value for money and that reading your story or watching your movie was worth the investment of their time. You should also aim to make the ending of a story memorable. You can't top what just happened in the climax, but you can help the reader discover the significance of what they have just seen, so that they go away feeling that your story was actually about something that was important to the characters involved, to you the writer, and to themselves as the reader.

If you ever leave a movie that was all action and spectacle but which left you feeling somehow unfulfilled, it will usually be because the story lacked any sense of thematic depth. It wasn't really about anything significant. It was, to steal a phrase from Shakespeare, a tale "Told by an idiot, full of sound and fury, Signifying nothing." Don't be that idiot. Give the ending of your story meaning. But keep it short. This should be the shortest section of your story. Ten minutes maximum in a screenplay, and half-a-dozen pages or so for a novel. But don't short-change the reader by making it too short – they need to be able to catch their breath, consider what they have just witnessed, and savour the moment. We don't want to be shooed out of the restaurant as soon as we've finished dessert. An ending should feel like an ending, rather than giving the reader a sense that the story has just stopped.

It is possible to ruin an otherwise great story by botching the ending, so take some time to think it through and get it right. Sometimes you read a story and get the impression that the author has spotted the finish-line and is sprinting to get the marathon over with. You want your reader to regret that your story is over, not feel relief that they have survived the ordeal. Your resolution and denouement should be dramatised in the same way as the rest of the story, and not be something that has been tacked on as an afterthought. Show what happens to your characters by showing them in action. A montage approach is fine, as long as it moves. You don't necessarily need complete scenes with their own climaxes – after all, at this point, we're indicating how life will go on now that the adventure is over. You need a great climax, but you also need a satisfying resolution and denouement. This can consist of a number of elements, though they're all likely to be bound up in a single scene or a small number of short scenes. Some of these might be covered by the climax of the story and need not be repeated in this final section. And sometimes you might want to add a final twist – but be careful with 'trick' endings – don't cheapen your story for the sake of a final laugh.

And for heaven's sake, avoid those awful 'freeze-frame on a grin' endings that used to end almost every American TV show after someone had made one final 'witty' comment. Avoid long speeches at the end of your story. This not the time for great chunks of exposition – in a great story, there is never a good time for great chunks of exposition. If you feel that there is a need to explain things to the audience, then there is a problem with your 'showing' earlier in the story. There should be no need for you to have characters talk about the resolution of the thematic argument: that outcome should have been demonstrated in the action of the climax and its immediate aftermath. In theatre, such explanations are referred to as 'curtain speeches. As Louis E. Catron says in *Elements of Playwriting*, "... make certain that the play's action expresses its meaning. If it does, no curtain speech is necessary; if it doesn't, no curtain speech will correct the problem."

The same applies to a stand-alone epilogue – unless your story *really* needs it, avoid having one. The only real reason for having one is if you need to show something that occurs in a very different time or place, or where you have a prologue and an epilogue that frame your story. Personally, I think having your main story in a framework or bracketed by another story, is a mistake as it is difficult to pull off effectively because it draws attention to the artificiality of the storytelling process.

What can be included in this final sequence of your story?

1. Reaction to the climactic events
2. Resolution
3. Validation and closure
4. New Equilibrium
5. Denouement
6. Final image or Paragraph

(1) Reaction to the Climactic Events

The aftermath of the climactic scene. This section may include a celebration of success, if that is appropriate. Or a realisation that even though the outcome wasn't what people hoped for or expected, things have turned out for the best. The physical or emotional battle is over, the hero stops and draws breath, looking around him and taking stock.

(2) Resolution

The aim here is to resolve the important issues, giving the reader enough information to fill in any missing details. Things that must be resolved include the relationship between the hero and the co-protagonist – the ally or lover. What will happen to the relationship between these two people? The reader also needs to know the answer to the major dramatic question: Does the hero achieve his story objective? People are also likely to want to know the ultimate fate of the opponent – the villain or rival. This will be tied in with the outcome of the thematic argument.

The resolution is the final payoff: the hero is rewarded (or punished) for his or her actions, in accordance with the thematic virtue of the story. Other characters may similarly receive their deserved fates, mirroring or counterpointing the fate of the hero, as any subplots not resolved at or before the climax are brought to a conclusion.

In his book *Anatomy of a Screenplay,* Dan Decker says that there are four elements that go towards making an emotionally satisfying resolution for a story:

i. What is the outcome of the hero and co-protagonist relationship?
ii. Does the hero achieve his story objective?
iii. What is the fate of the antagonist?
iv. Is the thematic argument of the story proved?

Resolving the hero and co-protagonist relationship is particularly important if this is a romantic subplot in the story. We said that if the hero broke his own code of conduct and used 'immoral' action during his moment of desperation, then the co-protagonist might abandon him. In many romance subplots, there is some event or misunderstanding that results in what Karen S. Wiesner, in *First Draft in 30 Days,* calls 'the relationship black moment.' Where this happens, part of the resolution will show whether these two characters can be reconciled. The hero may resolve the external story goal and achieve success but may fail to save the relationship. Or you could use Dwight V. Swain's 'false defeat' twist ending for this part of your ending.

(3) Validation and Closure

Here we often have some external, objective person or event that verifies that the thematic argument is, in fact, concluded and has been proved. There is something that, by implication, demonstrates that the hero's victory – if he has indeed 'won' – is valid. It's the equivalent of having the officials at the *Guinness Book of Records* verify your record-breaking attempt. Or having the Olympic anti-doping people confirm that your pee is untainted and your victory fairly won. There is an element here of showing that the successful outcome of the hero's quest isn't just a personal or even selfish victory, but rather something that benefits all of society. If the hero has corrected an injustice, then he has succeeded in a specific instance, and also – by demonstrating a universally approved behaviour – has helped to demonstrate that justice prevails in our society. His victory receives the social seal of approval.

In the hero's journey monomyth, this stage of the story involves the hero returning home with artefacts. Knowledge, truth or experience that will help to rebuild or mend the world. This might be an actual or a figurative 'healing elixir.' In other types of stories, we see some evidence that the corruption that was damaging the world has been uncovered and cut out so that our world can heal and become pure again. It is not enough that the hero triumphs, he must also bring back something that benefits his people. Closure means giving your reader enough information about the fate of the characters and their world so that they feel the story is actually over. An ambiguous ending might be okay for a short story, but the ending of a novel or screenplay out to be decisive and clear. Arguing that you want the reader or viewer to decide for themselves what happens to the characters is a cop out – they are paying you to tell them a story, and will expect you to let them know how it ends. You don't want their last feelings about your story to be ones of disappointment.

(4) New Equilibrium

Now that the destabilising element has been dealt with, what will the world and/or the hero's life be like going forward? What will everyday life be like from now on? The instability introduced in Act I has been settled, and balance has been restored. The world may be restored to exactly the same state it was in before. Or it may have been changed in some significant way. In either case, the hero is not the same person he was in Act I: he has been changed by his experiences. He has learned something about himself and about the way the world works, and can never see things in quite the same way again. He may have achieved personal fulfilment, overcoming the thing that was lacking in his own life. Or he may have made the first steps along a longer journey towards fulfilling that need. Or his need may remain tragically unfulfilled – it all depends on what you want to say in your story. This new equilibrium, the hero's new life, may be exactly as he dreamed of it and – perhaps – spoke of it in Section 5. Or it may be something radically different – something much better, something much worse, or something of equal value. Sometimes the fantasy life we wish we could have comes true, and we discover that it is not all that we hoped it would be. An ironic ending to a story might reflect this.

Sometimes there are rituals that need to be performed to demonstrate this return to equilibrium. Or there may be physical or emotional healing that needs to take place. A man returning from battle must take off the armour that he wore as a soldier, and assume the mantle of a man of peace. There is a need for readjustment, perhaps shown symbolically by a change of garments, or by washing the blood and dirt of battle from the hero's skin. In other types of story, there may be a 'putting away' of things that symbolise an old way of life, as a way of embracing the new. The hero's current adventure is over. This section of the story gives a glimpse of the answer to the question: What is he going to do for the rest of his life?

(5) Denouement

This is a tying up of loose ends – though technically it is a French word meaning to unknot or untie. We don't need to tidy up everything and show how every single character will live their lives going forward, but we would normally give some hint of what the future holds for those characters that the reader has been emotionally involved with in some way during the story – both the good guys and the bad. Check that you haven't left any important character unaccounted for. But don't feel that you have to give every character a happy ending. Mark Twain referred to the ending of a story as marryin' and buryin' which is as good a description of this section as any.

Christopher Keane, in *How to Write a Selling Screenplay,* warns against ending your story in a way that is too 'tidy,' and where all the strands are 'tied neatly into a little package of contrivance.' This type of ending, he says, is flat and predictable because they broadcast themselves early in the story. This reinforces what William Goldman said about giving the audience what they want, but not in the way they expect it.

I would advise against having your villain's henchman have a change of heart at the climax, and so 'earn' for himself a happy ending. At the end of *Moonraker* Jaws, the assassin with the steel teeth, shares a glass of bubbly with his girlfriend Dolly, and the audience reached for their sick bags.

Way back at the beginning of the book, I cautioned against using a prologue and epilogue to bracket or 'bookend' your story – I think these are a bit fake and draw attention to the artificiality of the storytelling process. And they're 'telling' and not 'showing.' And I think they risk falling into Christopher Keane's 'too tidy' category. But, like everything else in this book, you are free to take my advice or leave it. If you do go for the framing device, then you'll need to create something at the end that doesn't make your story seem like story hour for children. You're on your own with that one.

(6) Final Image or Paragraph

The last image on screen or the last paragraph of a novel should be something that sums up and concentrates the emotion of the ending of the story. It should visually echo what has gone before. It may be the opposite of the opening image. It might be exactly the same as the opening image. Or it could be the same scene, subtly or radically altered. It could signal that, in terms of the world of the story, we have come home. Or it could indicate that home no longer exists – there is no going home. Ideally, you want the final image to be something that the reader will remember long after they have finished reading your story.

Dwight V. Swain in *Techniques of the Selling Writer* says that in your final paragraph, what you should strive for is euphoria – "... a sense of well-being and buoyancy. It's the feeling that follows the draining off of the last vestiges of reader tension." To achieve it, you search for a final paragraph, "... and a line to end it, that will epitomise your character's or characters' fulfilment." This final paragraph should make it clear to the reader that the danger that the character has faced throughout the story, and the tension and upset that it has caused, are finally and completely ended.

Unless, of course, they are not...

The Series Novel or Screenplay

A story that is part of a series must succeed as a complete, satisfying, stand-alone work, while at the same time leaving the way open for the next story. There are a number of questions that you will need to consider before writing Act III (Sections 7 and 8) of your story.

Which characters must survive and go forward into the next story? In a detective thriller, the detective-hero must still be standing – if battered and bruised – and ready to take on another case. In a horror movie franchise, it might be the villain – or monster – that has to survive. Does the co-protagonist – the ally or lover – belong in the next story, or do we need to find a way to move them on to another life that doesn't include our main series character? Are there other secondary characters that are part of our franchise that have to go forward? Bond has his boss, M, and the guy who gives him his gadgets, Q, and the secretary he always flirts with, Miss Moneypenny.

What locations have to remain in place for future stories? If your series relies on one or more specific locations, then you may not have the option of blowing them up at the climax of your story. But having said that, I've lost count of the number of times the Starship Enterprise has been destroyed, so there are ways around this problem.

What aspects of the continuing story arc can you resolve? There may be an over-arching storyline that continues throughout the series, in which case you need to know what you can resolve and what you must leave open. This story arc may involve an on-again off-again relationship with another character – or in the case of Janet Evanovich's Stephanie Plumb, with two characters! Or a detective may be involved in a long-term investigation as well as his normal day-to-day cases.

If you are writing the first book in a series of novels, try and avoid cramming new stuff into the last section of the book in order to set up situations that can be developed in later stories. The elements are better set-up during Acts I and II and then mentioned as ongoing and unresolved in Act III. That way they will look less like blatant sequel set-ups. And remember that even if you are planning a sequel, or a series of sequels, each individual book must have a complete and satisfying ending of its own.

Symmetry and Plot Cohesion

We've said that the inciting incident sets off a chain-reaction of events, a series of decisions and actions that all have consequences which must then, in turn, be dealt with. This is one of the things that stops your story feeling like a series of unrelated and unmotivated incidents. Stories are criticised for being episodic, because they seem like a series of things happening one after the other, with no apparent link between them. *Why* something happens is probably more important to a reader or viewer than the event itself. Without an understanding of 'what caused this,' the action is meaningless. For events to have meaning, we need to know why someone did something – what did they hope to achieve; what was at stake for them?

But the linear and escalating chain reaction – the inverted check-mark in the diagram we saw at the beginning – is only one of the ways that we can make our plot feel like a cohesive whole. A second important structural device is symmetry: things that occur in the second half of the story mirror or echo ones that occurred in the first half. We've mentioned that the opening image and final image can perform this function, but there are other key moments during the plot that can be used to strengthen the sense of the story being a creative whole, rather than a collection of elements. This mirroring helps the reader or viewer see how much things have changed and how far the main character has come on his or her journey.

Often this symmetry occurs between events on either side of the midpoint:

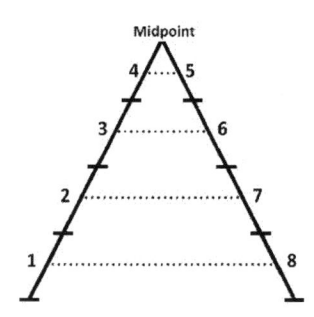

If you plot the eight sequences on a circle, you can visualise other possible links:

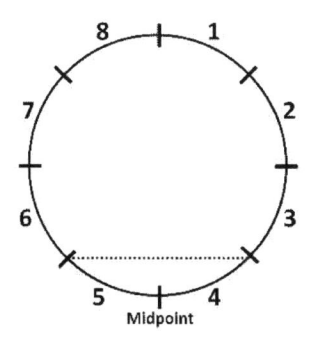

In his book *The Screenwriter's Workbook*, Syd Field says that in a standard 120-page screenplay, there is often a link between something that occurs at page 45 and something at page 75 – the end of Section 3 and the end of Section 5 in our diagram (see above).

You could draw lines from any point on the circle to any other point, and look for echoes or reflections. The 'inciting incident' or 'call to adventure' at the end of Section 1 is often mirrored in the situation that the main character must face at the crisis/climax of the story at the end of Section 7: in 1 he was afraid or reluctant to take action, but in 7 we often seem him prepared to risk everything. The commitment and 'crossing the threshold' at the end of Section 2 is often mirrored in a recommitment and 'entering the lion's den' moment at the end of Section 6, following the crisis.

These echoes in the story may take the form of actions taken or decisions made – typically the decision or action in the first half of the story contrasts starkly with the one in the second half. Or the echo can be a place or an image that gives a sense of before and after; a line of dialogue that takes on a new meaning (sometimes ironic) when repeated; or it can be in the form of the roles that characters fulfil – a student may become a master, or he may become a teacher; a child becomes the parent; a coward becomes the hero; or a trusted friend becomes a betrayer. The echo may also be something less tangible, occurring on a thematic level – good becomes bad, for example, or tragedy becomes hope. You can use irony to make the same words or actions have a very different meaning in different parts of the story.

You can also go beyond the idea of a before-after mirroring, and have the same (or similar) thing occur at three or four points in the story (or perhaps more, but don't overdo it) – this gives an opportunity for the reader or viewer to reflect on a more gradual change or an initial failure to change. This is another spot where the 'rule of three' might come into play.

Look for these links in the novels and screenplays you study, and try to find ways to insert reflections or echoes in your own stories.

Fade to Black...

It might seem like we've come a long way from 'Once upon a time there were three bears...' but it isn't really that far. What we have done is delved deep beneath the surface of story and poked around at the underlying structure. The mechanics of it all are pretty ancient, but I hope you've seen that there's a great deal of power in their simplicity. Four quarters and a midpoint; eight sequences.

Where do we go from here? I said back at the beginning that this structure underlies novels and screenplays in all genres: the obvious next step is to look at how to apply the eight sequences to specific genres. But that is a story for another day. That's all I have for you on the eight-sequence approach to plotting.

When you get to the end, stop – everything else is anti-climax.

THE END

Sources & Bibliography

I have divided the list below into two sections: items listed under *Sources* are quoted in the text, or they had a direct influence on my thinking about plot. Items in the more general *Bibliography* are items I read which broadened my understanding of the subject.

Sources

Aristotle, *The Poetics,* 335BC
Bell, James Scott, *Plot and Structure. Cincinnati,* Ohio: Writer's Digest, 2005
Burroway, Janet, *Writing Fiction: A Guide to Narrative Craft.* Longman, 2006
Campbell, Joseph, *The Hero With a Thousand Faces.* London: Fontana Press, 1993
Catron, Louis E., *The Elements of Playwriting.* Collier Books, 1993
Decker, Dan, *Anatomy of a Screenplay: Writing the American Screenplay from Character Structure to Convergence.* Chicago: The Screenwriters Group, 1998
Dibell, Ansen, *Plot,* in: *How to Write a Million.* London: Robinson, 1995
Dunne, Peter, *Emotional Structure: Creating the Story Beneath the Plot.* Quill Driver Books, 2006
Egri, Lajos, *Art of Dramatic Writing: Its Basis in the Creative Interpretation of Human Motives.* Touchstone, 2004
Field, Syd, *Screenplay: The Foundations of Screenwriting.* New York: Dell Publishing, 1979, 1982
Field, Syd, *The Screenwriter's Workbook.* New York: Dell Publishing, 1987
Foster-Harris, William, *The Basic Patterns of Plot.* University of Oklahoma Press, 1959
Frey, James, *How to Write a Damn Good Novel.* New York: St. Martin's Press, 1987
Griffiths, Stuart, *How Plays are Made.* Heinemann, 1982
Gulino, Paul, *Screenwriting: The Sequence Approach.* New York: Bloomsbury Academic, 2013
Halperin, Michael, *Writing the Second Act: Building Conflict and Tension in Your Film Script.* Studio City, CA: Michael Wiese Productions, 2000
Hauge, Michael, *Writing Screenplays That Sell.* London: Elm Tree Books, 1989
Herman, Lewis, *A Practical Manual of Screen Playwriting for Theatre and Television Films.* New York: New American Library, 1974
Keane, Christopher, *How to Write a Selling Screenplay* (previously published as *Keane on Screen*). Broadway Books, 1998
Kress, Nancy, *Beginnings, Middles, and Ends.* Chicago: Writer's Digest Books, 1995
Kübler-Ross, Elizabeth. *On Death and Dying.* New York: The Macmillan Company, 1969
McKee, Robert, *Story: Substance, Structure, Style and the Principles of Screenwriting.* London: Methuen Publishing Ltd., 1998
Mariner Software, *Contour: Step-by-Step Screenplay User Guide,* v1.0 (2009) www.marinersoftware.com
Marks, Dara, *Inside Story.* Three Mountain Press, 2007
Orr, Alice, *No More Rejections: 50 Secrets to Writing a Manuscript that Sells.* Cincinnati, Ohio: Writer's Digest Books, 2004
Ray, Robert J. & Bret Norris, *The Weekend Novelist.* London: A & C Black, 2005
Rockwell, F.A., *How to Write Plots that Sell.* Chicago: Contemporary Books, Inc., 1975

Root, Wells, *Writing the Script: A Practical Guide for Films and Television.* New York: Holt, Rinehart and Winston, 1980
Rossio, Terry, "The Big Finish" - *Screenwriting Column 13* www.wordplayer.com July 1997
Sargent, Epes Winthrop, *Technique of the Photoplay* (3rd ed.). New York: The Moving Picture World, 1916
Seger, Linda, *Making a Good Script Great.* Samuel French, 1994
Siegel, David, *The Nine-Act Structure Home Page* (archived at the address below) – https://web.archive.org/web/*/http://www.dsiegel.com/film/intro.html
Snyder, Blake, *Save the Cat! The Last Book on Screenwriting You'll Ever Need.* Studio City, CA: Michael Wiese Productions, 2005
Sokoloff, Alexandra, *Screenwriting Tricks for Authors: Stealing Hollywood.* Sokoloff / CreateSpace, 2015
Soth, Chris, *Million-Dollar Screenwriting: The Mini-Movie Method.* MillionDollarScreenwriting.com, 2014
Stefanik, Richard Michaels, *The Megahit Movies.* Fairfax, VA: RMS Productions Company, 2004
Swain, Dwight V., *Techniques of the Selling Writer.* Norman: University of Oklahoma Press, 1965, 1973
Tobin, Rob, *The Screenwriting Formula.* Cincinnati, Ohio: Writer's Digest Books, 2007
Uzzell, Thomas H., *Narrative Technique: a Practical Course in Literary Psychology.* New York: Harcourt, Brace and World 1964
Vogler, Christopher, *The Writer's Journey: Mythic Structure for Writers* (3rd ed.). Studio City, CA: Michael Wiese Productions, 2007
Wiesner, Karen S., *First Draft in 30 Days.* Cincinnati, Ohio: Writer's Digest Books, 2005
Williams, Stanley D., *The Moral Premise: Harnessing Virtue and Vice for Box Office Success.* Studio City, CA: Michael Wiese Productions, 2006

Bibliography

Archer, William, *Play-Making: A Manual of Craftsmanship* (3rd ed.). London: Chapman & Hall Ltd., 1926
Ayckbourn, Alan, *The Crafty Art of Playmaking.* London: Faber & Faber, 2002
Berman, Robert A., *Fade In: The Screenwriting Process (2nd ed.).* Studio City, CA: Michael Wiese Productions, 1997
Bickham, Jack M., *Scene and Structure.* Cincinnati, Ohio: Writer's Digest Books, 1993
Bickham, Jack M., *Setting,* in: *More About How to Write a Million.* London: Robinson, 1996
Block, Lawrence, *Writing the Novel: From Plot to Print.* Cincinnati, OH: Writer's Digest Books, 1985.
Bonnet, James, *Stealing Fire from the Gods: A Dynamic New Story Model for Writers and Filmmakers.* Studio City, CA: Michael Wiese Productions, 1999
Booker, Christopher, *The Seven Basic Plots: Why We Tell Stories.* Continuum International Publishing Group Ltd., 2004
Campbell, Walter S., *Writing: Advice and Devices.* New York: Doubleday, 1950.
Collier, Oscar & Frances Spatz Leighton, *How to Write and Sell Your First Novel.* Chicago: Writer's Digest Books, 1997
Epstein, Alex, Crafty *Screenwriting: Writing Movies That Get Made.* New York: Owl Books, 2002
Freytag, Gustav, *Freytag's Technique of the Drama: An Exposition of Dramatic Composition and Art* (4th ed.). Chicago: Scott, Foresman and Company, 1908

Garrison, Roger H., *A Creative Approach to Writing*. New York: Henry Holt & Company, 1951

Gerard, Philip, *Writing a Book That Makes a Difference*. Cincinnati, Ohio: Writers Book Society, 2000

Hall, Oakley, *How Fiction Works: The Last Word on Writing Fiction - From the Basics to the Fine Points*. Cincinnati, Ohio: Story Press, 2001

Hamlett, Christina, *Could it Be a Movie? How to Get Your Idea Out of Your Head and Up On the Screen*. Studio City, CA: Michael Wiese Productions, 2004

Harrison, Sarah, *How to Write a Blockbuster*. London: Allison & Busby Limited, 2003

Hiltunen, Ari, *Aristotle in Hollywood: The Anatomy of Successful Storytelling*. Bristol: Intellect Books, 2002

Hogrefe, Pearl, *The Process of Creative Writing*. New York: Harper & Row, Publishers, 1963

Howard, David & Edward Mabely, *The Tools of Screenwriting: A Writer's Guide to the Craft and Elements of a Screenplay*. New York: St. Martin's Griffin, 1995

Hunter, Lew, *Screenwriting*. London: Robert Hale, 1994.

Indick, William, *Psychology for Screenwriters: Building Conflict in Your Script*. Studio City, CA: Michael Wiese Productions, 2004.

Karetnikova, Inga, *How Scripts are Made*. Southern Illinois University, 1990

Katahn, T. L., *Reading for a Living: How to be a Professional Story Analyst for Film and Television*. Pacific Palisades, CA: Blue Arrow Books, 1990

Kelner, Jr., Stephen P., *Motivate Your Writing!* Hanover: University Press of New England, 2005

Klick, Todd, *Something Startling Happens: the 120 Story Beats Every Writer Needs to Know*. Studio City, CA: Michael Wiese Productions, 2011

Krevolin, Richard, *How to Adapt Anything into a Screenplay*. Hoboken, NJ: John Wiley & Sons, 2003

Lewinski, John Scott, *Alone in a Room: Secrets of Successful Screenwriters*. Studio City, CA: Michael Wiese Productions, 2004

Macauley, Robie & George Lanning, *Technique in Fiction*. New York: St. Martin's Griffin, 1987

Marshall, Evan, *The Marshall Plan for Novel Writing: A 16-Step Programme Guaranteed to Take You from Idea to Completed Manuscript*. Cincinnati, Ohio: Writer's Digest Books, 1998

Marshall, Evan, *The Marshall Plan Workbook: Writing Your Novel from Start to Finish*. Cincinnati, Ohio: Writer's Digest Books, 2001

Maass, Donald, *The Career Novelist: A Literary Agent Offers Strategies for Success*. Portsmouth, NH: Heinemann, 1996

Maass, Donald, *Writing the Breakout Novel*. Cincinnati, Ohio: Writer's Digest Books, 2001

Maass, Donald, *Writing the Breakout Novel Workbook*. Cincinnati, Ohio: Writer's Digest Books, 2004

Mayer, Bob, *The Novel Writer's Toolkit: A Guide to Writing Novels and Getting Published*. Cincinnati, Ohio: Writer's Digest Books, 2005

Meredith, Robert C. & John D. Fitzgerald, *Structuring Your Novel: From Basic Idea to Finished Manuscript*. New York: Quill, 2003

Morrell, David, *Lessons from a Lifetime of Writing: A Novelist Looks at His Craft*. Cincinnati, Ohio: Writer's Digest Books, 2002

Obstfeld, Raymond, *Novelist's Essential Guide to Crafting Scenes*. Cincinnati, Ohio: Writer's Digest Books, 2000

Parker, Philip, *The Art and Science of Screenwriting* (2nd ed.). Exeter: Intellect Books, 1999

Perry, Dick, *One Way to Write Your Novel*. Cincinnati, Ohio: Writer's Digest Books, 1972

Rabiger, Michael, *Developing Story Ideas* (2nd ed.). London: Focal Press, 2006

Raphaelson, Samson, *The Human Nature of Playwriting*. New York: The Macmillan Company, 1949

Reed, Kit, *Revision*, in: *More About How to Write a Million*. London: Robinson, 1996

Rockwell, F.A., *Modern Fiction Techniques*. Boston: The Writer, Inc., 1969

Seger, Linda, *Advanced Screenwriting*. Los Angeles: Silman-James Press, 2003

Swain, Dwight V. and Joye R. Swain, *Scriptwriting: A Practical Manual*. Boston: Focal Press, 1988

Truby, John, *The Anatomy of Story: 22 Steps to Becoming a Master Storyteller*. North Point Press, 2007

Uzzell, Thomas H., *The Techniques of the Novel*. New York: The Citadel Press, 1959

Woodford, Jack, *Trial and Error: A Key to the secret of Writing and Selling*. New York: Garden City Publishing Co., Inc., 1940

Woodford, Jack, *Plotting for Every Kind of Writing*. New York: Garden City Publishing Co., Inc., 1939

Zuckerman, Albert, *Writing the Blockbuster Novel*. London: Little, Brown and Company, 1994

Index

007, see *James Bond*
1930s murder mystery, 3
48HRS (film), 39, 74
abandonment, 64
abuse of power, negative trait, 57
acceptance, 22, 122
accepting the challenge, 62, **79**
Act I, **31**, 83, 132, 135, 136, 150, 152, 157
Act II, 83, **84-85**, 92-93, 96, 97, 105, 120, 122, 131, 134, 135, 145, 150, 157
Act II, functions of, **84**
Act III, 83, 92, **131-133**, 157
act of desperation, 126, **127**
act, irrevocable final, 146
action, 68
action taken in ignorance, 27, 87
action, opening with, 38
action, rising, 85
action-adventure, structure of, 17
actions towards goal, first, 87, **96-97**
actions, consequences, 100, 101, **103**, 106
actions, minor, 96
active antagonist, 112, **115-116**
active hero, 112, **115**
adventure story, structure of, 17
adventurer, character type, 17
aerial view of plot, 1
Agent Smith (*The Matrix* character), 78
allies and enemies, 87, **93-94**
ally, 73, **74**, 94, 95, 100
Anatomy of a Screenplay, 154
anger, 22, 122
antagonist, the villain or rival, 34, **55-59**, 77-78, 108, 112, **115-116**, 126, **130**, 138, 141, 144
antagonist acts, Sequence 7, 134, **138**

antagonist counter-attacks, 101, **102-103, 126**
antipathy for the villain, creating, **57**
Aristotle, 10, 147
art-house movies, 7
As Good as it Gets (film), 7, 18
A-story, 68
attack by co-protagonist, 126, **128**
attitude, negative trait, 58
backstory, 62, **66-68**
bad guys close in, 116
bad, worse, worst, **19**
balk (or baulk), hero's, see *first failure*
bar scene, 93
bargaining, 22, 122
Basic Patterns of Plot, The, 147
battle begins badly for hero, 134, **141**
Beaufort, Pamela Swynford de, 78
Beginnings, Middles and Ends, 31, 145
Bell, James Scott, 142
Bentham, Jeremy, 142
best friend, see *ally*
bestsellers, importance of plot in, 1
best-selling novel, formula, 8
betrayal, negative trait, 58
big finish, the, 150
Blaine, Rick (*Casablanca* character), 145
Blessed, Brian, 48
blockbuster movie, formula, 8
Bogart, Humphrey, 48, 124, 143, 145
Bond villain, 78
Bond, James, 16, 39, 44, 48, 63, 66, 77, 78, 125
bonding, hero and co-protagonist, 112, **117-118**
Book, John, 46
Brannagh, Kenneth, 48
Brasi, Luca, 78
breaking point, hero reaches, 126, **129-130**

B-story, subplot, 62, **68-70**, 87, **95-96**, 100, 107, **109**, 115, 118
buddy movie, structure of, 15
buddy, see *ally*,
building a climax, **144**
Burroway, Janet, 11
Burton, Richard, 41
call to adventure, see *challenge* and *inciting incident*
Campbell, Joseph, 9
cantina scene, *Star Wars*, 93
Carmichael, Hoagy, 48
Casablanca (film), 7, 18, 124, 143, 145
catalyst, 72
Catron, Louis E., 153
causally-liked events in a story, 6
cause and effect, 6
central question, see *major dramatic question*
chain-reaction of events, 6
challenge or inciting incident, **59-61**, 65
challenge, accepting, 62, **79**
change, coping with, 5, 21-22, 93, 122
change, decisive, 134
change, experience of in the hero's quest, **123**
change-curve, **22**, 27, 122, 134
character, 8
character arc, hero, 107, **109**, 120-121
character development arc, 1, 9, 18
character versus plot, 1
character, ability to judge, 93
character-based story, 18
characters, larger-than-life, 5
check-mark, inverted, diagram of story, 10
childhood trauma, 64
children's stories, themes, 56
children's stories, structure, 12
choose-your-own adventure, 47
chronological sequence, 6-7
Cinderella, 11, 12, 76

circular and linear endings, **144**
Clarice Starling, 40
Clark Kent, 63
Claudius, 57
cliché, 40, 48
climactic action, see *climax* and *final battle*
climactic events, reaction to, **153**
climax, 10, 12, 78, 131-133, 140, 144, 145, 146, 148, 152
climax, building a, **144**
climax, how big?, **148**
clock, ticking, 116, 134
closure and validation, 153, **154**, 155
cohesion, plot, 158
coincidence in a story, 6
coincidence versus pattern, 11
comedy, 76
commitment to co-protagonist by hero, 117
commitment to hero by co-protagonist, 117
commitment, new, 112, **113-114**
Compact Overview of European Film Theories, 24
competence, positive trait, 50
complexity of life vs. simplicity of fiction, 5
concern for hero's safety, 50
confidant/confidante, see *ally* and *co-protagonist*
Confidence (film), 40
conflict, 68, 92
conflict, foreshadowing, **53-54**
conflict, promise of in a story, 31-32
Connery, Sean, 48
conscience, 77
consequences of actions, 85, 91, 100, 101, **103**, 106
consequences of refusing the challenge, 62, **71**
Contour (software), 71
Cooper, Gary, 60, 125
co-protagonist, see also *romance* and *ally*, 74, 94, 100, 106, 107, 109, 154
co-protagonist and hero bonding, 112, **117-118**
co-protagonist and hero increased intimacy, 112, **117-118**
co-protagonist and hero unite against villain, 112, **118**

co-protagonist attacks hero, 126, **128**
co-protagonist commitment to hero, 117
countdown, see also *clock, ticking*, 116
courage, positive trait, 51
Craig, Daniel, 48
credits sequence, 36, 44
criminal mastermind, 78
crisis, the, 19-20, 120, 122, 123, **126-130**, 134, 136
crisis of faith, 76
crisis, responding to, 29
crossing the threshold, 63
Crouse, Russell, 37
C-story, **69-70**
cunning plan, 97
danger and desire, 31, 66
Daniel, Frank (František), 24
dark cave, see *villain's lair*
dark night of the soul, see *crisis*
dark side, villain as opposite, 56
Darth Vader, 57, 78
Dead Poets Society (film), 7
deadline, see also *clock, ticking*, 116, 134
Deadpool (film), 41
death and dying, 21
Death Star, 107
Deathwish (film), 46
debate, 62, 66
decision, 6, 27, 62, **79**, 135-136
decision to continue, 112, **113-114**
decisive action, see *final battle*
Decker, Dan, 126, 154
demon, 64
denial of problem, 22, 101, **103**, 106, 122
denouement, 30, 152, 153, **156**
dependability, positive trait, 50
depression, 22, 122
Desdemona, 52
desire and danger, 31, 64
desire versus need, 97
desperation, act of, 126, **127**
deus ex machina, 148, 151
Dibell, Ansen, 84, 150
Dickens, Charles, 38
dilemma, 66, 95, **134**, 135-136
Dirty Harry, 46
disaster, potential, 78
discovery or revelation, 28, 134, **138-139**
drama, 4

dramatic action, 31
dramatic significance, 27
dramatic writing, **4**
dreams, 64
Dunne, Peter, 87
dynamite, 37
E.T.: The Extra Terrestrial, 108
economy in story structure, 11
Egri, Lajos, 134
eight sequences, diagram, 26
eight sequences, list, 25
eighths, **24**
elegance in story structure, 11
Elements of Playwriting, 153
emotion, rising, 85
emotional loss, 64
emotional reaction to midpoint, **112-113**
emotional reaction to strange new world, **90**
emotional response, importance of evoking, 45
emotional significance, 27
Emotional Structure, 87
emotions, 45
empathy, 63
empathy and sympathy, **45**
empathy with antagonist, 59
end, the, 131-133
ending, trick, 151, 153
ending, types of, **143**
endings, satisfactory, 152
endings, wrong or bad, **150**
enemies and allies, 87, **93-94**
Englishman, Irishman, Scotsman joke structure, 10-11
Enterprise, USS, 157
enthusiasm, positive trait, 50
epilogue, 153
equilibrium, 32, 44, **155**
equipment, consideration of, 97
escapism, why people read stories, 4
Evanovich, Janet, 157
Excalibur, 77
expectations of story structure, 12
experience, 92, 97
external action, conflict, 100
failure, consequences, 78, 101
failure, hero's, see *first failure*, 101
fair-play, positive trait, 51
Fairy Godmother, Cinderella, 76
fall, the, 120, 122, 126, **128-129**

false solution, 126, **127**
fate and pre-determination, 6
fear, hero's greatest, 62, **63**, 78, 91, 93, 97, 103-104
Ferris Beuller's Day Off (film), 41
fiction vs. non-fiction, 5
Field, Syd, 12, 98, 116, 159
fight, promise of conflict in a story, 31-32
film reels, 25
final battle, 134, **140-141**, 146
final battle, outcome, 134, **142-143**
final image, 153
final paragraph, 153
first actions towards goal, 87, **96-97**
First Attempt, 28, 87, **97-98**, 100, **101**, 106, 116
First Attempt, planning, 87, **97-98**
First Draft in 30 Days, 154
first failure, 100, **101**
first impressions of a character, 47
first test, 87, **88-89**
first-person viewpoint, 37, 47
Fisher King myth, 43
five stages of grief, 21, 122
flashback, 7
flash-forward, 39, **40**
Flatland, 1
flaw or weakness, creating sympathy, 51
flaw, hero's, 105
flawed hero story, 7, 18, 51, 64, 105
flawed hero, story structure, 18
flaws and weaknesses, introducing, 49
Fleming, Ian, 48
Ford, Harrison, 46
foreshadowing, 34, 43, **53-54**
formula for stories/plots, 2
Foster-Harris, William, 147
freedom, theme, 52
Freeman, Morgan, 41
Frey, James, 132
Fulbright, Leo, 48
gadgets, 77
gauntlet, see *challenge* and *inciting incident*
genre, **8**, 34, **41**

genre expectations, 5
genre fiction, 7, 8, 9
genre iconography, 9
ghost from the past, 64
goal, first actions toward, 87, **96-97**
goal, hero's, 62, **80**, 97
goal, wrong, 80
Godfather, The (film), 46, 78
Goldman, William, 131, 143, 147
Good Will Hunting (film), 7
Gothic fiction, 8
grabber, see *hook*
greatest fear, hero's, 62, **63**, 78, 91, 93, 97, 103-104
Griffiths, Stuart, 149
growth, hero's personal, 107, **109**, 120-121
Guinness Book of Records, 154
Gulino, Paul, 24, 25
gurus / story theorists, 7
Halloween (film), 39
Halperin, Michael, 84
Hamlet, 57, 67, 82
Hannibal Lecter, 58
happy ending, **143**
Harrison, Harry, 36
Hauge, Michael, 37
healing a sick world, 43, 144
healing elixir, 144, 155
Henchman (character archetype), 73, 77
Henry, O., 151
herald, character archetype, 60
Herman, Lewis, 69
hero and co-protagonist bonding, 112, **117-118**
hero and co-protagonist increased intimacy, 112, **117-118**
hero and co-protagonist unite against villain, 112, **118**
hero as outsider, 87, **91**
hero balks, see *first failure*
hero pleads for second chance, 112, **117**
hero reaches breaking point, 126, **129-130**
hero redeems himself, 112, **115**
hero takes action, Sequence 6, **126**
hero tries to prove himself, 112, **114**
Hero with a Thousand Faces, Joseph Campbell, 9

hero, active, 112, **115**
hero, introducing, 34, **45**
hero's black moment, 149
hero's flaw, 18, 34, 53, 64-65, 105
hero's goal, 62, **80**, 97
hero's greatest fear, 62, **63**, 78, 91, 93, 97, 103-104
hero's journey, story model, 9, 43, 76
hero's lack or inner problem 18, 34, 53, 64-65, 105, 18, 34, 53, 64-65, 105
high concept, 5
High Noon (film), 60, 125
high stakes, 5, 135
high-brow fiction, 7
highest stakes, 134, **139-140**
Hitchcock, Alfred, 7, 16, 37, 47, 55, 79
Hoffman, Dustin, 41
Holmes, Sherlock, 150
hook, 34, **36**
hopes and fears, sharing, 117
How Plays are Made, 149
How to Write a Damned Good Novel, 132
How to Write a Selling Screenplay, 156
How to Write Plots That Sell, 135
humiliation, 64
Iago (*Othello* character), 52
iconography, genre, 9
ignorance, action taken in, 27, 87
Ilsa (*Casablanca* character), 145
immoral action or behaviour, 94, 127, 137, **140**, 144, 154
in medias res, 7
inciting incident (see also *challenge*), 34, 44, **59-61**
increased threat, Sequence 7, 134, **140, 142**
Indiana Jones, 39, 44, 66
initial reaction to challenge, 62, **63**
injustice, theme, 52
inner problem or lack, see also *internal conflict*, 18, 34, 53, 64-65, 105
insanity, negative trait, 58
Inside Story, 86, 112, 118
integration, 22, 122
interloper or usurper, negative trait, 58
internal conflict, 53, 100

intimacy, increased, hero and co-protagonist, 112, **117-118**
inverted check-mark, diagram of story, 10
ironic ending, **143**
J.D. (*Thelma & Louise* character), 98
James Bond, 16, 39, 44, 48, 63, 66, 77, 78, 125
James Bond film, structure of, 16
Jaws (film), 11, 22, 39, 76
Jaws (James Bond character), 57, 78, 156
jealousy, theme, 52
Jerry Maguire (film), 7
John Book, 46
joke structure, 10-11
Jones, Indiana, 39, 44, 66
journey versus guidebook, 19
judging character, ability for, 93
Justice, James Robertson, 48-49
justice, theme, 52
Karate Kid, The (film), 76
Keane, Christopher, 147, 156
Kenobi, Obi Wan, 76
Kent, Clark, 63
King, Stephen, 48
knowledge, 92, 97
Kratochvil, Miloš, 24
Kress, Nancy, 31, 84, 145
Kryptonite, 63
Kübler-Ross, Elisabeth, **21**, 27, 122, 134
lack, hero's inner problem, 18, 34, 53, 64-65, 105
lair, villain's, 123, **124-126**
land of the dead, see *villain's lair*
Lane, Lois, 63
larger-than-life characters, 5
laws and rules, learning, 93
Lazlo (*Casablanca* character), 145
learning, 87, 88, **93**, **107**
least likely person, 78
Lecter, Hannibal, 58
Leo Fulbright, 48
Lethal Weapon (film), 76
likeability, 63
likeable hero, creating, **49**
likeable hero, myth of, 46
Lindsay, Howard, 37
linear and circular endings, 144
lock-in, 62, **72**
Lois Lane, 63

lost in a book, 4
love interest, see *romance* and *co-protagonist*
love story, structure of, 15
lover, see *romance*
Luca Brasi (*The Godfather* character), 78
Lucas, George, 9
Luke Skywalker, 107, 108
M (James Bond character), 157
Macguffin, 16
Mafia, the, 56
magic elixir, 43, 77, 144, 155
magic potion, 77
magic sword, 77
mainstream fiction, 6,7
major characters, introducing, 62, **73**
major dramatic question, 33, 63
major turning point, **82**
major turning point, second, 130
Making a Good Script Great, 69
Maltese Falcon, The, 48
manipulating the reader, 5
Mariner Software, 71
Marks, Dara, 86, 112, 118, 137
Matrix, The (film), 78
McKee, Robert, 101, 137, 147
meaning, of events in a story, 6
meltdown, 126, **129-130**
Mentor (character archetype), 73, **76**
Merlin, 76
midpoint, 28, 80, 98, 100, **105-110**, 120-121
midpoint, emotional reaction to, **112-113**
midpoint, reacting to, **111-119**
Million Dollar Screenwriting, 24
mind's-eye, 49
mini movies, 24
minor actions to solve problem, 96
mirror (character archetype), see *ally*
miscommunications, 121
misjudgements, 121
Miss Moneypenny (James Bond character), 157
mistakes and transgressions, 87, **91**
misunderstandings, 96
Miyagi, Mr. (*The Karate Kid* character), 76

moment of revelation or discovery, 28
Moneypenny, Miss (James Bond character), 157
monomyth, Joseph Campbell, 9
montage, **40**, 152
Moonraker (film), 156
moral action or behaviour, 106, 127, 137, **140**, 144, 154
moral argument, see *thematic argument*
Moral Premise, The, 53
motivation, 17, 60, 62, 77, **79**, 147
motive, villain's, 57
Mr. Spock (*Star Trek* character), 142
multiple reel films, 25
murder mystery, 43
murder mystery, structure of, 16
Murphy, Eddie, 39, 74
mythology, 124
mythology, stories from, 9
narration, 39, **41**
narrative hook, see *hook*
Narrative Technique, 137
Nazis, 56, 145
need or desire, 97
need versus want, 102
need-girl versus want-girl, 64
Neeson, Liam, 41
nemesis, see *antagonist*
new equilibrium, 153, **155**
new world, 82, 85
Nicholson, Jack, 150
nine-act structure, 108
No More Rejections, 35-36
Nolte, Nick, 39, 74
non-fiction vs. fiction, 5
Norris, Bret, 132
North by North-West (film), 79
Obi Wan Kenobi, 76
obstacles, 92
odd couple, see *ally*
Oddjob (James Bond character), 57, 78
On Death and Dying, 21, 122
one-act plays, 2
opening image, 34, **35**
opening paragraph, 34, **35**, 38
opening scene, 34, **35**, 38
opening scene, types of, 39
opening sentence, 37
opponent, see *antagonist*
opportunity, 66

opposition, the antagonist, 34, 55-59, 123, **124**
ordeal, supreme, 123, **126-130**
ordinary world, 43, 44
original plot, no such thing, 4
Orr, Alice, 35-36
Othello, 52, 56
outcome of the final battle, 134, **142-143**
outsider, hero as, 87, **91**
Page 45, Pinch Point I, 87, **98-99**, 112, 116, 118
Page 75, Pinch Point II, 112, **116**
Pamela Swynford de Beaufort, 78
pantser versus plotter, 2
paradigm, screenplay structure (Syd Field), 13
Path to Film Drama, 24
pattern versus coincidence, 11
period of grace, 112, 118
personal growth, hero, 107, **109**, 120-121
personal tragedy, ending, **143**
personal triumph, ending, **143**
Pinch Point I, Page 45, 87, **98-99**
Pinch Point II, Page 75, 98, 112, **116**
Pitt, Brad, 98
planning the First Attempt, 87, **97-98**
planting, plot device, 77
plausibility, 96
plot, **6-7**
Plot, 84, 150
Plot and Structure, 142
plot, original – no such thing, 4
plot-based story vs. character-based, 7
plotting, what is it?, 4
Plotto, 2
Plum, Stephanie, 157
poetic justice, 132
Poetics, The, 10, 147
point of no return, 63, 82
point of view, hero's, 79
politics, local, 93
Popeye moment, 56
popular fiction / films, 6, 8
positive attitude, positive trait, 50
potential disaster, 78

power structure, local, 93
Practical Manual of Screen Playwriting for Theatre and Television Films, 69
pre-credits sequence, 36, 44
premise, high concept, 5
preparation for the ordeal, **123**
pressure to accept the challenge, 62, **71**
problem, character with a , 5
problem, hero's inner, 18, 34, 53, 64-65, 105
procrastination, 97
prologue, 36, **39**
promises, fulfilling, 132
promises, made in Act I, 31
proving himself, hero, 112, **114**
Psycho (film), 47
pulp fiction, 8
Q (James Bond character), 63, 77, 157
quarters, **14**
quest model for a story, 9
quick fixes, 27
Quint (*Jaws* character), 76
Raiders of the Lost Ark (film), 143
Rainman (film), 7
random events in life, 6
Ray, Robert J., 132
reaction to climactic events, **153**
reaction to midpoint, **112-113**
reaction to the crisis, **134-137**
reader involvement / contribution, 43
recruiting, 87, **94-95**
redeeming features, antagonist, 59
redeeming himself, hero, 112, **115**
Reeve, Christopher, 63
reflection (character archetype), see *ally*
refusal of the call or challenge, 62, **65**
refusing the challenge, consequences, 62, **71**
rejection, 64
religion, stories from, 9
reluctance to continue, 112, **113**
reluctant hero, 66
resentment, negative trait, 58
Reservoir Dogs, 40

resisting the call to adventure, **65**
resolution, 30, 131-133, 152, 153, **154**
resources, consideration of, 97
responding to change, 5
responding to the challenge, 27
responding to the crisis, 29
responding to the midpoint, 28
revelation or discovery, 28, 134, **138-139**
reversing the situation, climax, 149
reward, hero's, 149
Rick Blaine (*Casablanca* character), 145
rising action, 85
rising tension, 10, 12, 85
rival, see *antagonist*
Robin (*Batman* character), 94
Rockwell, F. A., 135, 136
Rocky (film), 7, 143
role-model, see also *ally*, *mentor*, *co-protagonist*, 106
Romance (character archetype), 73, **75**, 95
romance genre, antagonist, 55
romance, story type, 93
romantic comedy, 76
romantic interest, see *romance* and *co-protagonist*
Root, Wells, 37
Rossio, Terry, 150
rubber duck, 46
rule of three, **11**
rules and laws, learning, 93
sadism, negative trait, 59
saloon, Western, 93
Sam Spade, 48
same only different, 5
Sargent, Epes Winthrop , 25
satisfactory endings, 152
Save the Cat!, 48
scene objective, 81
schedule, planning, 97
Screenplay: The Foundations of Screenwriting, 12, 98
Screenwriter's Workbook, The, 98, 116, 159
Screenwriting Formula, The, 101
Screenwriting Tricks for Authors, 24
Screenwriting: The Sequence Approach, 24
ScriptLab.com, 24
S-curve of change, **22**, 27, 122, 134

Second Attempt, 29, 114, 119, **119-130**, 134
Second Attempt, planning, 112, **116**
second chance, hero pleads for, 112, **117**
second failure, 126, **128-129**
second major turning point, 130
secondary plotlines, 62, **68-70**
second-person viewpoint, 47
secret wish, **64**
Seger, Linda, 69, 83
self-confidence, positive trait, 50
self-definition or self-image, hero, 66, 135
self-sacrifice, 134, **142**
self-sacrifice, positive trait, 51
sensationalist fiction, 5
Sequence 1, 27, **34-61**
Sequence 2, 27, **62-83**
Sequence 2, 120
Sequence 3, 27, **86-99**, 120
Sequence 4, 28, **100-104**
Sequence 5, 28, **111-119**
Sequence 6, 29, **120-130**
Sequence 7, 29, **134-151**
Sequence 8, 30, **152-157**
series novel or screenplay, 157
setting, 34, **41**
set-up, 10, 12
Seven (film), 76
shadow, villain as opposite, 56
Shakespeare, William, 48, 52, 56, 57, 152
sharing hopes and fears, 117
Shaw, Robert, 76
Sherlock Holmes, 150
short stories, 2
showdown, see *final battle*
showing versus telling, 67, 156
Siegel, David, 108
Silence of the Lambs, The (film), 40
simplicity of fiction vs. complexity of life, 5
single-reel films, 25
sitcoms, 2
situation, setting up, 27
six major turning points, plus climax, 2
skills, 92, 97
Skywalker, Luke, 107, 108
Slayer of Dragons (novel), 9

slow-build opening scene, 38
SMART objectives, 81
Snyder, Blake, 48, 62, 84, 116
sociopath, negative trait, 58
Sokoloff, Alexandra, 24
Soth, Chris, 24
Soylent Green (film), 41
Spade, Sam, 48
Spinoza, Baruch, 45
Spock (*Star Trek* character), 142
stakes, 62, **78**
stakes, highest, 134, **139-140**
Star Trek, 157
Star Wars (film), 9, 41, 56, 76, 93, 107
Starling, Clarice, 40
Stealing Hollywood, 24
Stefanik, Joseph Michaels, 11
Stephanie Plum, 157
stereotypes, 11
story, **6**
Story (McKee, Robert), 101, 137, 147
story objective, see *goal, hero's*
story question, see *major dramatic question*
story theorists / gurus, 7
strange new world, 82, 85, **89-90**
subplots, 62, **68-70**
subplots, climax, 149-150
success, formula for, **97**
Superman, 63
surprising the reader, endings, **148-149**
Swain, Dwight V., 31, 37, 68, 146, 149, 154, 156
Sword in the Stone Dead, The (novel), 3, 48
symmetry, plot, 158
sympathy for the hero, 49, 63
teaching, 77
team, 117, 124
team, recruiting, 94
Technique of the Photoplay, 25
Techniques of the Selling Writer, 31, 37, 68, 149, 156
teen comedy, 120
television, 2
telling versus showing, 67, 156
tension, rising, 85
terminal diagnosis, 22
tests, 87, **92**
The Dead Zone (novel), 48
The Megahit Movies, 11
The Stainless Steel Rat, 36

Thelma & Louise (film), 98-99, 137
thematic argument, 8, 32, 35, **52**, 94, 106, 108, 127, 134, 137, **140**, 144, 154
thematic argument, hero-villain relationship, 56
theme, 8, 32, 35, **52**, 94, 106, 108, 127, 134, 137, **140**, 144, 154
Third Attempt, 29, 134, 140
Thirty-Nine Steps, The (film), 79
Three Bears, The, 12
Three Little Pigs, 11, 12
three-act structure, 10
Threshold Guardian (character archetype), 87, **88-89**
thriller, 73
thriller, structure of, 16
ticking clock, 116, 134
Tobin, Rob, 101, 126
Tonto (*Lone Ranger* character), 94
tools, gaining, 77
Tootsie (film), 7, 18, 41
tragic ending, **143**
tragic flaw, 76
training, 77, 97
traitor, 95
transformation moment, 137
transgressions and mistakes, 87, **91**
trauma, 66
Triads, the, 56
trick endings, 151, 153
true beginning, **40**
True Blood (TV series), 78
turning points, 63, **82-83**
turning points, six major plus climax, 2
twist endings, **149**
types of ending, **143**
tyranny, theme, 52
unconscious incompetence, 91
underworld, the, 123, **124-126**
uniting against villain, 112, **118**
unravelling, see *fall* and *crisis*
Usual Suspects, The (film), 40
usurper or interloper, negative trait, 58
Uzzell, Thomas H., 137
validation and closure, 153, **154**
Vantage Point (film), 11
vicarious experience, 45
vice, theme, 52

viewpoints, hero and antagonist, 134, **140**
villain gains an advantage, **71**
villain, see *antagonist*
villain's lair, 123, **124-126**
virtue, theme, 32, 35, 52, 64
virtues, of the villain, 59
Vogler, Christopher, 9, 43, 82, 88, 87, 122, 125 126
volunteer, positive trait, 51, 79
vulnerability, creating sympathy, 51, 63
want versus need, **64**, 102
want-girl versus need-girl, 64
War of the Worlds, 41
warrior, character type, 17
Watson (Sherlock Holmes character), 94
weakness, 63
weakness or flaw, creating sympathy, 51
weaknesses and flaws, introducing, 49
weapons, gaining, 77
Weekend Novelist, The, 132
Welles, Orson, 49
When Harry Met Sally (film), 9
whodunit, 7, 47, 67
Why doesn't he just...?, 96
Wiesner, Karen S., 154
Williams, Stanley D., 53
Witches of Eastwick, The (film), 150
Witness (film), 46
wordplayer.com, 150
worry about the hero, **50**

worse, bad, worst, **19**

worst possible thing that can happen, **18**, 62, 78

worthiness, hero proving, 88
Writer's Journey, The, 9, 43, 82, 87, 88, 122
writer's block, 3
Writing Fiction: A Guide to Narrative Craft, 11
Writing Screenplays That Sell, 37
Writing the Script, 37
Writing the Second Act, 84
wrong endings, **150**

wrong goal, 80, **108**

wrong path, 56
You know what your trouble is...?, 64
Young Sherlock Holmes (film), 150

About the Author

Paul Tomlinson is the author of novels in the mystery, crime, science fiction, and fantasy genres. He has also published articles and author interviews in print magazines and online.

Contact him via his website at **www.paultomlinson.org** or on Facebook @PaulTomlinson.org

Books by Paul Tomlinson

Fiction:

The Great Vicari Mysteries series:
The Sword in the Stone-Dead
Murder by Magic
The Missing Magician

The Thurlambria series:
Slayer of Dragons
Fortune's Fool
Dead of Night

Robot Wrecker
Who Killed Big Dick?

Non-Fiction:

Harry Harrison: An Annotated Bibliography

Made in the USA
Las Vegas, NV
24 June 2021